MATERIAL TESTING LABORATORY MANUAL
(For Quality Control)

By :
C.B. KUKREJA, KAUSHAL KISHORE, S.K. KAUSHIK, V.K. GUPTA

Revised & Enlarged by :

C.B. KUKREJA Ph.D

RAVI CHAWLA M.E.

Department of Civil Engineering
Thapar Institute of Engineering & Technology
(Deemed University) Patiala (Pb.) - 147 001.

STANDARD PUBLISHERS DISTRIBUTORS

Specialist in: Engineering, Medical, Dental, Nursing, Pharmacy, Computer, Agriculture, Management, Bio-Science and Imported Scientific Books

1705-B, NAI SARAK, P.O. BOX NO.-1066, DELHI-110006

Ph.: 3262700, 3285798, Telefax: 011-3243180
www.standardpubdist.com

www.indiamart.com/stpub
email : stpub@vsnl.com

Published by:
A.K. Jain
For Standard Publishers Distributors,
1705-B, Nai Sarak, Delhi-110006.

Showroom:
4581/15 G.F., Ansari Road,
Daryaganj, New Delhi-110002.
Ph.: 011-23281159

First Edition	:	1990
Fourth Edition	:	2015
Reprint	:	2018
Reprint	:	2026

Price: Rs. 200-00

ISBN : 978-81-8014-217-8

Printed by: Prabhat Offset Press.

PREFACE TO FIRST EDITION

This publication on experiments in structural design covers mainly all tests required to check the suitability of various construction materials used in buildings and other structures. It is hoped that this manual will fulfil the long felt need of the students for laboratory manual on tests for materials.

This manual mainly covers such experiments which are included in the syllabus for undergraduate students of Civil Engineering. Each experiment is intended to be completed in a duration of two hours class by students working in batches of 3 to 4 in numbers. In almost all tests, the recommended procedure is based on relevant Indian Standard Code of Practice which is the usual accepted method of performing the test and is backed by laboratory experience of the authors gained over number of years. It is however recommended that the students should come prepared to the class for performing the experiment. They should follow the recommended procedure or state specifically where he did not do so and record reasons. On the basis of experimental data the student is expected to write discussion and comments on his results and compare them with relevant I.S. Code specifications. All efforts have been made to make this manual self contained but by no means it is a complete testing manual.

Number of books, Indian Standard Codes have been referred to for the preparation of this manual. We are grateful to all such authors and particularly the authorities of Bureau of Indian Standard, New Delhi.

The authors are thankful to Shri Nem Chand Jain proprietor, Standard Publisher Distributors, Delhi for bringing out the manual in the present form.

Suggestions to improve the manual are welcome and errors, if any, may be pointed out to the authors.

S.K. Kaushik
C.B. Kukreja
V.K. Gupta
Kaushal Kishore

PREFACE TO THIRD EDITION

In preparing the second edition of this manual, the authors have been fortunate in receiving the comments from the student and teaching community, who have been kind enough in sending their comments and their ideas for the improvement of this manual.

The revision has involved the correction of errors, expansion of various sections and particularly the addition of the section on Building Limes. We hope that with the addition of section 8 on experiments on Building limes, the manual will get improved considerably and long felt demand of the builders, contractors, architects and particularly the student community will be fulfilled. This revised addition of the manual will more useful to teachers in general and to the students in particulars and to all those who are engaged in design, research and construction of Civil Engineering Structures.

Patiala

C.B. Kukreja
Ravi Chawla

CONTENTS

PART I—CEMENT

PART II—AGGREGATES

PART III—CEMENT CONCRETE

APPENDIX

PART I

CEMENT

EXPERIMENT NO. 1/1

FINENESS

1. **Object**–To determine the fineness of cement sample by (a) Dry Sieving (b) By Blaines Air Permeability method.

2. **Theory** :

Control of particle size of cement is important in practice because it has an influence on the behaviour of the cement. Cement which is more finely ground hardens more rapidly and has a higher rate of heat evolution at early ages. Fineness of grinding is of more importance in relation to the workability of concrete mixes. Greater fineness improves the cohesiveness the a concrete mix and the quantity of water rising to the surface of the concrete known as bleeding is reduced.

Shrinkage cracking is related to the rate of development of strength of concrete. In general cements which gain more strength rapidly are more apt to cracking. Increasing the fineness of any particular cement, raises its rate of development of strength and so indirectly increases the risk of shrinkage crack formation.

(a) DRY SIEVING :

1. **Apparatus**–I.S. : 90 micron sieve, Rice plate, weighing balance (Sensitive to : 0.1 gm).

2. **Procedure**–(a) Weigh accurately 100 gm of cement in a rice plate.

(b) Place is on a standard IS 90 micron sieve breaking down any air-set lumps in the cement sample with finger.

(c) Continously sieve the sample by holding the sieve in both the hands. Sieve with a gentle wrist motion for a period of 15 minutes, rotating the sieve continuously throughtout the sieving, involving no danger of spalling the cement.

(d) Weigh the residue after 15 minutes of sieving.

(e) Repeat the procedure for two more such samples.

3. **Observations and calculations**

Weight of cement taken on IS : 90 micron Sieve = 100 gms.

Weight of residue after 15 minutes of sieving = ...gm.

TABLE 1·1

Sample No.	*Weight of Sample (gms)*	*Weight of Residue (gms)*	*Fineness*
1.	100		$\frac{\text{Wt of residue}}{\text{Wt of sample}}$ (percent)
2.	100		
3.	100		
		Average =	Percent.

4. **Results**–Fineness of cement by dry sieving is =...%

5. **Precautions**– (1) Before sieving, air set lumps of cement should be broken.

(2) Sieving should be done by rotating the sieve and not by translation.

6. **Discussion of Test Result**–Give your comments on the result obtained above and discuss about the suitability of this cement to be used on a construction site.

FINENESS

(b) BLAINES AIRPERMEABILITY METHOD:

1. **Apparatus**– The Blaine's air permeability apparatus consists essentially of a means of drawing a definite quantity of air through a prepared bed of cement of definite porosity. The number and size of the pores in a prepared bed of cement of definite porosity is a function of the size of the particles and determines the rate of air flow through the bed (Fig. 1.1) The apparatus consists of permeability cell, disc, plunger, filter paper, manometer, manometer liquid, timer, mercury, weight box, analytical balance, watch glass, camel hair brush, and stop watch.

2. **Procedure:**

(a) Calculate the bulk volume of compacted bed of standard*

$$V = \frac{W_A - W_B}{D}$$

Where–

W_A = gms of mercury required to fill the permeability cell

W_B = gms of murcury required to fill the portion of the cell not occupied by the bed of cement formed by 2.8 gms of standard cement sample.

D = Density of mercury at temperature of test.

(b) Determine the weight of the standard sample (W) required to produce a bed having porosity of 0.500 ± 0.005 (e) as follows :

$$W = 3.15\,V\,(1\text{-}e)$$

where V= Bulk volume of compacted cement powder

and e = Desired porosity of bed of cement (0.500 ± 0.005)

(c) Determine the time taken by the manometer liquid to fall from second mark from the top to the third mark on the manometer when air is allowed to permeate through the compacted bed of cement using the quantity of standard cement calculated in (b).

(d) Calculate the constant of the apparatus (k) by using the following formula

$$S_s = K\sqrt{T_s}$$

where $K = \dfrac{S_s}{\sqrt{T_s}}$

Where S_s is the fineness of standard portland cement in Sq. Cm/gm.

(e) Using the same quantity (w) of the cement sample find the time (T_s) in seconds required for the manometer liquid to fall from second mark to third mark

(f) Calculate the specific surface of cement in Sq. cm/gm using the formula

$$S = K\sqrt{T_s}$$

3. **Observations and calculations**

(i)	Weight of empty crucible	= gms
(ii)	Weight of crucible + mercury filling permeability cell	= gms
(iii)	Weight of mercury filling cell, (ii)-(i)-(WA)	= gms
(iv)	Weight of crucible + mercury filling portion above cement bed	= gms
(v)	Weight of mercury filling cell above cement bed of 2.80 gm of standard cement (W_B) (iv)-(i)	= gms
(vi)	Temperature of the laboratory	= ^{0}C

---

* Cement powder (V) by the following formula

(*vii*) Time taken by the manometer liquid to fall from Second to third mark (T*s*) 2nd to 3rd = Secs.

4. **Results**– The fineness of given cement sample = Sq.cm/gm

5. **Precautions :**

(1) The volume of the compacted cement should be calculated accurately

(2) The time taken by the manometer liquid to fall from one mark to the other should be measured very accurately

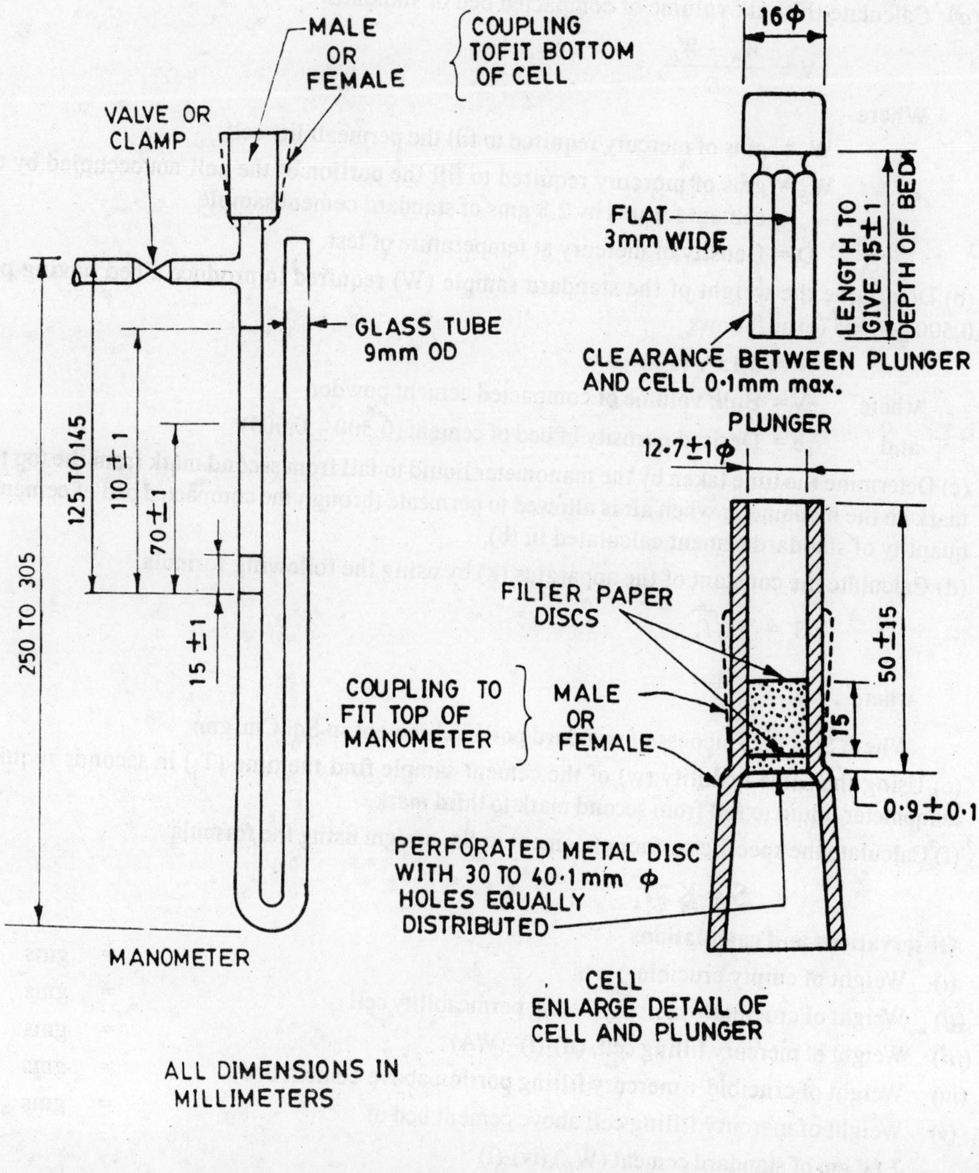

Fig. 1.1 Blaine's Air Permeability Apparatus

6. **Comments–Comment on the value of specific surface of the cement sample and compare with the value given in the relevant I.S. code**

7. **Questions :**

(a) What is fineness of cement ? State the IS specifications for fineness in terms of its specific surface (Sq. cm/gm)

(b) What is the importance of this test ?

(c) How is the fineness expressed when using the IS 90 micron Sieve ?

(d) What effect does the additional fineness has upon the rate of development of strength ?

(e) Define specific surface area of cement. Name the popular method to determine the specific surface.

(f) What precautions do you take while performing this experiment ?

(g) How many openings are there per square Cm in the IS 90 micron sieve ?

(h) What precautions will you take in transporting and storing the cement ?

(*i*) Explain the statement in relation to the arrival of cement at the construction site 'First arrived first used.'

(*i*) Correct the following statements :

(*ii*) Finer the cement, lesser is the surface area.

(*iii*) Finer the cement, lesser the strength it will attain.

EXPERIMENT NO. 1/2

STANDARD CONSISTENCY AND SETTING TIMES

1. **Object**–To determine (a) Standard consistency (b) initial and final setting times of a cement sample,

2. **Theory**–since different batches of cement differ in fineness, pastes with the same water content may differ in consistency when first mixed. For this reason the consistency of the paste is standardized by varying the water content until the paste has a given resistance to penetration, when it is first mixed. When testing the portland cement it is necessary to carry-out trial mixes until a mix of the required consistency is obtained. The quantity of water required to produce a paste of standard consistency, is needed for the determination of the water content of mortar for tensile test, soundness test and setting time test.

   It is essential that cement set neither too rapidly nor too slowly. In the first case there might be insufficient time to transport and place the concrete before it becomes too rigid. In the second case too long a setting period tends to slow up the work unduly, also it might postpone the actual use of the structure because of inadequate strength at the desired age. Setting should not be confused with hardening, which refers to the gain in mechanical strength after the certain degree of resistance to the penetration of a special attachment pressed into it. Two periods of times are used to assess the setting behaviour. These are called the "initial setting time" and the "final setting time".

3. **Apparatus**–Vicat's apparatus with Vicat's plunger, vicat's needle and vicat's mould, Gauging trowel, measuring jar, weighing balance, stop watch, rice plate.

(A) STANDARD CONSISTENCY

4. **Procedure**–Standard consistency of cement paste is defined as the consistency which will permit the Vicat's plunger to penetrate to a point 5 to 7mm from bottom of the Vicat mould. For preparing one mould, take 400 gms of cement and prepare a paste of the cement with a weighed quantity of water, taking care that the time of gauging is not less than 3 minutes and not more than 5 minutes.

   (b) Gauging time is counted from the time of adding water to the dry cement until commencing to fill the mould. Fill the Vicat mould with this paste, the mould resting upon non porous plate.

   (c) After completely filling the mould, smoothen off the surface of the paste, making it level with the top of the mould. The mould may be slightly shaken to expel air.

   (d) Place the test block in the mould (Fig. 1.2 with the non-porous plate resting under the rod, bearing the plunger (G) lower the plunger gently to touch the surface of the test block and quickly, release, allowing it to sink into the paste.

   (e) Prepare trial paste with varying percentages of water (firstly at an interval of 4%, that is of 28%, 32% and 36% and then at an interval of 1% and 0.25% between the percentage range determined by the previous test) and test as described in step (a) to step (d) until the amount of water necessary for making up the standard consistency as defined is found.

(B) INITIAL AND FINAL SETTING TIMES

(a) Take 400 gms of cement and prepare a neat cement paste with 0.85P of water by weight of cement where P = standard consistency of cement as found in part (A).

(b) Gauge time is kept between 3 to 5 minutes. Start the stop watch at the instant when the water is added to the cement.

(c) Fill the Vicat mould with cement and smoothen the surface of the paste making it level with the top of the mould. The cement block thus prepared is known as the test block.

(d) For initial setting time place the test block confined in the mould and resting on non porous plate under the rod bearing the needle -C, lower the needle gently in contact with the surface of the test block.

(e) In the beginning the needle completely pierces the test block. Repeat this procedure until the needle

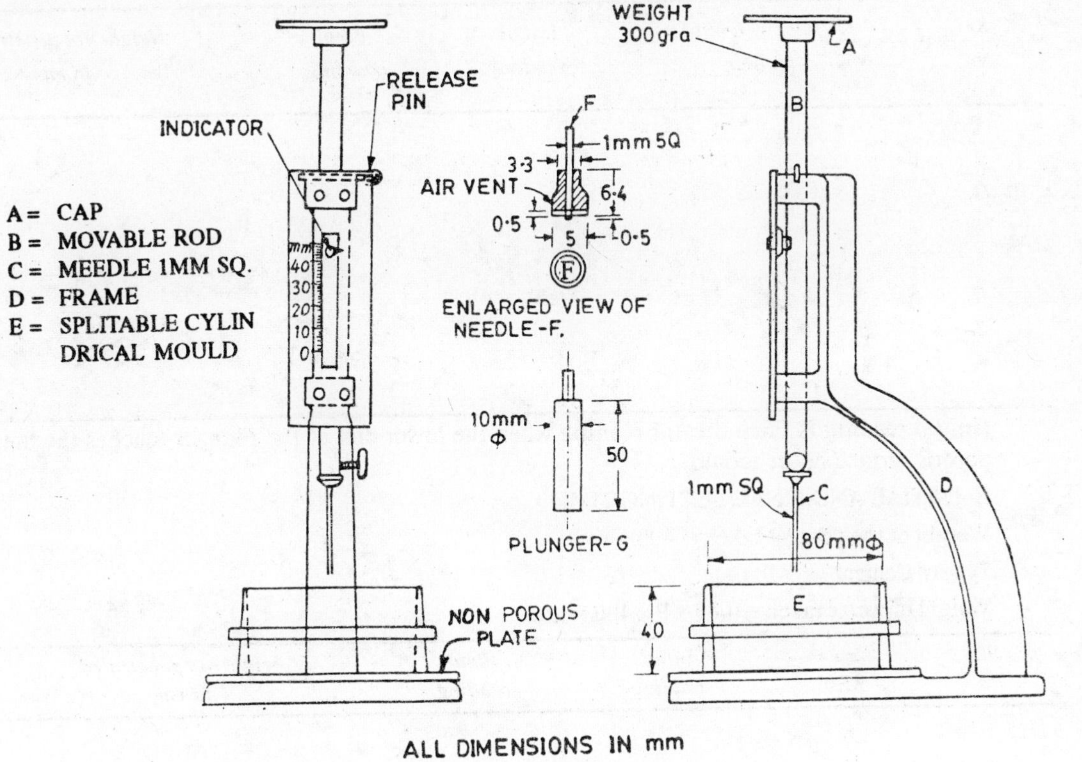

Fig. 1.2 Vicat's Apparatus

fails to pierce the block for about 5mm measured from the bottom of the mould.

(f) The period elapsing between the time when water is added to the cement and the time at which the needle fails to pierce the test block by about 5mm is the initial setting time.

(g) For determining the final setting time, replace the needle of the Vicat's apparatus by the needle with an annular attachment. (Needle-F)

(h) The cement is considered finally set when upon applying the final setting needle gently to the surface of the test block, the needle makes an impression thereon, while the attachment fails to do so. The period elapsing between the time when water is added to the cement and the time at which the needle makes an impression on the surface of test block while the attachment fails to do so shall be the final setting time.

In the event of a scum forming on the surface of the test block, use under side of the block for the determination of final setting time.

5. Observations and Calculations

A–STANDARD CONSISTENCY

Weight of Cement taken for one mould=400 gms.

Type of Cement

Sr. No.	*% of weight of water*	*Initial reading*	*Final reading*	*Height not penetrated in mm*
1.				
2.				
3.				
4.				
5.				
6.				
7.				
8.				

(Initial reading is the indicator reading when the lower-end of the plunger touches the bottom non porous surface of the mould).

B–INITIAL AND FINAL SETTING TIME

Weight of the cement taken = 400 gms.

Type of Cement ....

Weight of water taken = 0.85 x P x 400 = gms.

Sl. No.	*time in Min.*	*Intial reading*	*Final reading*	*height not penetrated in mm*
1.				
2.				
3.				
4.				
5.				
6				

6. Results

(a) Standard consistency of cement = %

(b) Initial setting time of the cement = Mins.

Final setting time of the cement = Mints.

6. Precautions

(a) The cement balls if any should be powdered before adding water to the cement.

(b) While preparing the test block do not press the cement in the mould.

(c) Release the initial and final setting times needles gently.

(d) The experiment should be performed away from vibrations and other disturbances.

8. Comments

Comment on test results obtained by you in laboratory. Compare your values with the standard values for the type of cement used by you. Give your comments on the suitability of using the cement sample tested by you on a construction site.

9. Questions

(a) What do you understand by the terms 'standard consistency, initial setting time and final setting time of a cement sample ?

(b) What is the importance of the above three tests ?

(c) What precautions do you observe in performing the above tests ?

(d) What is gauge time ? What is its importance ?

(e) What are the I.S. Specifications for setting times of various types of cements recommended for use on a construction site.

(f) What is the weight of the moving part of the Vicats apparatus and what are the dimensions of the plunger and initial setting time needle ?

(g) What is the amount of water required for initial setting time.

(h) How is the rate of setting of portland cement controlled in manufacturing process ?

(i) What is difference between setting and hardening ?

EXPERIMENT NO. 1/3

SOUNDNESS

1. **Object**–To determine the soundness of given cement by (i) Lechatelier's method (ii) autoclave Test.
2. **Theory**–Once of the most important properties of cement is its soundness. Unsoundness in cement is caused by undue expansion of some of the constituents like free lime produced in the manufacturing process of cement. Another possible cause of unsoundness is the presence of too high a magnesia content in the cement. As the cement absorbs moisture, free lime expands to many times its original volume and develops considerable heat both of which are injurious to concrete. The immediate hydration of free lime may not take place because lime after the cement is set and since lime expands manifold and with considerable force when hydrated, its delayed hydration may readily disrupt the mass. One advantage of slow setting cement is that more time is given to hydrate the lime before the mass becomes rigid.

   In the soundness test a specimen of hardened cement paste is boiled for a fixed time so that any tendency to expand is speeded up and can be detected.

1. LECHATELIER'S METHOD

3. **Apparatus**–Lechatelier's apparatus, two glass plates, temperature control water bath, scale.

   Lechatelier's apparatus is shown in Fig. 1.3. It consists of a small split cylinder of spring Brass of other suitable metal of 0.5mm thickness forming a mould of 30mm internal diameter and 30mm high. Either end of the split are attache to two indicators with pointed ends AA, the distance from these ends to the centre of the cylinder being 165mm. The mould shall kept in good condition with not more than 0.5mm apart.
4. **Procedure**

   (a) Place the mould on a glass sheet and fill it with the cement paste formed by gauging cement with 0.78 times the water required to give a paste of Standard consisting (approximately 30%), keeping the edge of the mould gently together.

   (b) Cover the mould with another glass plate, placing a small weight on the covering glass plate and immediately submerge the whole assembly in water at a temperature of 27 ± 2^0C and keep there for 24 hours.

   (c) Measure the distance D_1 between the indicator points after 24 hours and again submerge the mould in the water at a temp. given in step (b).

   (d) Bring the water to boiling in 25 to 30 minutes and keep it boiling for 3 hours.

   (e) Remove the mould form the water, allow it to cool and measure the distance D_2 between the indicator points.

   (f) The difference (D_2–D_1) between the two measurements give expansion of cement and it should not be more than 10mm according to IS specifications.
5. **Observations and Calculations**

   Type of cement

   Intial distance between the indicator points D_1 = mm

   Final distance between the indicator points D_2 = mm

   Expansion of Cement D_2–D_1 = mm
6. **Results**

   Soundness of cement = mm

7. **Precautions :**

(a) Note the measurements D_1, D_2, D_3 . accurately.

(b) Do not apply extra pressure while filling the moulds.

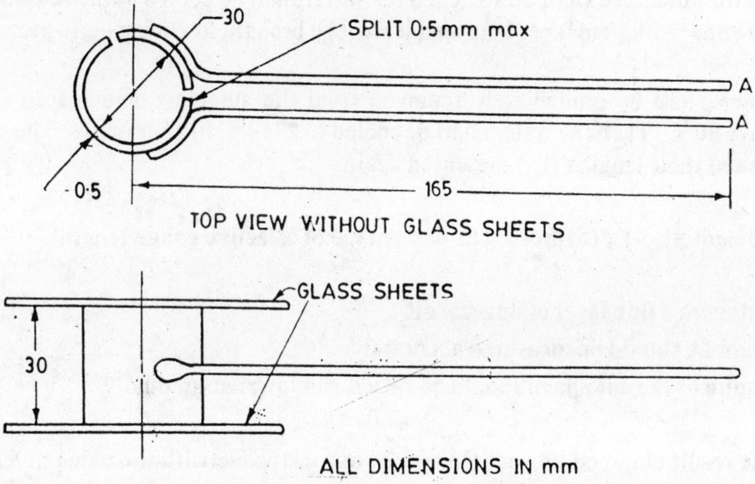

Fig. 1.3 Apparatus for 'Lee chatelier' Test

(c) Cooling the samples should be gradual.

8. **Comments**

Comment on the test results and compare your values with those given in IS specifications. Do you recommend the use of the cement sample tested by you in your laboratory for Civil Engineering construction.

II. AUTOCLAVE TEST

1. **Apparatus–**

Scale, weights, graduated glass cylinders; trowel, length comparator, moulds 25 × 25 × 250 mm size.

2. **Procedure :**

This method of test is intended for determining the soundness of port-land cement by means of an autoclave test on a 25 × 25 × 250 mm neat cement specimen.

(a) Moulds shall be thinly covered with mineral oil. Then the reference point which are clan and free from oil shall be set.

(b) 500 gm of cement shall be mixed with sufficient water to given a paste of standard consistency.

(c) After mixing, the moulds shall be filled in one or two layers by pressing the paste into corners by thumb. Then the top level shall be smoothened by trowel.

(d) After preparing the mould, they shall be stored in a moist room and after 24 hours the specimens shall be taken out of the mould.

(e) At 24 ± ½ hrs. after moulding, the specimen shall be removed from the moist atmosphere, measured for length and placed into the autoclave at room temperature in a rack so that the four sides of each specimen shall be exposed to saturated steam. The autoclave shall contain enough water to maintain an atmosphere of saturated steam vapour during the entire period of test. Ordinarily 7 to 10% of the volume of the autoclave shall be occupied by the water.

(f) To permit air to escape from the autoclave during the early portion of the heating period, the vent value shall be left open until stem begins to escape. The valve shall then be closed and the temperature of the autoclave shall be raised at such a rate as will bring the gauge pressure of the steam to 2.1 N/mm^2 (21 kg/cm^2) in 1 to 1½ hrs. from the time the heat is turned on. The 2 ± 0.1 N/mm^2 (20± 1 kg/cm^2) pressure shall be maintained.

(g) After 3 hrs. the autoclave shall be switched off and it shall be cooled at the rate so as to lower the pressure by 0.1 N/mm^2 (1 kg/cm^2) per hour and it shall be brought to atmospheric pressure by opening the vent valve.

(h) The specimen shall be immediately removed from the autoclave and placed in the water of temperature above 90^{0}C. Then the water shall be cooled to 27±2^{0}C in 15 minutes. The specimens shall be surface dried and their lengths (L_2) measured again.

3. Results :

Soundness of cement =L_1–L_2 (expressed as percentage of effective gauge length).

4. Precautions :

(a) Oil the moulds with a thin layer of mineral oil.

(b) Lengths L_1 and L_2 should be measured accurately.

(d) The temperature of the autoclave should be raised and lowered gradually.

5. Comments :-

Comment on the result obtained by you. Compare your test value with the value given in the Indian Standard code for the type of cement tested by you.

6. Questions :

(a) What do you mean by soundness of cement ?

(b) What is the diameter of Lechateliers apparatus ?

(c) What is meant by unsoundness and how it is caused ?

(d) What is likely to cause unsound cement ?

(e) What is the importance of soundness of cement ?

(f) How is the hydration accelerated in the experiment ?

(g) What precautions does a manufacturer take to prevent unsound cement ?

(h) Distinguish between expansion and shrinkage of cement paste.

(i) What is the cause of free lime in cement ?

(j) Why it is necessary to keep the cement paste moist in this test while it is setting ?

(k) What is the maximum expansion for ordinary portland cement ?

EXPERIMENT NO. 1/4

COMPRESSIVE STRENGTH

1. **Object :**

To determine the compressive strength of cement.

2. **Theory :**

The mechanical strength of hardened cement is the property of the material that is needed in structural design. Strength tests are not made on a neat cement paste because of difficulties of moulding and testing with a consequent large variability of test, results. The strength of cement is usually determined from tests on mortar made with cement. The compressive strength of cement is determined as represented by compressive strength tests on mortar cubes compacted by means of a standard vibration machine. The standard sand shall be used in the test which shall conform to IS ; 650-1966. The specimens shall be in the form of cubes 70.6mm × 70.6mm × 70.6mm. The parts of the mould when assembled shall be positively held together and suitable methods of ensuring this, both during the filling and on a subsequent removal of the filled mould from the vibration machine shall be provided in order to prevent the moulded specimen from damage.

3. **Apparatus :**

70.6mm x 70.6mm ($50 cm^2$) cube moulds, apparatus for gauging and mixing mortar, compression testing machine etc.

4. **Procedure :**

(a) Gauge a mixture of cement and regraded Indian Standard sand in the proportion of 1 : 3 by weight using (P/4 + 3.0) percent of water where P is the percentage of water required to produce a paste of standard consistency.

(b) Fill the cube moulds by compacting it for 2 minutes on a vibrating machine at a speed of 12,000±400 vibrations per minute.

(c) Smoothen the top surface of the cubes with flat side of a trowel.

(d) Immediately upon completion of moulding, place the cube moulds in an atmosphere of $27^0C \pm 2^0C$ and relative humidity over 90%. After 24 hours, remove the specimens from the moulds and keep them in water till testing.

(e) Test the cubes at 3 days and 7 days age in the compression testing machine at such a rate that maximum load is reached in 80-100 seconds.

(f) Report the average compressive strength in N/mm^2 (kg/cm^2).

5. **Observations and Calculations**

Weight of cement for one cube = 200 gms

Weight of sand (3 particlé sizes

200 + 200 + 200 = 600 gms.) for one cub = 600 gms.

Weight of water for one cube = $\left(\frac{P}{4} + 3.0\right)\%$

Area of cube face = $50\ cm^2 = 5000\ mm^2$

Where **P** = Standard consistency of cement as determined earlier by Standard consistency test of cement.

Sample No.	At 3 day's Age			At 7 day's Age		
	Load (Newtons)	Camp. Stress (N/mm^2)	Average	Load (N)	Camp. Stress (N/mm^2)	Average
1						
2						
3						

6. Results :

The average value of compressive strength of cement sand mortar cubes at 3 and 7 days age were found to be = ... N/mm^2 at 3 days

=........... N/mm^2 at 7 days.

7. Precautions :

(a) The moulds should be oiled before use.

(b) The weighings should be done accurately.

(c) The temperature and humidity must be accurately controlled.

(d) Increase the load during testing gradually.

8. Discussion :

Comment on the 3 days' and 7 days' results obtained by you and compare with the standard values recommended by IS Code. Do you recommend the use of the cement sample tested by you on a construction site ?

9. Questions :

(a) What is the percentage of water required for preparing 1:3 cement sand mortar for compressive strength test ?

(b) What is the significance of this test ?

(c) What are the IS specifications for compressive strength of 1:3 cement sand mortar after 3 days and 7 days?

(d) What is the minimum number of specimens to be made for each age of testing ?

(e) How is the curing of a test specimen done ?

(f) Why should not the specimen be allowed to dry until they are tested ?

(g) What is the rate of loading ?

(h) How can you be sure that the cement and sand are thoroughly mixed ?

(i) Is it true that the cement, sand and water are mixed together ?

EXPERIMENT NO. 1/5

SPECIFIC GRAVITY

1. **Object**–To determine specific gravity of a cement sample.
2. **Theory**–The specific gravity of a cement is not a property normally determined for its own sake, but it is required in the measurement of its specific surface. The specific gravity is defined as the ratio between the weight of a given volume of cement and weight of an equal volume of water. The test for finding the specific gravity of Portland cement was originally considered to be of value in detecting adulteration and underburning, but is no longer thought to be of much importance in view of the fact that other tests lead to more definite conclusions. The most popular method of determining the specific gravity of cement is by the use of a liquid such as water free kerosene which does not react with cement. A specific gravity bottle or a standard Le-chatelier flask may be used.
3. **Apparatus**

   Specific gravity bottle, Le-chatelier flask, kerosene free from water, weighing balance, constant temperature water bath etc.
4. **Procedure**

   A-Using specific gravity bottle (Fig. 1.4)

   (a) Weigh the specific gravity bottle dry (W_1)

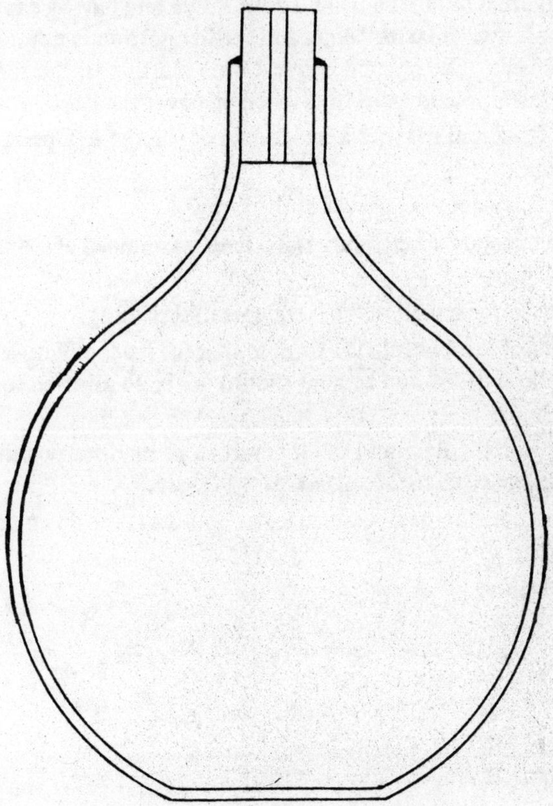

Fig. 1.4–Specific Gravity Bottle

(b) Fill the bottle with distilled water and weight the bottle (W_2)

(c) Dry the specific gravity bottle and fill it with kerosene and weight (W_3)

(d) Pour some of the kerosene out and introduce a weighed quantity of cement (say about 60 gms.) into the bottle. Roll the bottle gently in the inclined position until no further air bubble rise to the surface. Fill the bottle to the top with kerosene and weigh it (W_4)

5. **Observations and Calculations**

(a) Weight of empty dry bottle (W_1) = gms

(b) Weight of bottle + water (W_2) = gms

(c) Weight of bottle + Kerosene (W_3) = gms

(d) Weight of bottle + Cement + Kerosene (W_4) = gms

(e) Weight of cement (W_5) = gms

Specific gravity of kerosene = g = $\dfrac{W_3 - W_1}{W_2 - W_1}$

Specific gravity of cement = G = $\dfrac{W_5(W_3 - W_1)}{(W_5 + W_3 - W_4)(W_2 - W_1)}$

B - Using Le chatelier Flask (Fig. 1.5)

The Le-chatelier flask is made of thin glass having a bulb (having nearly 250ml capacity) at the bottom. The diameter of the bulb is 78mm. The stem is graduated in millilitres. The zero mark is placed at a distance of 8mm from the top of the bulb. Then from zero a distance of 10mm is measured and divided into ten parts. After leaving 10mm distance more, there is another bulb of length 35mm and having capacity of 17mls. Again after 10mm length of stem, the stem is marked with 18mls and further portion is graduated upto 24mls. The total capacity of stem and bulb is 24mls. The portion above 24mls mark is in the form of a funnel having top diameter equal to 50mm. A glass nipple is fitted in the stem to cover the flask.

(a) Dry the Le-chatelier flask and fill with kerosene oil or Naptha to a point on the stem between zero and one ml.

(b) Dry the inside of the flask above the level of the liquid.

(c) Immerse the flask in a constant temperature water bath maintained at room temperature for sufficient time.

(d) Record the level of the kerosene oil in the flask as initial reading.

(e) Introduce about 60gms of cement into the flask so that the level of kerosene rises to about say 22ml mark. Splashing should be avoided and cement should not be to allowed to adhere to the sides of the flask above the liquid.

(f) Insert the glass nipple into the flask and roll it gently in an inclined position to free the cement from air until no further air bubble rises to the surface of the liquid.

(g) Keep the flask again in constant temperature water both and note down the new liquid level as final reading.

Observations and Calculations

(a) Air temperature = ^{0}C

(b) Weight of Cement used = gms

(c) Initial reading of flask = mls

(d) Final reading of flask = mls

(e) Volume of cement particles (d–c) = mls

(f) Weight of equal volume of water = gms

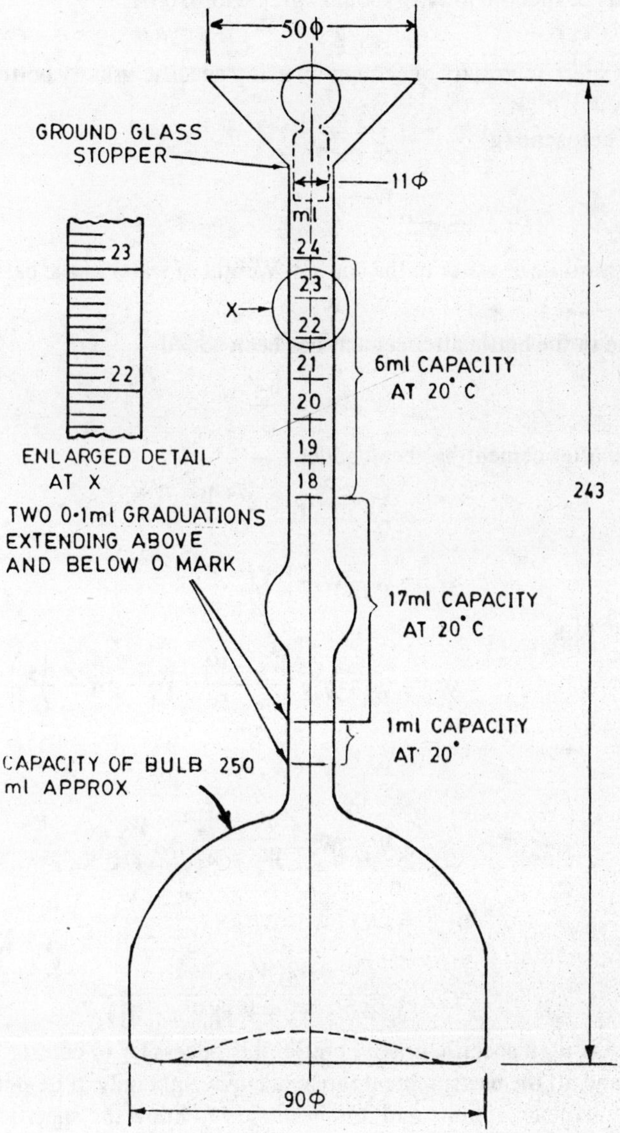

Fig. 1.5–Le-chatelier Flask

(g) Specific gravity $= \dfrac{\text{Weight of cement of given volume}}{\text{Weight of equal volume of water}}$

6. **Precautions**

(a) While pouring cement in the specific gravity bottle or Le-chatelier flask, care should be taken to avoid splashing and cement should not adhere to the inside of the flask above the liquid.

(b) The kerosene or Naptha should be completely free from water.

(c) The specific gravity bottle or the Le-chatelier flask should be kept in a constant temperature water bath sufficiently long to ensure same temperature before each weighing is made.

(d) Duplicate results of specific gravity should agree within 0.01.

7. **Comments**

The expression for specific gravity of cement by using specific gravity bottle is derived as below :

Specific gravity of kerosene (g) $= \frac{W_3 - W_1}{W_2 - W_1}$

Volume of Cement $= \frac{W_5}{G}$

Volume of bottle = Volume of water in the bottle = Weight of water in the battle

$= W_2 - W_1$

Volume of kerosene in the bottle after cement has been added

$= W2 - W1 - \frac{W_5}{G}$

Weight of kerosene after cement has been added

$$= \left(W_2 - W_1 - \frac{W_5}{G} \right) \text{x } g$$

Therefore $W_4 = W_1 + W_5 + \left(W_2 - W_1 - \frac{W_5}{G} \right) g$

Substitute the value of g

$$W_4 = W_1 + W_5 + \frac{W_3 - W_1}{W_2 - W_1} \left(W_2 - W_1 - \frac{W_5}{G} \right)$$

$$= W_1 + W_5 + W_3 - W1 - \frac{W_3 - W_1}{W_2 - W_1} \text{ X } \frac{W_5}{G}$$

$$= W5 + W3 - \frac{W_3 - W_1}{W_2 - W_1} \text{ X } \frac{W_5}{G}$$

Or $\frac{W_5}{G} = (W5 + W3 - W4) \text{ X } \frac{W_2 - W_1}{W_3 - W_1}$

Or $G = \frac{W_5(W_3 - W_1)}{(W_5 + W_3 - W_4)(W_2 - W_1)}$

While conducting test with specific gravity bottle, it is necessary to determine the specific gravity of kerosene or naptha used and all the measurements are made in weight only. If Le-chatelier flask is used, some of the measurements are made by volume and it is necessary to know the specific gravity of kerosene, the usual value of which is 0.8. The specific gravity of portland cement varies from 3.1 to 3.15 and that of portland blast furnace cement varies from 3.0 to 3.05.

8. **Questions**

(a) Differentiate between density and specific gravity of a material.

(b) State the importance of this test.

(c) Out of the above two methods, which method you will prefer.

(d) What is the effect on the specific gravity value if the air bubbles are not removed completely.

(e) Why constant temperature bath is used in this experiments.

(f) Why do we use kerosene or naptha in this experiment. ?

EXPERIMENT NO. 1/6

HEAT OF HYDRATION OF LOW HEAT PORTLAND CEMENT

1. **Object**–To determine the heat of hydration of low Heat Portland Cement.
2. **Theory**–The silicates and aluminates of Cement react with water to form a binding medium, which solidifies into a hardened mass. This reaction by virtue of which portland cement becomes a binding medium is termed hydration. The hydration of cement is exothermic with approximately 120 Cal/g being liberated.

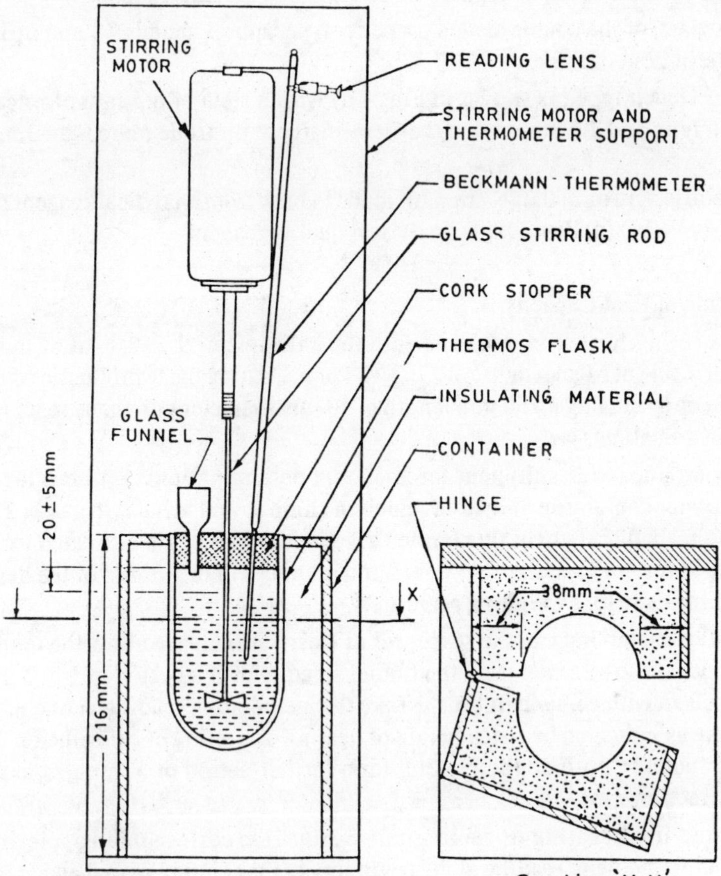

FIG.1.6.

Fig. 1.6

In the interior of a large concrete mass, the hydration can result in a large rise in temperature. At the same time the exterior of the concrete mass looses some heat so that a steep temperature gradient may be established and during the subsequent cooling of the interior, severe cracking may occur. On the other hand, the heat of hydration may be advantageous in preventing the freezing of water in the capillaries of freshly placed concrete in cold weather.

The heat of hydration is the quantity of heat in calories per gram of unhydrated cement, evolved upon its complete hydration at a given temperature. The conventional way of determining heat of hydration is by measuring the heats of solution of unhydrated and hydrated cement in a mixture of nitric and hydroflouric acids. The difference of the heat of solutions of the two is the heat of hydration of the cement. The heat of hydration of the cement shall be calculated at 7 and 28 days and to the nearest 0.1 calorie.

3. Apparatus–Calorimeter, a thermometer, stirrer and funnel, Analytical Quality Reagents.

The calorimeter (Fig. 1.6) consists of an open-mouthed thermos flask of about 150 x 70 mm dia. with a cork lid 38 mm thick, an insulated container for the flask, a Beckmann thermometer (range 6^0C) with reading lens, a constant speed stirrer, and a funnel for introducing the sample. If flask 150 x 70 mm is not obtainable, a flask 150 x 75 mm shall be substituted.

The container consists of insulating layer of cork, cotton wood or the like, at least 25 mm thick, completely enclosing the flask, and shall also provide support for the flask and the stirrer motor.

The stirrer is of glass, of the double bladed propeller type, approximately 38 mm in dia, and shall extend to within 38 mm of the bottom of flask.

The funnel is of Gooch type (as shown in Fig. 1.6) with a stem of 6.5 mm of internal dia and a body approximately 25 mm long and 2.5 mm in dia. the stem shall not protrude more than 3 mm beneath the cork stopper.

Reagents –(a) Nitric acid of 2±0.05N strength made in bulk from analytical reagent quality materials (b) Hydrofluoric acid (40% W/W) (c) Zinc Oxide analytical quality reagent.

4. Procedure

(a) Determination of Heat Capacity :-

Inspect the wax lining for faults. Measure into the calorimeter 9.6±0.1 ml of hydrofluoric acid and 388±0.1 ml of 2.0N nitric acid at a temperature of 27±2^0C. For measuring the hydrofluoric acid, a small measuring cylinder shall be made up by sealing a 150 mm length of 10 mm diameter polythene resin tube to a flat plate of the same material with a small gas jar.

Take a quantity of zinc oxide sufficient for about six determinations. Ignite it for one hour at 900 to 950^0C. Cool in a desiccator containing anhydrous calcium chloride and grind it to pass a 250 micron IS Sieve. For each determination, about 7.0 gm of this ignited zinc oxide shall again be heated to 900^0 to 950^0C for 5 minutes and then cooled for not less than 2 ½ hours and not more than 5 hours in the desiccator containing anhydrous calcium chloride before weighing accurately.

Assemble the calorimeter and run the stirrer for at least 5 minutes to allow the temperature to become uniform. Then introduce the zinc oxide from the funnel steadily over a period of 1 to 2 minutes. The funnel shall then be brushed clean with camel hair brush. Take the temperature reading at one minute intervals until the solution is complete as indicated by a steady rate of heating or cooling of calorimeter. The solution period shall not exceed 20 minutes. Continue the reading for a further period of 5 minutes to determine the final heating or cooling correction.

Plot the initial and final heating or cooling rate against the corresponding calorimeter temperature, namely, the Beckmann thermometer reading at the beginning of the solution period and at the end respectively. Join the two points by a straight line (Fig. 1.7). From this graph, the corrections are read off for each temperature reading during the solution period.

(b) Calculation of heat capacity :-

Heat capacity (cal/^{0}C)

$$= \frac{\text{Weight of Zno (g)}}{\text{Corrected temperature rise}} \times [(256.1 + 0.1\,(30 - \phi) + 0.1\,(\phi_0 - \phi)]$$

Where 256.1 is the heat of solution of Zinc Oxide at 30^0C and 0.1 the negative temperature co-efficient of the heat of solution, ϕ is the final temperature of the calorimeter and contents in ^{0}C, the second 0.1 is the specific heat of Zinc Oxide and ϕ_0 is the room temperature in ^{0}C.

This expression simplifies to

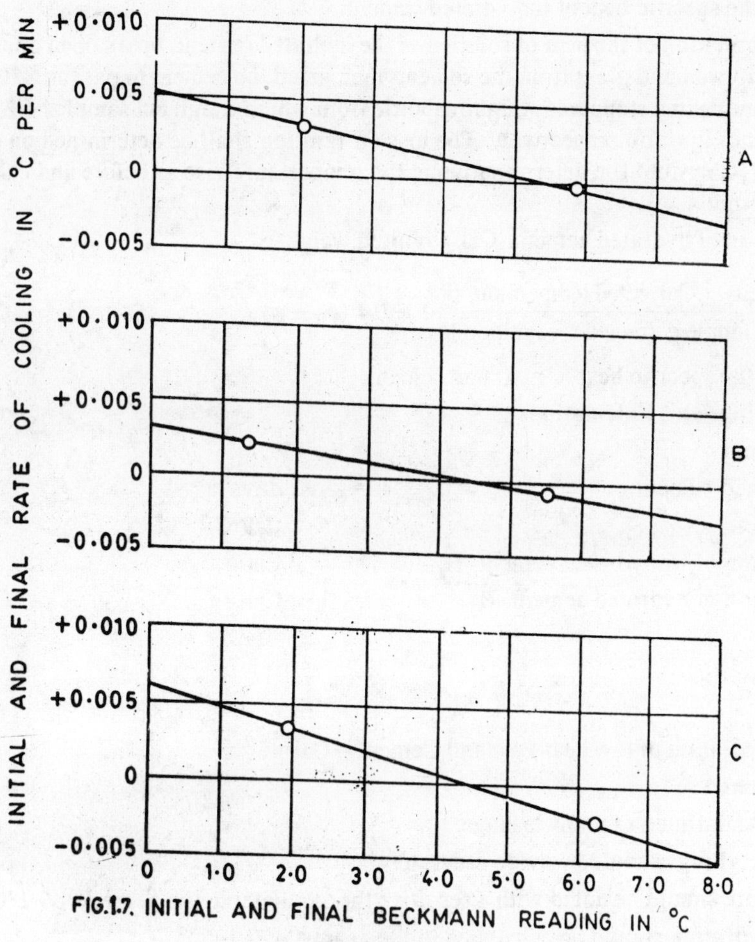

Fig. 1.7

$$\text{Heat Capacity (Cal/}^0\text{C)} = \frac{\text{Weight of ZnO } (259.1 - 0.2\phi + 0.1\phi)}{\text{Corrected temperature rise}}$$

(c) Preparation of Cement Sample :-

Mix by hand for 4 minutes 60 gm of cement and 24 ml of distilled water which shall be between 15^{0}C and 25^{0}C. Fill with this mixture 3 glass specimen vials 100 × 20mm, cork and then seal with wax. Store the specimen vials with a mixture in a vertical position at 27 ± 2^{0}C.

(d) Determination of the heat of solution :-

For the determination of heat of solution of unhydrated cement, weigh a sample of about 3 gm. At the same time weigh out another quantity approximately 7 gm for the loss on ignition. Both the weighings shall be correct to the nearest 0.001 gm. Carry out the determination of temperature rise exactly as described for zinc oxide. Calculate the heat of solution from the formula. Heat of solution (cal/g) of unhydrated cement :

$$= \frac{\text{Heat capacity x Corrected temp. rise}}{\text{Weight of sample corrected for Ignition Loss}} - 0.2(\phi_0 - \phi)$$

where 0.2 is the specific heat of unhydrated cement.

For the determination of the heat of solution of the hydrated cement, break open one of the glass vials. Remove the adherent wax and glass from the cement, then grind the cement to pass an 850 micron IS Sieve. Keep the ground sample in a stoppered weighing bottle from which weigh out samples 4.2 and 7 gm for heat of solution and loss of ignition respectively. The loss off ignition shall be determined on each sample used for heat of solution. Carry out the determination at the temperature-rise as before and calculate the heat of solution from the formula.

Heat of solution of hydrated cement (Cal/g ignited weight)

$$= \frac{\text{Heat capacity x Corrected temperature rise}}{\text{Weight of sample corrected for ignition loss}} - 0.4\ (\phi_0 - \phi)$$

Where 0.4 is the specific heat of hydrated cement.

5. Observations and Calculations

Type for cement	=	
Age of hydrated cement	=	days
Heat capacity	=	Cal/^{0}C
Heat of solution of Unhydrated cement, H_1	=	Cal/g
Heat of solution of hydrated cement, H_2	=	Cal/g
Ignition loss	=	
Heat of hydration	=	$\dot{H} = H_1 - H_2$ Cal/g

6. Results

Heat of hydration of low heat Portland Cement = Cal/g

7. Precautions

(a) Check the calorimeter for any leakage.

(b) All the weighings should be made accurately.

(c) Temperature should be noted with a sensitive thermometer to the nearest of 0.1^{0}C.

(d) Heat of hydration should be calculated to the nearest of 0.1 calorie.

8. Comments

Comment on the results obtained by you and compare these values with those of IS Specifications.

9. Questions

(a) Define heat of hydration of a cement.

(b) Why do you perform this experiment ?

(c) Define heat capacity and Ignition loss.

(d) Explain how thermal stresses are introduced in massive structures due to cement hydration ?

(e) Which compounds of cement contribute more to its heat of hydration ?

(f) Will a Portland Pozzolana cement exhibit a higher or lower value of heat of hydration ? And why ?

EXPERIMENT NO. 1/7

DRYING SHRINKAGE OF PORTLAND POZZOLANA CEMENT

1. **Object**–To determine drying shrinkage of Portland Pozzolana Cement.
2. **Theory**–Withdrawl of water from concrete stored in unsaturated air causes drying shrinkage. When concrete is cast and cured under wet conditions and then after stipulated time it is dried, it shrinks during drying process. This property is called drying shrinkage. The importance of shrinkage in structures is largely related to cracking. Strictly speaking the engineer is concerned with the cracking tendency as the advent or absence of cracking depends not only on the potential contraction but also on the extensibility of concrete, its strength and its degree of restraint to the deformation that may lead to cracking.
3. **Apparatus**–Scale, weights, trowel, length comparator, flow table etc.
4. **Procedure**

(a) Moulds of the size 25 x 25 mm in section and 250 mm long are prepared which are coated with thin layer of mineral oil.

(b) Dry materials for the standard test mortar shall be portland pozzolan cement : standard sand in proportion of 1 :3 by weight is taken.

(c) The materials for each batch of moulds are mixed separately using the quantities of dry materials, conforming to the proportion given in step (b) above and the quantity of water as determined in accordance with the procedure given in the test for determination of compressive strength of masonary cement.

(d) Mixing is done mechanically.

(e) Immediately after mixing the ingredients, the test specimen is moulded in two layers, each layer being compacted with the thumbs and forefingers by pressing the mortar into the corners, until a homogeneous specimen is obtained. After the top layer has been compacted, the mortar shall be levelled off flush with the top of the mould and the surface smoothed with a few strokes of the trowel. During the operations of mixing and moulding, the hands shall be protected by rubber gloves.

(f) After filling the moulds, place them immediately in a moist room or moist closet for 24 ± 2 hours. Then remove the specimens from the moulds and immediately immerse in water at $27^0 \pm 2^0$C and allow them to remain there for six days.

(g) Remove the specimens from the water and measure its length using a length comparator. Protect specimens against loss of moisture prior to reading for initial length.

(h) Store the specimens in a closet or room maintained at $27^0 \pm 2^0$C and 50 ± 5 percent relative humidity. Measure the length of the specimens again at 28 days after the initial measurement.

(i) Place the specimens in the comparator with respect to the position of the specimens as when the initial measurement was made. When making the measurements, the specimens, comparator, and the reference bar shall be at a temperature of 27 ± 2^0C.

5. **Observations and Calculations**

	I	II	III
Initial length of specimen (in mm) (at the Age of 7 days)			
Final length of Specimen : (at the Age of 35 days)			
Difference in length of Specimen :			
Average difference in length of			

three specimen = ________ mm.

6. **Results**

Drying shrinkage of portland pozzolana cement = ________mm

7. **Precautions**

(a) At the materials should be weighed to an accuracy of 1 in 1000.
(b) The moulds should be oiled lightly before use.
(c) Compaction of the specimen should be done by pressing it with the thumbs and forefingers.
(d) The specimen should not be allowed to dry.
(e) All the dimensions of the specimen should be noted accurately.

8. **Comments**

During setting very slight expansion due to hydration of cement takes place but on subsequent drying, it shrinks. Most of the drying shrinkage takes place during the first few weeks.

9. **Questions**

(a) Define drying shrinkage of cement.
(b) What is the effect of this shrinkage on concrete members ?
(c) How is shrinkage affected by the curing conditions ?
(d) How is the shrinkage of cement paste related to its fineness ?
(e) Explain the term carbonation shrinkage.
(f) Differentiate between shrinkage and creep.

EXPERIMENT NO. 1/8

WATER RETENTIVITY OF MASONARY CEMENT

1. **Object**–To determine the water retentivity of masonary cement.

2. **Theory**–Masonary cement used in mortar in brickwork is made by intergrinding very finely ground Portland, Cement, limestone and an air entraining agent, or alternatively portland cement and hydrated lime, granulated slag or an inert filler, and an air entraining agent. Masonary cements make a more plastic mortar than ordinary Portland Cement. They also have a greater water retaining power and lead to lower shrinkage. The strength of masonary cements is lower than that of ordinary portland cement, particularly since a high air content is introduced. But this low strength is generally an advantage in brick construction. Masonary cement must not be used in structural concrete.

3. **Apparatus**– Apparatus Assembly, straight Edge, Mixing apparatus.

   Apparatus Assembly for the water retention consists of a water aspirator or other source of vacuum controlled by a mercury column relief and connected by way of a three-way stopcork to a funnel upon which rests a perforated dish (see fig. 1.8). The perforated dish shall be made of metal not attacked by masonary mortar. The metal in the base of the dish shall have a thickness of 1.7 to 1.9 mm. The bore of the stopcock shall be 4 mm diameter and the connecting glass tubing shall have a minimum inside diameter of 4 mm. A mercury manometer, connected as shown in Fig. (1.8) indicates the vacuum. A synthetic rubber gasket shall be permanently sealed to the top of the funnel and is lightly coated with petrolium or light cup grease during a test to ensure a seal between the funnel and dish. Hardened filter paper of a grade equivalent to Whatman No. 50 filter paper is used.

4. **Procedure**

   (a) Adjust the mercury relief column so as to maintain a vacuum of 50mm as measured on the manometer. Seat the perforated dish on the greased gasket of the funnel.

   (b) Place a wetted filter paper in the bottom of the dish.

   (c) Turn the stopcock to apply the vacuum to the funnel and check the apparatus for leaks and to determine that the required suction is obtained.

   (d) Turn stopcock to shut off the vacuum from the funnel.

   (e) Mix the mortar consisting of one part of masonary cement and 3 parts of standard sand; by volume to a consistency to give a flow of 110 ± 5.

   (f) Immediately after making the flow test, return the mortar on the flow table to the mixing bowl and remix the entire batch for 15 seconds at medium speed.

   (g) Immediately after remixing of the mortar, fill the perforated dish with the mortar to slightly above the rim.

   (h) Tamp the mortar 15 times with the tamper. The tamping pressure shall be just sufficient to ensure filling of the dish. On completion of tamping, the top of the mortar should extend slightly above the rim of the dish.

   (i) Smooth off the mortar by drawing the flat side of the straight edge across the top of the dish.

   (j) Cut off the mortar to a plane surface flush with the rim of the dish by drawing the straight edge with a sawing motion across the top of the dish in two cutting strokes, starting each cut from near the centre of the dish. If the mortar is pulled away from the side of the dish during the process of drawing the straight edge across the dish, gently press the mortar back into contact with the sides of dish using the tamper.

   (k) Turn the stopcock to apply the vacuum to the funnel. The time elapsed from the start of mixing the cement and water to the time of applying the vacuum shall not exceed 8 minutes.

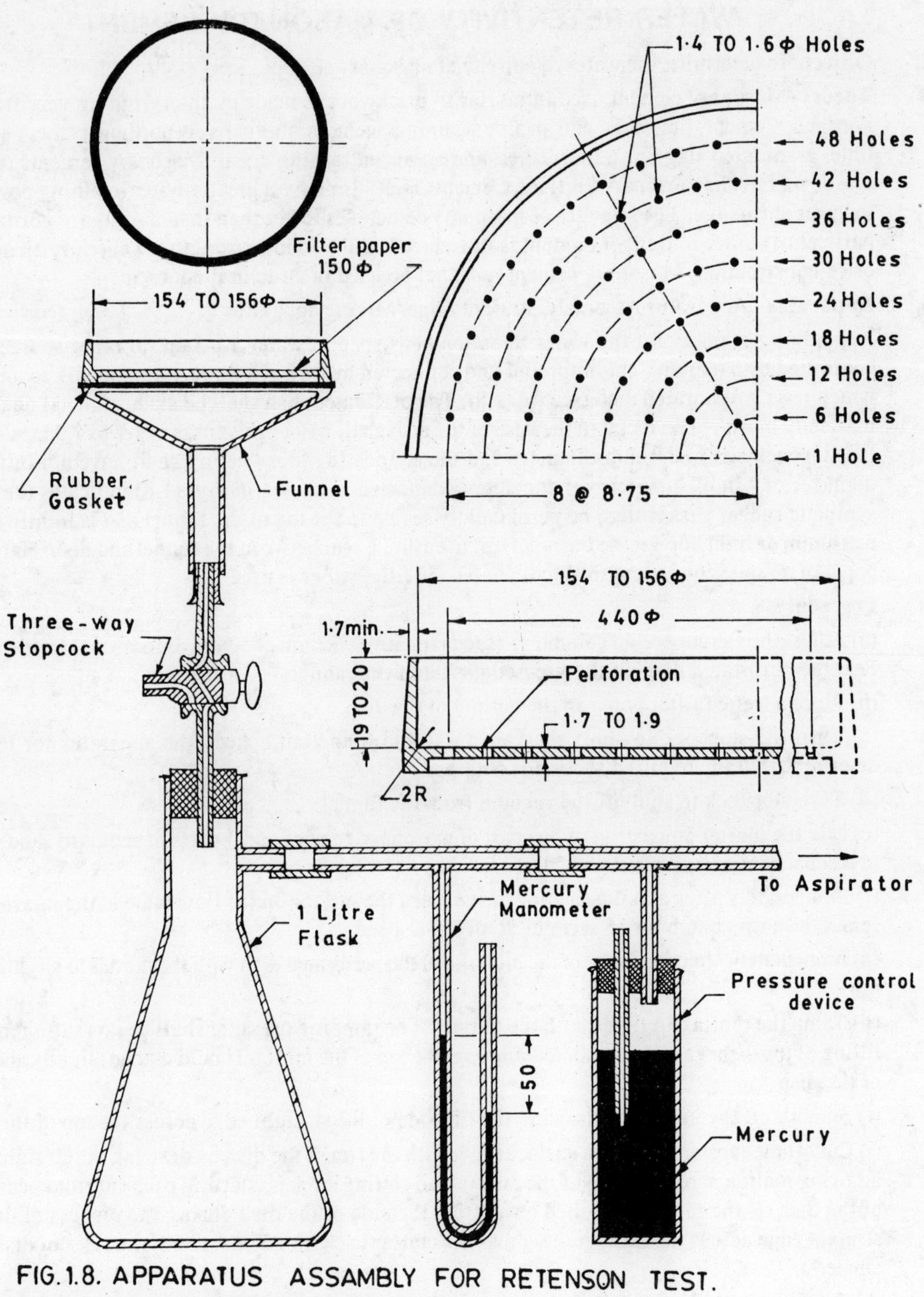

FIG. 1.8. APPARATUS ASSAMBLY FOR RETENSON TEST.

Fig. 1.8

(l) After suction for 60 seconds quickly turn the stopcock to expose the funnel to atmospheric pressure. Immediately slide the perforated dish off from the funnel, touch it momentarily on a damp cloth to remove droplets of water and set the dish on the table.

(m) Using the bowl scraper plow and mix the mortar in the dish for 15 seconds. Upon completion of mixing, place the mortar in the flow mould and determine the flow. The entire operation shall be carried out without interruption and as quickly as possible and shall be completed within an elapsed time of 11 minutes after the start of mixing the cement and water for the first flow determination.

5. Observations and Calculations

Flow immediately after mixing = A

Flow after suction = B

Water retention value $= \frac{B}{A} \times 100$

6. Results

%age of water retention of masonary cement = __________%

7. Precautions

(a) Check the water retention assembly for any leakages before use.

(b) The mercury should not split out of the manometer.

(c) Check the seal of the gasket at the top of the funnel.

(d) Use only hardened filter paper.

(e) After applying vacuum for 60 seconds quickly turn the stopcock to expose the funnel to atmospheric pressure.

8. Questions

(a) Define water retentivity of masonary cement.

(b) What is the significance of performing this experiment.

(c) How does fineness of cement affect the water retentivity property of the cement.

(d) How does water retentivity of cement affect the preparation of cement mortar.

(e) What are the ingredients of a masonary cement ?

(f) why the strength of masonary cement is lower than that of Portland Cement ?

(g) Why masonary cement is preferred for brick construction ?

REFERENCE

(1) I. S. 269–1976 - Specifications for ordinary, Rapid hardening and low heat portland cement. Published by Bureau of Indian Standards (BIS) New Delhi

(2) I. S. 4031–1968 - Method of Physical tests for Hydraulic Cement. BIS, New Delhi.

(3) I. S. 4845–1968 - Definitions and terminology relating to hydraulic cement. BIS New Delhi.

(4) I. S. 4032–1968 - Methods of Chemical analysis of hydraulic cement. BIS New Delhi.

(5) I. S. 1727–1967 - Methods of test for Pozzolanic materials. BIS New Delhi.

(6) I. S. 1469–1967 - Methods of test for Pozzolanic materials. BIS New Delhi.

(7) I.S. 1469–1987 – Handbook on Mix Design BIS, New Delhi

(8) Jai Krishna and Jain O.P. Plain Reinforced Concrete. Vol. I Published by Nem Chand and Brothers, Roorkee.

(9) Concrete Manual U.S.B.R. Publication.

(10) National Building Organization Handbook for Building Engineers N.B.O., New Delhi.

(11) F. M. LEA - The chemistry of cement and concrete. Published by Science Book Agency Calcutta.

(12) Satyendra Chandra Lodh-Chemistry for Engineers. Published by Science Book Agency Calcutta.

(13) Concrete Handbook Published by the Concrete Association of India, Bombay.

PART II

AGGREGATES

INTRODUCTION

Aggregate is a general term applied to those inert (chemically inactive) material which when bonded together by cement form concrete. Most aggregates used in our country are naturally occurring aggregates, such as, sand, crushed rock and gravel.

Aggregates are commonly classified into two sizes, fine and coarse, the dividing line being the 4.75 mm size. Material which is mainly retained on 4.75 mm I.S. Sieve is classed as 'coarse aggregate, whereas material mainly passing as fine aggregate.

Sampling of Aggregates for Test:

The samples of aggregates for various tests should be a representative sample of the stock-pile. To ensure this the sample which is sent to Laboratory should be made up from about twelve smaller samples taken from various parts of the stock pile and thoroughly mixed. This main sample should be reduced to a quantity as per table 2.1 (Minimum smaller size to be available in Laboratory) by the method of quartering.

Method of Quartering:

(a) Spread the main sample into a layer about 70 mm. thick.

(b) Divide this layer into four equal parts by means of a cross.

(c) Discard two diagonally opposite quarters and remix the remainder.

(d) Repeat this process until the sample is reduced to the amount required to be sent to the Laboratory for testing.

The sample available for Laboratory testing shall beoven dried (Except for the aggregates whose moisture content is required) at a temperature of 100 to 110°C, cooled to room temperature and test samples made from this main sample by the method of quartering or by sample divider. Table 2.1 to 2.5 are very useful tables to guide the students in selecting the aggregate sample for various tests.

Table 2.1: Size of samples required for various tests (I.S. 2386 - 1963)

Test	*Minimum Sample Size*	
	To be available in the Lab Kg	*To be tested Kg*
(1)	(2)	(3)
Sieve Analysis		
Maximum size present in substantial proportions		
63 mm	100	50
50 mm	100	35
40 mm	50	15
25 mm	50	5
20 mm	25	2
12.5 mm	12	1
10 mm	6	0.5
6.3 mm	3	0.2
4.75 mm	2	0.2
2.36 mm	2	0.1
Determination of Materials Finer than 75 Micron:		
Maximum size present in substantial proportions		
40 mm or above	20	5
20 mm	10	2.5
10 mm	10	2.0

(1)	(2)	(3)
4.75 mm	5	0.5
Estimation of organic impurities	5	0.5
Determination of Specific Gravity and water Absorption		
Aggregate larger than		
10 mm	10	2
10 mm - 4.75 mm	5	1
Smaller than 4.75 mm	3	0.5
Determination of bulk Density and Voids:		
Maximum size of aggregate		
Over 40mm	150	60
40mm - 4.75mm	100	30
Less than 4.75 mm	20	30
Determination of Aggregate Crushing Value:	30	7
Determination of Aggregate Impact Value:	5	1
Determination of Aggregate Abrasion Value by use of the Deval Machine	30	6
Determination of Aggregate Abrasion Value by use of Los Angles Machine :	300	50
Determination of Aggregate Soundness:		
Coarse aggregate	60	10
Fine Aggregate	10	1

Table 2.2 I.S. Sieves for sieve analysis of aggregates for concrete

Type	*Sieve designations*
Square hole, perforate plate:	80 mm, 63 mm, 50 mm, 40 mm, 31.5 mm, 25 mm. 20mm, 16 mm, 12.5 mm, 10 mm, 6.3 mm, 4.75 mm.
Fine mesh, wire cloth:	3.35 mm, 2.36 mm, 1.18 mm, 600 micron, 300 micron, 150 micron, 75 micron.

Table 2.3: Maximum weight to be retained at the completion of sieving

IS Sieve	*Coarse agg regate Max. weight for*		*Fine aggregate*	
	45 cm dia sieve (Kg)	*30 cm dia sieve (Kg)*	*I.S. Sieve*	*Maximum weight for 20 mm dia sieve (gm)*
(1)	(2)	(3)	(4)	(5)
50 mm	10	4.5	2.36 mm	200
40 mm	8	3.5	1.18 mm	100
31.5 or 25 mm	6	2.5		
20 mm	4	2.0	600 micron	75
16 mm or 12.5 mm	3	1.5	300 micron	50
10 mm	2	1.0		
6.3 mm	1.5	0.75	150 micron	40
4.75 mm	1.0	0.50	75 micron	25
3.35 mm	-	0.30		

Table 2.4: Grading limits for fine aggregate (IS. 383-1970)

I.S. Sieve *designation*	*Percent Passing* Grading *Zone I*	Grading *Zone II*	Grading *Zone III*	Grading *Zone IV*
10 mm	100	100	100	100
4.75 mm	90-100	90-100	90-100	95-100
2.36 mm	60-95	75-100	85-100	95-100
1.18 mm	30-70	55-90	75-100	90-100
600 micron	15-34	35-59	60-79	80-100
300 micron	5-20	8.30	12-40	15-50
150 micron	0-10	0-10	0-10	0-15

Table 2.5 : Grading limits for coarse aggregates (I.S. 383-1970)

I.S. Sieve *designation*	*Percentage passing for single size* aggregate of nominal size						*Percent passing for graded* aggregate of nominal size			
	63mm	*40mm*	*20mm*	*16mm*	*15.5mm*	*10mm*	*40mm*	*20mm*	*16mm*	*12.5mm*
80 mm	100	-	-	-	-	-	100	-	-	-
63 mm	85-100	100	-	-	-	-	-	-	-	-
40 mm	0.30	85-100	100	-	-	-	95-100	100	-	-
20 mm	0-5	0.20	85-100	100	-	-	30-70	95-100	100	100
16 mm	-	-	-	85-100	100	-	-	-	90-100	-
12.5 mm	-	-	-	-	85-100	100	-	-	-	90-100
10 mm	0.5	0.5	0-20	0.30	0-45	85-100	10-35	25-55	30-70	40-85
4.75 mm	-	-	0-5	0-5	0-10	0-20	0-5	0-10	0-10	0-10
2.36 mm	-	-	-	-	-	0.5	-	-	-	-

EXPERIMENT NO.2/1

TO DETERMINE MATERIAL FINER THAN 75 MICRON

1. **Object** –To determine material finer than 75 micron in aggregate by washing.
2. **Theory**–The method of test deals with the procedure for determining the total quantity of material finer than 75 micron IS Sieve in aggregate by washing. Clay particles that are dispersed by wash water as well as water soluble materials will be removed from the aggregate during the test.
3. **Apparatus**–The balance or scale shall be of sufficient capacity and sensitivity and shall have an accuracy of 0.1 percent of the weight of thc test sample.

   (b) **Sieve**–A net of two sieves, the lower being 75 micron I.S. Sieve and the upper approximately 1.18 mm IS Sieve.

   (c) **Container**–a pan or vessel of a size sufficient to contain the sample covered with water and to permit vigorous agitation without inadvertent loss of any part of the sample or water.

   (d) **Oven**-An oven of sufficient size capable of maintaining a uniform temperature of 100° * 5°C.

   (e) **Sample**-The test sample shall be as given in table 2.1
4. **Procedure:**

   (a) The test sample shall be dried to constant weight at a temperature of 100° * 5°C and weighed to the nearest 0.1 percent.

   (b) The test sample after being dried and weighed shall be placed in the container and sufficient water added to cover it.The contents of the container shall be agitated vigorously.

   (c) The agitation shall be sufficiently vigorous to result in the complete separation and suspension of particles finer than 75 micron from the coarse particles. Care shall be taken to avoid, as much as possible, the decantation of the coarse particles of the sample. The operation shall be repeated until the wash water is clear.

   (d) The wash water containing the suspended and dissolved solids shall be immediately poured over the nested sieves arranged with the coarser sieve on the top.

   (e) All material retained on the nested sieves shall be returned to the washed sample. The washed aggregate shall be dried to constant weight at a temperature not exceeding 110° and weighed to the nearest 0.1 percent.
5. **Observations and Calculations**–The amount of material passing the 75 micron I.S. Sieve shall be calculated as follows:

$$A = \frac{B-C}{C} \times 100$$

   Where,

   A = Percentage of material finer than 75 micron

   B = Original dry weight, ...gm

   C = Dry weight after washing...........gm.
6. **Result**-% of material of finer than 75 micron. = %
7. **Precautions:** (a) Weigh the samples very accurately.

   (b) Dry the washed sample at the constant temperature.
8. **Comments** Comment on the result obtained by you in the laboratory. Do you recommend this sample for use on a construction site.
9. **Questions:**

   (a) What is the importance of this test?

   (b) What is the aperture size of 75 micron sieve?

EXPERIMENT NO. 2/2

TEST FOR ORGANIC IMPURITIES

1. **Object**–To test the fine aggregate for organic impurities.
2. **Theory**–The aggregate must be checked for organic impurities such as decayed vegetation, humus, coal dust. etc. Colour test is a reliable indicator of the presence of harmful organic matter in aggregates except in areas where there are deposits of lignite.
3. **Apparatus**–Glass bottle, 3% solution of caustic soda, sodium Hydroxide, distilled water.
4. **Procedure**

   (a) Fill 1 350 ml clear glass medicine bottle upto 75ml mark with a 3% solution of Caustic Soda or sodium hydroxide. A 3% solution of caustic soda is made by dissolving 3gm of sodium hydroxide (which can be purchased from any chemist) in 100ml of water (preferably distilled). The solution should be kept in glass bottle tightly closed with a rubber stopper., Handling sodium hydroxide with moist hands may result in serious burns. Care should b taken not to spill the solution for it is highly injurious to clothing, leather and other materials.

   (b) The sand is next added gradually until the volume measured by the sandy layer is 125ml. The volume is then made up to 200ml by the additional of more of the solution. The bottle is then corked and shaken vigorously and allowed to stand for 24 hours.

   (c) At the end of this period, the colour of the liquid will indicate whether the sand contains a dangerous amount of matter or not. A colourless liquid indicates a clean sand free from organic matter. A straw-coloured solution indicates some organic matter but not enough to be seriously objectionable. Darker colour means that the sand contains injurious amounts and should not be used unless it is washed and a re-test then shows that it is satisfactory.

4. **Observation :**

   Colour of the liquid observed = Colourless/straw colour/darker colour.

5. **Precautions**

   (a) Use every possible care while handling sodium hydroxide solution.

   (b) The sand and the sodium hydroxide should be shaken vigorously to get good results.

6. **Comments:**

   Give your comments on the colour of the liquid. Do you recommend this sand for a construction site.

7. **Questions :**

   (a) What do you understand by organic impurities in aggregates?

   (b) Does this impurity occur in finer or coarse aggregate or in both?

   (c) How a 3% solution of caustic soda is prepared?

   (d) Under what colour of liquid the organic impurity is ascertained in aggregates?

   (e) What effect will dirty aggregates have on the strength of the concrete.

   (f) Define fine aggregate and coarse aggregate.

   (g) What are the characteristic of a good aggregate.

EXPERIMENT NO. 2/3

BULK DENSITY AND PERCENTAGE VOIDS

1. **Object**–To determine the Bulk density and percentage voids in aggregates.
2. **Theory :**

Unit weight (Bulk density) is the weight of a Unit volume of aggregate, usually stated in Kg per litre. In estimating quantities of materials and in mix computations, when batching is done on a volumetric basis, it is necessary to know the conditions under which the aggregate volume is to be measured viz (a) loose or compact (b) dry, damp or inundated. For general information and for comparisons of different aggregates, the standard conditions are dry and compact. For scheduling volumetric batch qualities, the unit weight in the loose, damp state should be known.

With respect to a mass of aggregate the term "Voids" refers to the spaces between the aggregate particles, Numerically this void space is the difference between the gross or overall volume of the aggregate mass and the space occupied by the aggregate particles alone. The percentage of voids between the particles in a given gross or overall volume of the aggregate can be determined from the following expression.

$$\text{Voids percentage} = \frac{\text{Specific gravity} - \text{Bulk density}}{\text{Specific gravity}} \times 100$$

3. **Apparatus**–(a) A balance sensitive to 0.5% of the weight of sample to be weighed, Cylindrical containers (having capacities of 3, 15 and 30 litres), tamping rod 16mm in dia and 60mm long rounded at one end, piece of glass plate for use in calibration of container.

(b) Caliberation of Container–The container shall be calibrated by determining the weight of water at 27°C required to fill it such that no meniscus is present above the rim of the container. The capacity in litres shall be obtained by dividing the weight of water in one litre at 27°C, which may be taken as ten newton (1 kg.).

TABLE 2.6–Size of container for Bulk Density test.

Size of larger particles	*Nominal capacity (Litres)*	*Inside dia (mm)*	*Inside height (mm)*	*Thickness of metal (Min.) (mm)*
4.75 mm and under	3	150	170	3.15
Over 4.75 mm to 40 mm	15	250	300	4.00
Over 40 mm	30	350	310	5.00

(c) Sample–The quantity of sample shall be as given in Table 1,

4. **Procedure :**

(a) Condition of Specimen :

The test shall be carried out on dry material when determining the voids, but when bulk density tests are required material with a given percentage of moisture may be used.

(b) Rodded or Compacted Weight–The measure shall be filled about 1/3rd full with thoroughly mixed aggregate and tamped with 25 strokes of the rounded end of the tamping rod. A further similar quantity of aggregate shall be added and a further tamping of 25 strokes given. The measure shall finally be filled to over-flowing, tamped 25 times and the surplus aggregate struck off, using the tamping rod as a straight edge. The net weight of the aggregate in the measure shall be determined and the bulk density calculated in Newtons per litre.

(c) **Loose Weight**–The measure shall be filled to over-flowing by means of a shovel, the aggregate being discharged from a height not exceeding 50 mm above the top of the measure. Care shall be taken to prevent, as far as possible, segregation of the particle size of which the sample is composed. The surface of the aggregate shall then be levelled with a straight edge. The net weight of the aggregate in the measure shall then be determined and the bulk density calculated in Newtons per litre (kilogram per litre).

5. **Observations and Calculations :**

(a) Weight of empty container + Glass plate	=	Newtons (Kg)
(b) Weight of container filled with water and glass plate	=	Newtons (Kg)
(c) Weight of water in container (b-a)	=	Newtons (Kg)
(d) Weight of empty container	=	Newtons (Kg)
(e) Weight of container filled with loose aggregate	=	Newtons(Kg)
(f) Weight of looser aggregate in container (e-d)	=	Newtons (Kg)
(g) Weight of container filled with compacted aggregate	=	Newtons (Kg)
(h) Weight of compacted aggregate (g-d)	=	Newtons (Kg)

Bulk density loose $= \frac{(f)}{(c)} =$ N/Litre (Kg/Litre)

Bulk density compacted $= \frac{(h)}{(c)} =$ N/Litre (Kg/Litre)

Percentage of voids $= \frac{G_s - Y}{G_s} \times 100 =$ %

where,

G_g = Specific gravity of the aggregate, and

Y = Bulk density in N/litre (Kg/litre).

6. **Results**–The bulk density shall be reported in N/litre (Kg/Lit.) to the nearest (0.1 N 0.01 Kg).
The voids shall be reported as a percentage to the nearest whole number.
The conditions of aggregate at the time of test shall be stated, i.e. (a) Oven dry (b) Saturated and surface dry (c) with a given percentage of moisture.

7. **Precautions :**

(a) All the weighings should be done very accurately.

(b) While performing compacted bulk density test, there should be uniform rodding of the sample.

(c) Risk of segregation of particles should be avoided while performing loose bulk density test.

8. **Comments :**

Comment on the results obtained by you. Compare the values of bulk densities and percentage. Voids with the usual values of the aggregates recommended for normal concreting work.

9. **Questions:**

(a) Define Bulk density.

(b) What do you understand by voids in aggregates?

(c) What is the importance of bulk density?

(d) Define specific gravity of aggregate.

(e) What are the units of bulk density.

(f) What is the importance of voids in aggregates and what are their limits for good aggregates.

EXPERIMENT NO.2/4

SPECIFIC GRAVITY AND WATER ABSORPTION OF FINE AGGREGATE

1. **Object**–To determine specific gravity and water absorption of a fine aggregate sample.

2. **Theory :**

The specific gravity of a substance is the ratio of the unit weight of the substance to the unit weight of water. In the SI system, the unit weight of water (under standard conditions) may be taken as 9.81 KN (1000 in the m.k.s. system). Hence the Unit weight of a substance in KN is numerically equal to the specific gravity. Applied to aggregate, the term specific gravity refers to the density of the individual particles and not to the aggregated mass as a whole.

As regards moisture content, the various stages in which the aggregate may exist are (a) over dry (b) Air dry (c) Saturated surface dry (d) damp or moist. On the construction site, the fine aggregate usually carry some free moisture. Total internal moisture content of an aggregate in the saturated surface dry condition maybe termed as "Absorption capacity" although it is some times referred to simply as the absorption. The amount of water required to bring an aggregate from the air dry condition to the saturated surface dry condition is termed as "effective absorption". The absorption is determined by finding the weight of a surface dried sample after it has been soaked for 24 hours and again finding the weight after the sample has been dried in an over, the difference in weights, expressed as a percentage of dry sample weight, is the absorption capacity.

3. **Apparatus :**

(a) A pycnometer of 1 lit capacity fitted with a glass disc.

(b) A balance having a capacity of 2Kg. and sensitive to 0.1gm.

(c) A filter pump with the necessary pipe connection and gage for removing the entrapped air.

(d) A water storage jar of about 20 lit capacity for maintaining the water at room temperature.

(e) A sample splitter and a thermometer.

Calibration of Pycnometer–It will be convenient to have the pycnometer jar calibrated for various water temperatures, say from 5° to 45°C. This is done by filling the jar with water of a known temperature, applying a vacuum or agitating the water to remove entrapped air, and weighing the filled jar with disc in place. A curve may be plotted through the points obtained with weight as the ordinate and temperature as the abscissa. The weight (W_c) of the pycnometer, with water at a specific temperature, can then be selected from the curve.

4. **Procedure :**

(a) The sand sample shall be immersed in clean water for 24 hours and dried to Saturated and surface dry condition.

A representative sample of 12 to 15 Newtons (1200 to 1500 gm) of the above saturated surface-dry material is obtained by a sample splitter or other satisfactory means. The sample is divided into approximately equal parts from which two samples are weighed having identical weights from 6 to 7 N (600 to 700 grams). This weight of saturated and surface-dry materials is recorded as B.

(b) One sample is placed in an oven and dried to constant weight and the weight is recorded as A.

(c) The pycnometer is filled about three-quarters full of water of known temperature and the saturated surface dry sand sample B is added. Entrapped air is removed either by a vacuum applied to the top of the jar or by rolling the jar or otherwise agitating the sand. The jar is then filled with water and covered with a glass disc by sliding the disk across the top of the jar. The jar is shaken rigorously to remove all remaining entrapped air, after which the disk is removed and the jar carefully refilled with water. The disk is then replaced, making sure no air voids remains, and the outside surface is dried. The jar with disc in place is weighed and the weight recorded as W.

5. **Observations and Calculations :**

A = Weight of oven dry sample = N(gms.)

B = Weight of saturated surface-dry sample = N(gms.)

W_c = Weight of pycnometer filled with water at same temperature as water used in test = N(gms.)

W = Weight of pycnometer with water and sand sample = N(gms.)

(a) **Specific Gravity**–The bulk specific gravity is calculated by one of the following formula :

Specific gravity on dry basis $= \dfrac{A}{W_c + B - W} =$

Specific gravity on saturated surface dry basis $= \dfrac{B}{W_c + B - W} =$

(b) **Absorption** – The absorption is computed by the following formula :

Absorption percent $= \dfrac{B-A}{A} \times 100$

6. **Results :**

(a) Sp. gr. on dry basis =

(b) Sp. gr. on saturated surface dry basis =

(c) Absorption = percent

7. **Precautions :**

(a) Remove the entrapped air completely.

(b) All the weighings should be done accurately.

(c) While covering the pycnometer with glass disc, ensure that no air bubbles are entrapped.

8. **Comments :**

Comment on the results obtained by you in the laboratory and compare your values with the values for various types of sands.

9. **Questions :**

(a) Define specific gravity of a fine aggregate.

(b) Differentiate between bulk density and specific gravity.

(c) Where do we need the value of specific gravity of fine aggregate.

(d) Why should we test a fine aggregate sample for water absorption?

(e) Give the average figure for specific gravity of a fine aggregate sample.

EXPERIMENT NO.2/5

SPECIFIC GRAVITY AND WATER ABSORPTION OF COARSE AGGREGATE

1. **Object**–To determine the specific gravity and water absorption of a coarse aggregate sample.

2. **Theory**–In connection with concrete mix calculations, it is desired to know the space occupied by the aggregate particles within the relatively thick cement paste regardless of whether or not pores or internal voids exist within the particles. Hence there it is determined what is called the bulk specific gravity of the particles. The bulk specific gravity is defined as the ratio of the weight in air of a given volume of a material at the standard temperature to the weight in air of an equal volume of distilled water at the standard temperature. In concrete testing 20°C is taken as the standard reference temperature.

   Apparent specific gravity is the ratio of the weight in air of a given volume of the impermeable portion of a permeable material (i.e. the solid matter including its impermeable pores or voids) at a stated temperature to the weight in air of an equal volume of distilled water at a stated temperature.

   On the job, the fine aggregates usually carry some free moisture. Freshly washed coarse aggregates contain free water but since they dry quickly, they are ordinarily partially dry when used. Coarse aggregates are considered to be surface dry when they have been wiped free of visible moisture films with a cloth. The absorption capacity is a measure of the porosity of an aggregate. It is also used as a correction factor in determinations of free moisture by the oven drying method.

3. **Apparatus**–(a) A balance having a capacity of 20N (2 Kg) and sensitive to 0.1 gm.

   (b) A wire basket of 2.36 mm aperture approximately 200 mm in diameter and 60 mm in height. If it is continual use, the basket should be constructed of copper galvanized material.

   (c) A suitable container for immersing the wire basket in water and suitable apparatus for suspending the wire basket from centre of scale pan balance.

   (d) **Sample**–A representative sample is obtained by quartering and the following weights are used in the tests for the various sizes of aggregate:

Size of aggregate	Weight N (gms)
4.75 mm to 10 mm	10N to 15N (1000 to 1500 gm)
10 mm to 20 mm	15 N to 20N (1500 to 2000 gm)
20 mm to 40 mm	A sufficient amount to make a representative sample.

4. **Procedure**–(a) The sample is immersed in water having a temperature of 22°C to 32°C and the mixture thoroughly agitated to remove dust or other coatings from the surface of the particles and then allowed to absorb water for 24 hours. The sample is then removed from the water and rolled in a large cloth until all visible films of water are removed, although the surface of the particles still appear to be damp. The larger fragments may be individually wiped. Care should be taken to avoid evaporation from surface dry particles. The weight of the sample in the saturated surface dry condition is then obtained. This and all subsequent weights should be determined to the nearest of 0.5 gm.

   (b) After weighing, the saturated surface dry sample is placed immediately in the wire basket and its weight in water determined.

   (c) The sample is then dried to constant weight at a temperature of 100 to 110°C cooled to room temperature and weighed.

6. **Observations and Calculations :**

A = Weight of oven dry sample in air, = N(gms)

B = Weight of saturated surface dry sample in the air, = N(gms)

C = Weight of saturated surface dry sample in water, gm = N(gms).

(a) **Specific gravity**-The bulk specific gravity is calculated by one of the following formulas :

$$\text{Specific gravity on dry basis} = \frac{A}{B - C} =$$

$$\text{Specific gravity on saturated surface dry basis} = \frac{B}{B - C}$$

(b) **Absorption** - The percentage of absorption is calculated by the following formula :

$$\text{Absorption percent} = \frac{B - A}{A} \times 100 =$$

7. **Result :**

1. Sp. gr. on dry basis =
2. Sp. gr. on saturated surface dry basis =
3. Absorption = %

8. **Precautions :**

(a) Keep in mind that the saturated surface dry sample is the condition when all the visible films of water are removed from the sample.

(b) All the weighings must be done carefully and accurately.

9. **Comments :**

Comment on the results obtained by you in the laboratory and compare them with the normal ranges for the coarse aggregates used on a construction site.

10. **Questions :**

(a) As regards moisture content, discuss the various states in which an aggregate may exist.

(b) Does hardness affect specific gravity of an aggregate?

(c) State the average values of specific gravity for (a) Gravel (b) Granite (c) Lime stone aggregate.

(d) Why should we test a coarse aggregate sample for water absorption?

(e) Why are we interested in the value of specific gravity of a coarse aggregate?

(f) Out of specific gravity and bulk density, which is used in concrete mix design calculations.

EXPERIMENT NO.2/6

PARTICLE SIZE DISTRIBUTION AND FINENESS MODULUS

1. **Object**–To determine the particle size distribution and fineness modulus of coarse and fine aggregates.

2. **Theory**–The aggregate most of which passes IS 4.75 mm sieve is classified as fine aggregate. The fine aggregates obtained from Natural disintegration of rocks and deposited by streams are known as natural sands. Fine aggregates resulting from crushing of hard stone and natural gravel are known as crushed stone sand and crushed gravel sand respectively.

   Aggregate most of which is retained on IS 4.75 mm sieve is known as coarse aggregate. It may be in the form of uncrushed gravel or stone resulting from natural disintegration of rocks. Crushed gravel or stone aggregate is obtained by crushing gravel or hard stone. Mixture of the above two is classified as partially crushed gravel or stone.

   Sieve analysis is carried out for the determination of particle size distribution of fine, coarse and all-in-aggregates by sieving or screening. Sieves of size 80mm, 40mm, 20mm, 10mm, 4.75mm, 2.36mm, 1.18mm, 600 micron, 300 micron and 150 micron conforming to IS 460 specifications are used.

3. **Apparatus :**

   (a) **Balance**–The balance or scale shall be such that it is readable and accurate to 0.1% of the weight of the test sample.

   (b) **Sieves**–Sieves of the sizes given in Table 2.7 and 2.8 conforming to I.S. 460.1962 specification for Test Sieves (Revised) shall be used.

   (c) **Sample**–The weight of sample available shall be not less than weight given in Table 2.1. The sample for sieving shall be prepared from the larger sample either by quartering or by means of a sample divider.

4. **Procedure**–The sample shall be brought to an air-dry condition before weighing and sieving. This may be achieved either by drying at room temperature of by heating at a temperature of 100° to 110°C. The air-dry sample shall be weighed and sieved successively on the appropriate sieves starting with the largest size. Care shall be taken to ensure that the sieves are clean before use.

   Each sieve shall be shaken separately over a clean tray for a period of not less than 2 min. The shaking is done with a varied motion backwards and forwards, left and right, circular clock-wise and anticlockwise and with frequent jarring so that the material is kept moving over the sieve surface in frequently changing directions. Find the weight of aggregates retained on each sieve taken in order.

   If sieving is carried out with a nest of sieves on a machine, not less than 10 minutes sieving will be required for each test.

5. **Observation and Calculation :**

TABLE 2.7 Sieve Analysis of Coarse Aggregate

Date of testing................., Sample No...............

Weight of coarse aggregate taken for sieving = N(kgms)

I.S. Sieve size	*Weight Retained*	*% weight retained*	*% weight passing*	*Cumulative % wt. retd.*	*Remarks*
I.S. 80mm					
40mm					
20mm					
10mm					
4.75mm					
Residue					
Check					
				C =	

Fineness modulus of coarse aggregate $\frac{C + 500}{100}$

TABLE 2.8 Sieve Analysis of Fine Aggregate

Date of testing..................., Sample No...............

Weight of fine aggregate taken for sieving = N (Kg)

Sieve Size I.S.	*Weight Retained*	*% weight retained*	*% weight passing*	*Cumulative % weight retained*	*Remarks*
4.75mm					
2.36mm					
1.18mm					
600 Micron					
300 Micron					
150 Micron					
Residue					
Check					
				F =	

Fineness Modulus of fine aggregate = $\frac{F}{100}$

6. **Precautions :**

(a) Each sieve shall be shaken for a period of at lest 2 minutes if hand sieving is used.

(b) Sieving should be in a circular clockwise and anticlockwise directions.

(c) If serving is done in a shaker, at lest 10 minutes sieving per test must be used.

(d) The sample to be sieved should be in air dry condition.

7. **Comments :**

Draw a curve between percentage passing and the sieve size for both coarse and fine aggregate. Study and give comments on these curves.

8. **Comments :**

Discuss the suitability of the fine aggregate and coarse aggregate used by you in the laboratory for a construction site.

9. Questions :

(a) Define fineness modulus of an aggregate and what is its importance.
(b) What is the significance of grading of aggregates and what is meant by good grading ?
(c) How should aggregate be stockpiled on a construction site ?
(d) What are common maximum size of course aggregates available in the market ?
(e) What are the aggregates referred to as filler materials ?
(f) Why are the light weight aggregates used for certain jobs ?
(g) Differentiate between fine aggregate, coarse aggregate and mixed aggregate.
(h) What are different sieve systems used in India, U.K. and U.S.A. for grading of aggregates ?
(i) The fineness modulus of a concrete sand should lie within what range of limits.
(j) How does the size of an aggregate affect its fineness modulus ?
(k) What is a grading curve and where it is used ?
(i) What are usual limits of fineness modulii of coarse aggregates and mixed aggregates ?
(m) What are the fineness modulus limits of fine sand and coarse sand ?

EXPERIMENT NO. 2/7

BULKING OF FINE AGGREGATES

1. **Object**–To determine Bulking of fine aggregate
2. **Theory**–Dry and fully saturated sand does not bulk. As the sand become finer the bulking of the sand increases. The bulking of the sand is caused by the film of moisture which tends to keep the particles of sand apart. The bulking factor w.r.t. dry loose sand is the ratio of unit weight of dry loose sand and unit weight of dry sand contained in wet loose sand

$$\left(\frac{W_d}{W_{d^w}}\right)$$

The bulking factor w.r.t. dry compacted sand is the ratio of unit weight of dry compacted sand and unit weight of dry sand contained in wet loose sand $\left(\frac{W_d}{W_{d^w}}\right)$

Unit weight of dry sand contained in wet loose sand, is given by

$W_d^{\omega} = \dfrac{W_{\omega}}{1+\dfrac{X}{100}}$ Where W_w = Unit weight of loose wet sand and X is the percentage moisture content.

Percentage bulking = (Bulking factor-1) x 100

3. **Apparatus**–Weighing balance sensitive to 0.1 percent of the weight of the sample to be weighed, Cylindrical metalpot of fixed volume 150 mm dia and 150 mm in height, 100 cm graduated cylindrical measure, mixing pan and tamping rod 16 mm dia and 600 mm long bullet pointed at one end.
4. **Procedure**–Work out the quantity of sand in N(Kg) required to fill the pot in compacted state. Take representative sample of dry and approximately more than 10 percent of the calculated quantity. Weight it and put in the mixing pan. This quantity of the sand should be continued throughout the experiment. Care shall be taken that no sand shall be lost at the time of filling and emptying of pot back to the mixing pan.

   Weigh empty dry cylinderical pot, fill it with water and take its weight. Dry the pot and then fill it with dry sand loosely to overflowing, taking care that the sand is discharged from a height not exceeding 50mm above the top of measure. Level the surface at the top with the tamping rod and weight the pot with loose sand filled. Similarly find the weight of pot with compacted sand filled. The compaction of sand is done in layers of about 5cm height, each layer being tamped 25 strokes uniformly distributed over the surface by the standard tamping rod. Determine unit weights of dry loose and dry compacted sand as W_d and W'_d respectively. Place the dry sand back into the mixing pan and add known percentage of water by weight to the sand. Mix water thoroughly with sand by hand till it appears uniform. Fill the cylindrical pot with moist sand of known moisture content loosely and find the weight of the pot filled with moist sand. Vary the moisture content starting from 2% in Steps of 2,4,6,8,10,16,20, 25 percent and repeat as before to determine the unit weight of loose wet sand W_w. Calculate the bulking factors with respect to compacted dry and loose sand and plot a graph giving curves for percentage bulking and moisture content.
5. **Observations and Calculations**:

   (a) Weight of representative sand sample = N(Kg)

   (b) Weight of empty pot = N(Kg)

   (c) Weight of pot filled with water = N(Kg)

(d) Weight of pot + loose dry sand = N(Kg)

(e) Weight of pot + compacted dry sand = N(Kg)

(f) Unit weight of loose dry sand = W_d = N/lit(Kg/Lit)

(g) Unit weight of compacted dry sand = W'_d = N/lit(Kg/lit)

(h) Unit weight of loose wet sand = W_w = N/lit(Kg/lit)

Table 2.9

Percentage water	W_{dw}	*Bulking Factor Loose*	*Percent bulking loose*	*Bulking Factor compacted*	*Percent bulking compacted*
X	$= \dfrac{W_w}{1+\dfrac{X}{100}}$	$\dfrac{W_w}{W_{dw}}$	(B.F.–1) × 100	$\dfrac{W_w}{W_{dw}}$	(B.F.–1) × 100
2					
4					
6					
8					
10					
15					
20					
25					
27					

Table 2.10 Bulking of sand for various moisture contents

Moisture *Percent*	Percentage bulking		
	Fine sand	*Medium sand*	*Coarse sand*
1	16	8	6
2	26	16	12
3	32	22	15
4	36	27	17
5	38	29	18
6	37	28	18
8	35	26	16
10	32	22	12
12	28	19	8
15	22	12	2
17	18	7	0
20	9	0	0
27	0	0	0

6. **Results :**

(a) Percentage Bulking of loose sand =

(b) Percentage Bulking of Compacted sand =

7. **Precautions :**

(a) All the weighings should done very accurately.

(b) No sand particles should be lost while filling or emptying the pot.

(c) Mix the water in the sand uniformly.

8. **Comments :**

Comments on the percentage bulking value obtained in the laboratory.

9. **Questions :**

(a) State the importance of this test.

(b) State the relative bulking tendencies of fine and coarse sands.

(c) Explain void content as it implies to fine aggregate.

(d) How would you test sand for silt and organic matter?

(e) How bulking of fine aggregate is taken into account while designing a concrete mix.

(f) What is the reason for bulking of sand.

EXPERIMENT NO.2/8

SILT CONTENT OF FINE AGGREGATE

1. **Object**–To determine the silt content of a fine aggregate sample.
2. **Theory**–It is important to use clean aggregate for concrete. If the aggregates are coated with dirt, silt or clay, it will result in a poor concrete because the dirt will prevent the cement from setting and also weaken the bond between the aggregates and the cement paste.

   In the hand test, simply pick up a little sample of sand and rub it between your hands. If your palm stays clean the sand is alright from the cleaniness point of view. If it is stained, something is wrong and you must proceed to perform the silt test.
3. **Apparatus**–Measuring cylinder of 200cc capacity, Salt (NaoH)
4. **Procedure** :

   (a) Fill a measuring cylinder with sand upto 100cc mark and add water up to 150cc. To perform this test, more correctly better dissolve a little salt in the water (1 tea spoonful to 250cc is the right proportion).

   (b) Shake the sample vigorously for one minute and the last few shakes being in a side wise direction to level off the sand.

   (c) Allow the cylinder to stand for three hours during which time any silt present will settle in a layer on the top of the sand and its thickness can be read off on the cylinder itself. There should not be more than 6cc or silt of about 6 to 10 percent of the amount of the sand.
5. **Result :**

   Silt content = percent
6. **Precautions**

   (a) Shaking of the sample should be upside down and side wise so that water reaches every location of the sample.

   (b) Perform the experiment away from shocks and vibrations.
7. **Comments**

   Comment on the suitability of the sand sample for use on a construction site. If the sample is not suitable for use, suggest the measures to be taken.
8. **Questions :**

   (a) State the importance of this test.

   (b) What is the upper limit of silt content of a sand sample.

   (c) What is the effect of excessive silt content on the strength of concrete containing this sand.

   (d) State the rough method of approving a sand sample on a construction site.

EXPERIMENT NO. 2/9

MOISTURE CONTENT (SURFACE MOISTURE) OF CONCRETE AGGREGATE

1. **Object**–To determine moisture content (surface moisture) of aggregates.
2. **Theory:**
In a concrete mix, if the aggregates are not fully saturated some of the mixing water is absorbed by them that is free moisture on the surface of the aggregate particles becomes a part of the mixing water. In computations of the net or effective ratio of water to cement and in calculations relating to proportions of mixes by weight, the saturated surface dry conditions is used as the basis.
On a construction site, the fine aggregates usually carry some free moisture. Freshly washed coarse aggregates contain free water but since they dry quickly, they are ordinarily partly dry when used.
The total internal moisture content of an aggregate in the saturated surface dry condition may be termed as the absorption capacity, although it is sometimes refered to simply as the absorption. The amount of water required to bring an aggregate from the air dry condition to the saturated surface dry condition is here is termed as effective absorption.
3. **Apparatus:**
(a) Balance–having a capacity of 20N (2 kg) or more and sensitive to 1gm or less.
(b) Flask–A suitable container or flask preferably of glass or non corrosive metal. The container may be a psycnometer or a graduated volumetric flask or other suitable measuring device. The volume of the container shall be 2 to 3 times the loose volume of the sample.
4. **Procedure (I) For fine Aggregates:**
(a) Select a representative sample of fine aggregate to be tested for surface moisture content. It shall weigh not less than 2N (200 gms). Larger samples will yield more accurate results.
(b) Fill the container to the mark with water and determine its weight.
(c) Empty the container.
(d) Introduce the aggregates sample into the container and add enough water to cover the sample.
(e) Remove the entrained air by side rolling.
(f) Fill the container to the original mark and weight it.
5. **Observations and Calculations:**
Calculate the amount of water displaced by the sample as follows:
$V_s = M_c + M_s - M$
Where V_s = Weight in N (gms) of water displaced by the sample.
M_c = Weight in N (gms) of container filled upto the mark with water.
M_s = Weight in N (gms) of the sample.
M = Weight in N (gms) of the sample and container filled to the mark with water.
The percentage of surface moisture in terms of the saturated surface dry fine aggregate and in terms of the weight of wet fine aggregate shall be calculated as follows:

$$P_1 = \frac{V_s - V_d}{M_s - V_s} \times 100$$

$$P_2 = \frac{V_s - V_d}{M_s - V_d} \times 100$$

Where P_1 = percentage surface moisture in terms of saturated surface dry fine aggregate.

V_s = Weight in N (gms) of water displaced

V_d = Weight of the sample (M_s) divided by the specific gravity on saturated and surface dry basis.

M_s = Weight in N (gms) of the sample

P_2 = Percentage surface moisture in terms of the weight of wet fine aggregate.

(II) For Coarse Aggregate–The same procedure with appropriate changes in the size of the sample and dimensions of the container may be applied to coarse aggregates.

6. Results :

Surface moisture of fine aggregate = percent

Surface moisture of coarse aggregate = percent

7. Precautions :

(a) All the weighings should be done to the nearest 0.1g.

(b) As far as possible the entraped air should be removed completely.

8. Comments–The accuracy of the method depends upon the accurate information on the specific gravity of the material in a saturated surface dry condition. The finer the aggregate, the more free water it will carry. Comment on these two statements.

9. Questions :

(a) Why do you perform this test?

(b) What are the various moisture conditions in which an aggregate can exit,

(c) What do you understand by free moisture of an aggregate.

(d) What do you understand by absorption capacity of an aggregate.

(e) What is meant by saturated surface dry condition of an aggregate.

(f) State the approximate absorption capacities of the following type of aggregates.

- (*i*) Average concrete sand.
- (*ii*) Crushed lime stone.
- (*iii*) Porous sand stone.
- (*iv*) Very light and porous aggregates.
- (*v*) Trap rock granite.

(g) State the approximate surface moisture contents of the following types of aggregates.

- (*i*) Moist gravel of crushed stone.
- (*ii*) Moist sand
- (*iii*) Moderately wet sand
- (*iv*) Very wet sand.

EXPERIMENT NO.2/10

AGGREGATE CRUSHING VALUE

1. **Object**–To determine the aggregate crushing value.

2. **Theory–The strength of concrete cannot exceed that of the bulk of aggregate it contains. Therefore, so long as the strength of aggregate is an order of magnitude stronger than that of the concrete made with the, it is sufficient. The aggregate crushing value gives a relative measure of the resistance of an aggregate in bulk to crushing under a gradually applied compressive load. However, it is not a true measure. Crushing value is defined as the ratio of fines passing a standard sieve, produced by crushing under standard conditions to the weight of course aggregate, expressed as a percentage.**

   Aggregate crushing value as determined by the IS Code method shall not exceed 30 for aggregates to be used for making concrete for wearing surface such as roads and runways and 45 for uses other than wearing surfaces.

3. **Apparatus**

   (*i*) An open-ended 150 mm cylindrical cell with appropriate base plate and plunger (Fig. 2.1) metal measure and tamping rod conforming to relevant IS standard.

   (*ii*) A balance of capacity 30 N (3kg).

   (*iii*) IS-Sieve 12.5 mm, 10mm and 2.36 mm

   (*iv*) A compression testing Machine.

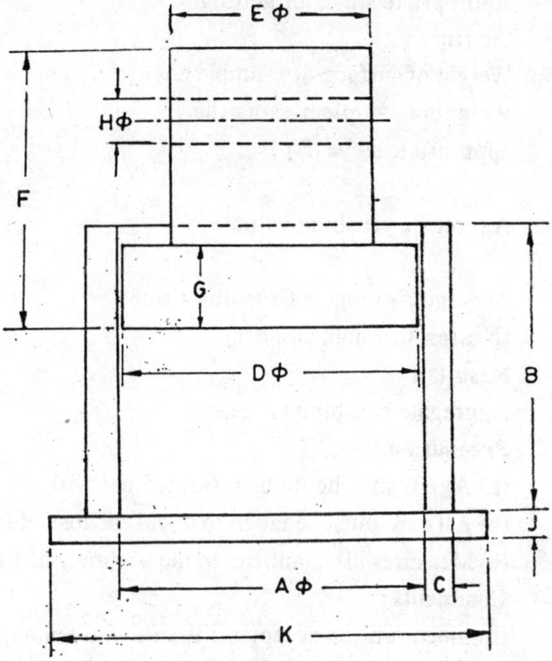

CYLINDRICAL CELL.

Fig. 2.1

4. **Procedure :**

   (a) The aggregate sample shall consists of particles passing on a 12.5 ,mm and retained on a 10 mm Sieve. When aggregate of the required size is not available, test may be conducted on the available sample, the specifications for cylinder and sieve separating the fines may be taken from the Table.2.1

   (b) The aggregate shall be tested in a saturated surface dry condition.

   (c) The quantity of aggregates should be such that the depth of the material in the cylinder after tamping shall be about 100mm.

   The appropriate quantity may be found conveniently by filling the cylindrical measure in three layers of approximately equal depth, each layer being tamped 25 times with the rounded end of the tamping rod, and finally levelled off.

   This weight of the tamping rod comprising the test sample shall be determined (weight A) and same weight of sample shall taken for repeat test.

(d) The cylinder of the test apparatus shall be put in position on the base plate and the test sample be added in thirds, each part being subjected to 25 strokes from the tamping rod. The surface of the plunger shall be carefully levelled and the plunger, inserted so that it rests horizontally on this surface, care being taken to ensure that the plunger does not jam in the cylinder.

(e) The apparatus with the test sample and the plunger in position shall then be placed between the platens of the test machine and loaded at a fairly uniform rate so that the total load of 400 KN is reached in 600 seconds.

(f) The load shall then be released and the whole of the material removed from the cylinder and sieved on a 2.36 mm IS-Sieve or the appropriate sieve if the sample size is not a standard one. The fraction passing the sieve shall be weighed (Weight B).

(g) Repeat the whole procedure for another set.

5. Observations and Calculations

Aggregate sample passing Sieve	=	mm
Aggregate retained on sieve	=	mm
Appropriate sieve for getting the fines	=	mm
Weight of surface-dry sample (A)	=	N(kg)
Weight of sample passing the appropriate sieve (B)	=	1. = B_1 = N(kg)
		2. = B_2 = N(Kg)
Aggregate crushing value	=	1. = $B_1/A \times 100$ =
	=	2. = $B_2/A \times 100$ =
Average Aggregate Crushing value (Nearest to whole number)	=	

6. Results :

Aggregate crushing value =

7. Precautions :

(a) Aggregate should be saturated but with dry surface.

(b) All care must be taken to avoid the loss of fines.

(c) Measures all quantities to the accuracy of 1 in 1000.

8. Comments :

Comment on the acceptability of the given aggregates for different purposes such as road, runways and buildings. Compare the values with standard values.

9. Questions

(a) What is difference between crushing load and impact load?

(b) What is the significance of this test?

(c) Why the strength tests on the stones cores are not usually resorted to?

(d) Why the moisture content of the sample is specified?

(e) Is the crushing value a true measure of resistance of aggregates to crushing? Why?

EXPERIMENT NO. 2/11

AGGREGATE IMPACT VALUE

1. **Object**–To determine aggregate impact value of the given course aggregate.

2. **Theory**–Toughness is the property of a material to resist impact. It is characterised by the energy absorbed before failure. Aggregate in bulk is used in structural concrete, pavements or in the railway tracks. Impact forces may result from moving vehicles, falling weights etc. Individual aggregate particles may fracture at corners or edges, or some elongated particles may fracture in the middle due to such impact forces. The impact value of bulk aggregates seeks to measure the extent of formation of smaller particles by resistance of bulk aggregates under impact loading. The impact results in fragmentation in a manner similar to that produced by the pressure of the plunger in the Aggregate crushing value test. For majority of aggregates, the aggregate impact value and the aggregate crushing values are numerically similar within fairly close limits, but the fine grained siliceous aggregate are less resistant to impact than static crushing load. The impact value should be 30 for aggregates to be used for wearing courses and 45 for the other surfaces.

3. **Apparatus**–Impact testing machine, a cylindrical measure, tamping rod, IS Sieves, balance and oven.

   (*i*) Impact Testing Machine:-It consists of a metal base with a plane lower surface supported well on a firm floor, without rocking. A detachable cylindrical steep cup of internal diameter 102 mm and depth 50 mm is rigidly fastened centrally to the base plate. A metal hammer of weight between 135 N(13.5kg) and 140N(14kg) having the lower end cylindrical in shape, 100mm in diameter and 50 mm long, with 2 mm chamfer at the lower edge is capable of sliding freely between vertical guides, and fall concentric over the cup. There is an arrangement of raising the hammer and allowing it to fall freely between vertical guides from a height of 380 mm on the test specimen in the cup, the height of fall being adjustable upto 5 mm. A key is provided for supporting the hammer while fastening or removing the cup (Fig. 2.2).

   (*ii*) Measure:-Cylindrical metal measure having internal diameter 75 mm and depth 50 mm for measuring aggregates.

   (*iii*) **Tampering** rod: Straight metal tamping rod of circular cross section, 10 mm in diameter and 230 mm **long**, rounded at one end.

   (*iv*) Sieves: IS sieve of sizes 12.5 mm, 10 mm and 2.36 mm.

   (*v*) Balance: A balance of capacity greater than 500g with least count of 0.1g.

   (*vi*) Oven: A thermostatically controlled drying oven capable of maintaining constant temperature between 100°C to 110°C.

4. **Procedure :**

   (a) Take a test sample of coarse aggregate the whole of which passes through a 12.5 mm IS Sieve and is retained on a 10 mm IS Sieve.

   (b) Fill the measure to about one third full with aggregates and tamp it with rounded end of the tamping rod with 25 strokes, Further add one third quantity and tamp it. The measure shall finally be filled to overflowing, tamped 25 times and surplus aggregates struck off using the tamping rod.

   (c) The net weight of the aggregate in the measure should be determined to the nearest gram (weight A.)

   (d) The cup of the Impact machine should be fixed firmly in position on the base of the machine and the whole of the test sample placed in it and compacted by a single tamping of 25 strokes.

   (e) Raise the hammer until its lower face is 380 mm above the upper surface of the aggregate in the cup and allow to fall freely on the aggregate. Make 15 such blows at the rate of one per second.

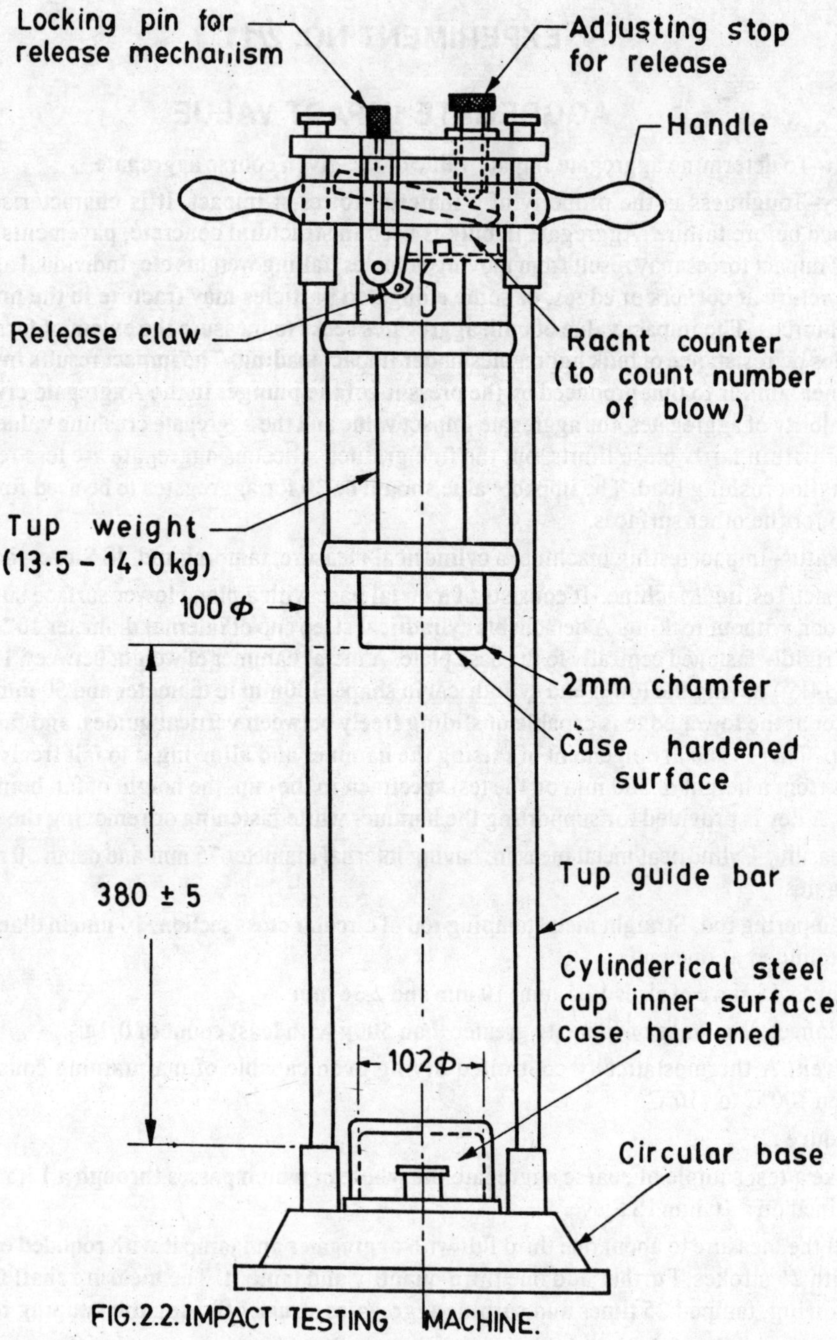

FIG.2.2. IMPACT TESTING MACHINE.

Fig. 2.2

(f) Remove the crushed aggregates from the cup and the whole of it be sieved on the 2.36 mm sieve until no further significant amount passes in one minute.

(g) The fraction passing the 2.35 mm Sieve is weighted (Weight B) and the fraction retained is also weighed (Weight C).

(h) The value is expressed as a whole number and is the average of three tests. If the difference A-(B+C) is more than one gram, the test shall be repeated.

5. Observations & Calculations

Weight of fraction passing 2.36 mm IS Sieve = B

Weight of Oven dried Sample = A

$$\text{Aggregate Impact value} = \frac{B}{A} \times 100\ \%$$

6. Results

Impact value is --------------- %

7. Precautions

(a) All weighing should be done on a sensitive weighting machine to an accuracy of 1 in 1000.

(b) Proper sieve should be used for preparing the sample.

(c) The sample should to subjected to standard number of blows i.e. 15 in number, at not less than one second interval.

(d) To avoid any accident while giving blows check that the metallic cup is tightly bolted to the base plate.

(e) The safety lock should always be in position, except while giving blows.

8. Comments

It is generally seen that aggregate crushing value agree with the aggregate Impact value. But some more brittle rocks give impact value which is relatively poorer. Solid samples of rocks like quarzite and Gravel give higher impact value than the crushing value.

In practice, we are more interested in finding crushing values of aggregates as compared to impact value.

9. Questions

(a) What do you mean by Impact load?

(b) What is the significance of this test?

(c) What are the various factors which affect the aggregate Impact value?

(d) How is Impact value expressed?

(e) What are the desirable limits of aggregate Impact value for different types of works?

(f) Value of Impact test for a specimen X is 25 and that of specimen Y is 45, which one is better for surface course of a pavement. Why?

EXPERIMENT NO. 2/12

ABRASION RESISTANCE USING DEVAL'S MACHINE

1. **Object**–To test the coarse aggregates for resistance to abrasion using Deval's Machine.
2. **Theory**–When concrete is used in pavements, then due to the movement of traffic, aggregates are subjected to wearing action at the top. Resistance to wear or hardness is hence an essential property for aggregates. Hence in order to test the suitability of coarse aggregates to resist the abrasing action due to traffic loads, this test is carried out in the laboratory. An aggregates sample which shows a low loss in this test is said to be generally hard, tough and strong.
3. **Apparatus**–Deval machine, 1.7 mm IS Sieve, Oven.

Deval Machine:–The deval abrasion testing machine consists of one or more (generally two) hollow cast iron cylinders closed at one end and provided with iron cover at the other end, capable of fitting tightly (Fig. 2.3). The inside diameter of the cylinder is 200 mm and length is 340 mm. The cylinders are mounted on a shaft at an angle of 30 degrees with the axis of rotation. Cast iron or steel spheres of about 48 mm diameter and 390 to 445 gm weight are used as abrasive charge. Six such spheres are used as abrasive charge, their total weight being 2500 ± 10 gms.

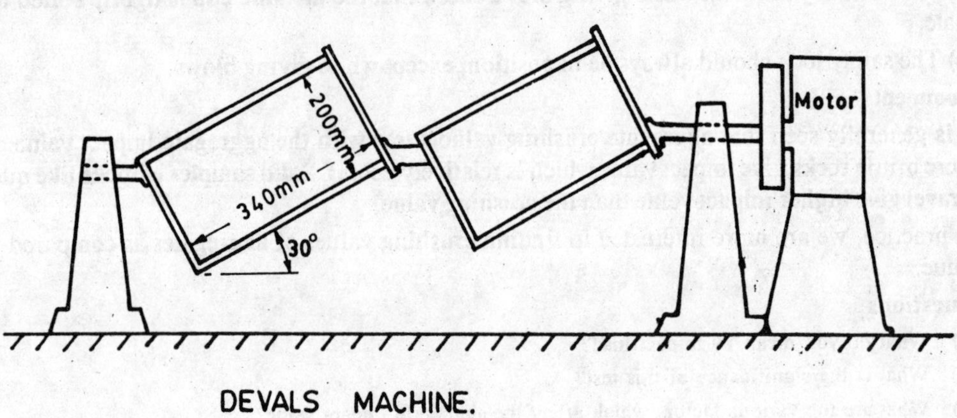

Fig. 2.3

4. **Procedure**

(a) Take a sample of about 5 kg ± 10 gm (most commonly taken) of stone consisting of nearly 50 pieces, which have been broken and tested to pass through 60 mm hole.

(b) The sample and the abrasive charge of 6 spheres of total weight 2500 ± 10 gm are placed in the Deval abrasion testing machine and the cover is tightly fixed.

(c) The machine is rotated at a speed of 30 to 33 rpm for 10,000 revolutions.

(d) After the completion of 10,000 revolution, the material is removed from the machine and is sieved on a 1.70 mm IS Sieve.

(e) The material retained on sieve is washed, dried and weighed to the nearest gram.

5. **Observations and Calculations –**

Original weight of the sample, W_1 (gm) = (gm)

Weight of material retained on 1.70 mm I.S. Sieve after the abrasion test, W_2 (gm) = (gm)

%age wear or Deval abrasion value = $= \frac{W_1 - W_2}{W_1} \times 100\ (\%)$

6. Results

Percentage wear of Aggregate is = ------------- %

7. Precautions

(a) The sample should be weighed accurately to an accuracy of 1 in 1000.

(b) The sample should be washed properly before putting it in the oven for drying.

(c) The drying of sample should be done between 105 to 110°C.

(d) All care must be taken to avoid loss of fines while weighing.

8. Comments

The sample taken in this test is of dry aggregate and therefore it is also known as dry test. The difference in %age of wear for different types of generally used stone aggregates is not much in this test. With the grading of the sample the losses may vary.

9. Questions

(a) What is the use of this test?

(b) How do you express the wear of aggregates?

(c) Lesser value of the test should indicate strong aggregate comment.

(d) What are the important factors which affect the percentage of wear?

EXPERIMENT NO. 2/13

ABRASION RESISTANCE USING LOS-ANGELES MACHINE

1. **Object**–To determine resistance to Abrasion for the course Aggregates using Los-Angeles machine.
2. **Theory**–In addition to strength and toughness, hardness or resistance to wear is an important properly of concrete used in roads and in floor surfaces subjected to heavy traffic. Several tests are available and it is possible to cause wear by abrasion i.e. by rubbing of a foreign material against the stone under test or by attrition of stone particles against one another.
3. **Apparatus**–Los-Angeles abrasion testing machine, 1.7 mm I.S. Sieve.

Los Angeles Machine: The Los-Angeles abrasion (Fig. 2.4) testing machine consists of a hollow steel cylinder, closed at both ends, having an inside diameter 700 mm and an inside length of 600mm, mounted on stub shafts about which it rotates on a horizontal axis. An opening is provided in the cylinder for the introduction of the test sample. A removable steel shelf projecting radially 88 mm into the cylinder and

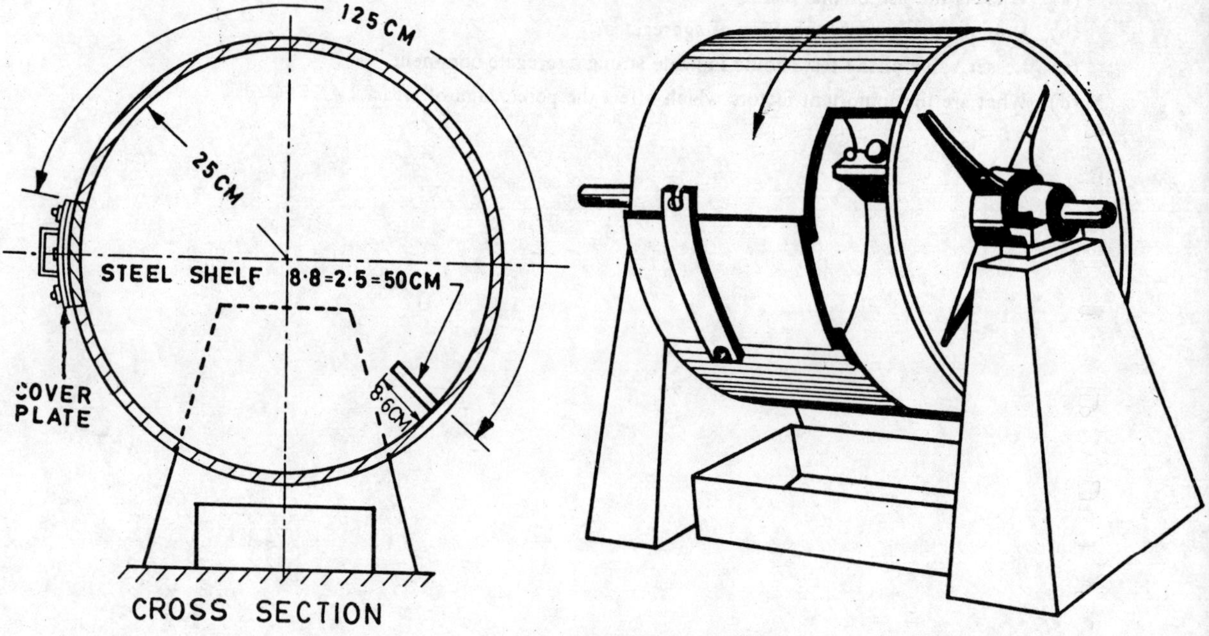

Los Angeles Machine

Fig. 2.4

extending to the full length of it, is mounted on the interior surface of the cylinder rigidly, parallel to axis. Abrasive charge, consisting of cast iron spheres approximately, 48 mm in diameter and 390 to 445 gm in weight are used. The weight of the sphere used as the abrasive charge and the number of spheres to be used are specified depending on the gradation of the aggregates tested. The aggregate grading have been standardised as A,B,C,D,E,F and G for this test and IS Specifications for the grading and abrasive charge to be used are given in Table 2.11

Table 2.11

Grading	*Weight in grams of each test sample in the size range, mm (Passing and retained on square holes.)*										*Abrasive charge*	
	80–63	63–50	50–40	40–25	25–20	20–12.5	12.5–10	10–6.3	6.3–4.75	4.75–2.36	*Number of spheres*	*Weight of charge, g*
A	–	–	–	1250	1250	1250	1250	–	–	–	12	5000±25
B	–	–	–	–	–	2500	2500	–	–	–	11	4584±25
B	–	–	–	–	–	–	–	25000	2500	–	8	3330±20
D	–	–	–	–	–	–	–	–	–	5000	6	2500±15
E	2500*	2500*	5000*	–	–	–	–	–	–	–	12	500±25
F	–	–	5000*	5000*	–	–	–	–	–	–	12	5000±25
G	–	–	–	5000*	5000*	–	–	–	–	–	12	5000±25

* Tolerence of ± 2 percent is permitted.

4. Procedure

(a) Clean aggregate dried in an oven at 105° - 110°C to constant weight, confirming to any one of the grading A to G, as per table 2.11, is used for the test.

(b) Aggregates weighting 50 N (5 kg) for grading A,B,C or D and 100 N (10 kg) for grading E, F or G may be taken and is placed in the cylinder.

(c) The abrasive charge is also chosen from Table 2.11 and is placed in the cylinder.

(d) The cover is fixed dirt-tight and the machine is rotated at a speed of 30 to 33 r.p.m.

(e) The machine is rotated for 500 revolutions for grading A,B, C and D and 1000 revolutions for E,F, and G.

(f) Material is discharged from the machine taking care to take out entire stone dust.

(g) Using a sieve of size-larger than 1.70 mm IS Sieve, the material is first separated into two parts and the finer portion is taken out and sieved further on a 1.7 mm IS Sieve.

(h) The portion of material coarser than 1.7 mm size is washed and dried in an over at 105 to 110°C to constant weight and weighed correct to one gram.

5. Observations and Calculations

Number of revolutions provided =

Original weight of aggregates = $W_1(g) =$

Weight of aggregates retained on 1.7 mm I.S. Sieve after the test = $W_2\,(g) =$

Loss of weight due to wear = $(W_1 - W_2)\,g =$

Loss Angeles abrasion value, % = Percentage wear = $\dfrac{W_1 - W_2}{W_1} \times 100$

6. Results

Percentage wear of Aggregate is = --------------%

7. Precautions

(a) To minimize wear of 1.7 mm Sieve use a higher grade sieve first.

(b) No spillage of aggregates should be there while putting the sample in the machine or while taking it out.

(c) All the weighting should be done accurately.

8. Comments

It is seen that percentage of wear increases if the aggregate used is flat and elongated. This is true for soft material also. But percentage of wear really depends upon the grading, number of steel balls (Abrasive charge), number of revolution of drum and the mass of the sample.

9. Questions

(a) Define Abrasive charge?

(b) Define the term 'Abrasion'.

(c) What is the significance of this test?

(d) On what factors does the abrasive charge depends?

(e) How is grading of aggregate done?

(f) How is wear expressed?

(g) Enumerate the factors which affect the percentage of wear of aggregates

EXPERIMENT NO. 2/14

FLAKINESS AND ELONGATION INDICES

1. **Objective**–To determine the flakiness and Elongation indices of coarse aggregates.
2. **Theory**–The particle shape of aggregate is determined by the percentage of flaky and elongated particles contained in it. According to IS Code an aggregate having least dimensions less than three fifth of its mean dimension is termed as flaky and particles having the largest dimension (length) greatest than 9/5 times the mean size are termed elongated. The presence of excess flaky and elongated particles in concrete aggregates decreases the workability appreciably for a given W/C ratio, therefore they require larger amounts of sand, cement and water. The percentage of flaky and elongated particles should be limited to 10 to 15.
3. **Apparatus** –Standard thickness gauge shown in Fig. 2.5, standard length gauge shown in Fig. 2.6, IS Sieve of sizes 63, 50, 31.5, 25, 20, 16, 12.5, 10 and 6.3 mm and a balance.
4. **Procedure**

(*i*) For determining flakiness index:

(a) Take quantity W_f gm of coarse aggregates so as to provide at least 200 pieces of any fraction.

(b) Sieve out the sample by hand by shaking each sieve in order; for a period not less than 2 minutes.

(c) Pass the separated aggregate as retained on the Sieves in Step (b) through the corresponding slots in the thickness gauge shown in Fig. 2.5

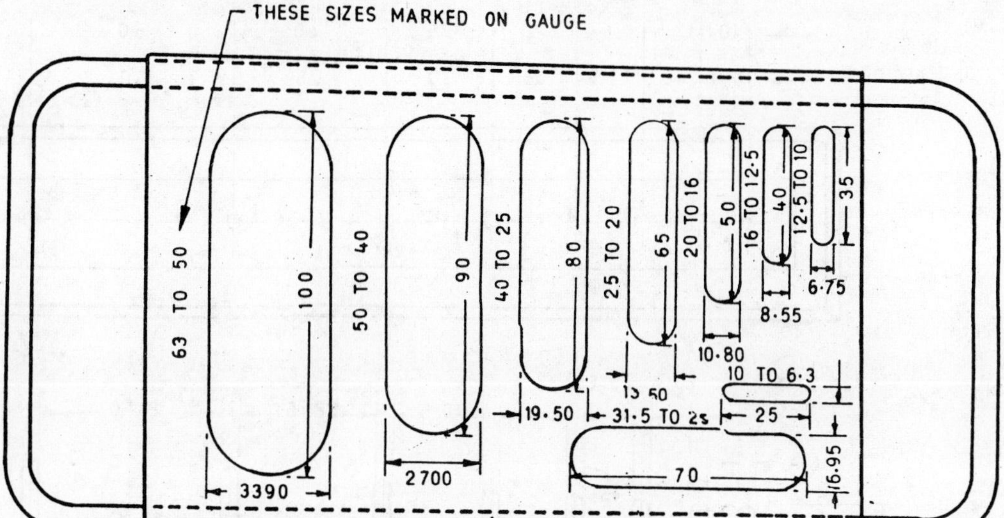

THICKNESS GAUGE.

Fig. 2.5

For example: The material passing through 25 mm sieve and retained on 20 mm sieve is passed through

$\frac{1}{2}(25+20) \times \frac{3}{5} = 13.5$ mm slot.

(d) Determine the weights of aggregates passing through each of the slots.

(e) Calculate the total weight W'_f of the materials passing through the slots of the thickness gauge and finally calculate the flakiness index as defined: The flakiness index is an empirical factor expressing the total materials passing through the slots of the thickness gauge as the percentage of the weight of sample taken for testing.

(*ii*) For determining Elongation Index:

(a) Steps a and b remains same as above. Let the weight of sample be designated as W_e

(b) Pass the separated aggregates as retained above through the corresponding length gauge size shown in Fig. 2.6.

For example: The material passing through 25 mm sieve and retained on 20 mm sieve is passed through

$\frac{1}{2}\,(25 + 20)\,\frac{9}{5} = 40.5$ mm slot.

(c) Determine the weights of aggregates passing through each of the slots.

(d) Find the total mass W'_e of the material retained on the length gauge and finally calculate the elongation index as percentage material retained by the length gauges of the total material taken for testing.

5. **Observations and Calculations**

(*i*) Flakiness index of coarse aggregates:

Weight of Aggregates, W_f . . . . (gm)

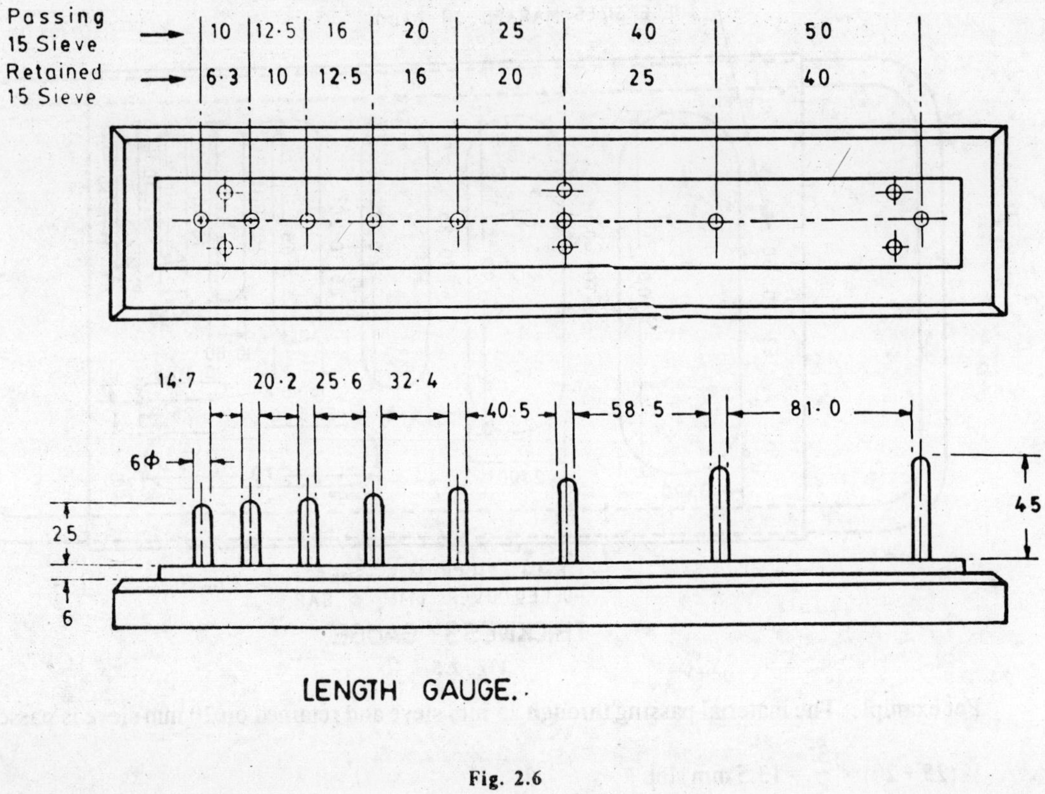

Fig. 2.6

S.No	Size of Aggregate			Weight of Aggregates retained on the length gauge (gm)
	Passing through IS : Sieve, mm	Retained on IS: Sieve, mm	Length gauge size, mm	
1.	63	50	33.90	
2.	50	40	27.00	
3.	40	31.5	19.50	
4.	31.5	25	16.95	
5.	25	20	13.50	
6.	20	16	10.80	
7.	16	12.5	8.55	
8.	12.5	10	6.75	
9.	10	6.3	4.89	

Flakiness index of coarse aggregates = $\frac{W'_f}{W_f} \times 100 = \%$ $\sum W = W'_f$

(ii) Elongation index of coarse aggregates:

Weight of Aggregates, W_e = (gm)

S.No	Size of Aggregate			Weight of Aggregates retained on the length gauge (gm)
	Passing through IS : Sieve, mm	Retained on IS: Sieve, mm	Length gauge size, mm	
1.	63	50	—	
2.	50	40	81.0	
3.	40	31.5	58.5	
4.	31.5	25	—	
5.	25	20	40.5	
6.	20	16	32.4	
7.	16	12.5	25.6	
8.	12.5	10	20.2	
9.	10	6.3	14.7	

$\sum W = W'_e$

Elongation Index of Coarse Aggregate = $\frac{W'_e}{W_e} \times 100$

6. Results

Flakiness Index = %

Elongation Index = %

7. Precautions

(a) Take the sample by quatering.

(b) Do not force to pass the particle from the thickness gauge or length gauge.

(c) Measure the mass of aggregate retained, accurately.

8. **Comments**

Elongated or flaky particles in excess of 10 to 15 percent are generally not desirable. These tests are not valid for particle sizes smaller than 6.3 mm.

9. **Questions**

(a) Define flakiness index. What is its significance?

(b) Define Elongation Index. What is its significance?

(c) How are the flakiness and elongation indices expressed?

(d) What is quatering of aggregates? How it is done?

(e) What is the effect of flakiness and elongation indices on the resulting concrete.

REFERENCES

1. I.S. 383-1970 - Coarse and fine aggregate from natural sources for concrete.
2. I.S. 460-1962 - Test sieves.
3. I.S. 2386-1963 - Methods of test for aggregate for concrete.
   Part-I–Particle size and shape.
   Part-II–Estimation of deleterious materials and organic impurities.
   Part-III–Specific gravity, density, voids, absorption and bulking.
   Part-IV–Mechanical properties.
   Part-V–Soundness.
   Part-VI–measuring mortar making properties of fine aggregate.
   Part-VII–Alkali aggregate reactivity.
   Part VIII–Petrographic examination.
4. I.S. 2430-1969–Methods for sampling of aggregate for concrete.
5. Concrete Technology–Student Manual Published by D.B. Taraporevala and Sons, Bombay-1.
6. IS 650-1966–Specification for standard sand for testing of cement B.I.S. New Delhi.
7. Concrete Hand book–Published by the concrete Association of India, Bombay.
8. Composition and properties of concrete by Goerge Karl Troxell and Harmer E. Davis Published by Mc Graw Hill Book Co. New York

PART III

CONCRETE

EXPERIMENT NO. 3/1

DESIGN OF A CONCRETE MIX BY TRIAL AND ERROR METHOD

1. **Object :** To design a concrete mix by trial and error method for:

   (*i*) 28 days cube compressive strength = 15 N/mm^2 (150 kg/cm^2)

   (*ii*) Slump = 40mm (4 cm)

2. **Theory :** Mix design can be defined as the process of selecting suitable ingredients of concrete and determining their relative quantities with the object of producing concrete as economically as possible, with certain minimum properties notably consistency, strength and durability.

   The present experiment is based on the principle that fine aggregate should fill all the voids in the coarse aggregate and the cement paste should fill all the voids in the fine aggregate. The aggregates having less voids give stronger concrete. The fine aggregate and coarse aggregate particles have nearly same density, the mixture giving maximum weight will have maximum solid matter and hence least voids. Such a combination of fine and coarse aggregate will require minimum amount of cement and will be most economical for a given water-cement ratio and slump.

   The proportion of fine to coarse aggregate which gives maximum weight of combined aggregate can be obtained by trial. By actual trial, the quantity of cement required to give the desired slump can be found out. The actual amounts of cement, fine aggregate, coarse aggregate and water to meet the requirements of strength, workability and economy can be calculated.

3. **Apparatus :** measuring cylinder, weighting machine, container of constant volume, tamping rod, slump test apparatus, Compression testing machine.

4. **Procedure:**

   (a) Take a container of given volume and weigh it.

   (b) Find the unit weight of mixed aggregates for various percentages of fine aggregate (Say 20, 25, 30, 35, 40, 45 & 50).

   (c) Fill the container full with dry mix of fine aggregate and coarse aggregate in three layers, lightly ram each layer and strike level the top of container by means of a straight edge. Weight the container full of aggregates.

   (d) Plot a curve between unit weight and percentage of fine aggregate.

   (e) Pick up the optimum percentage of sand from the above plot giving maximum unit weight.

   (f) Select a W/C ratio for the required strength of concrete from graphs (Fig. 3.1).

   (g) Determine workability in terms of slump for a particular job (40 mm for the present case).

   (h) Prepare the slurry of cement and water for the above W/C ratio.

   (i) Take the dense mixed aggregate and mix it with cement-water slurry, gradually increasing the slurry till a slump of 40m is obtained.

   (j) Weigh the slurry residue and find the weight of slurry used for the mix by difference.

   (k) Prepare three cubes of 150mm (15 cm) size and test them wet after 28 days of curing and check for the desired compressive strength.

5. **Observations and Calculations**

   (a) Calibration of container :

Weight of empty container	=	N (kg.)
Weight of container full of water	=	N (kg.)

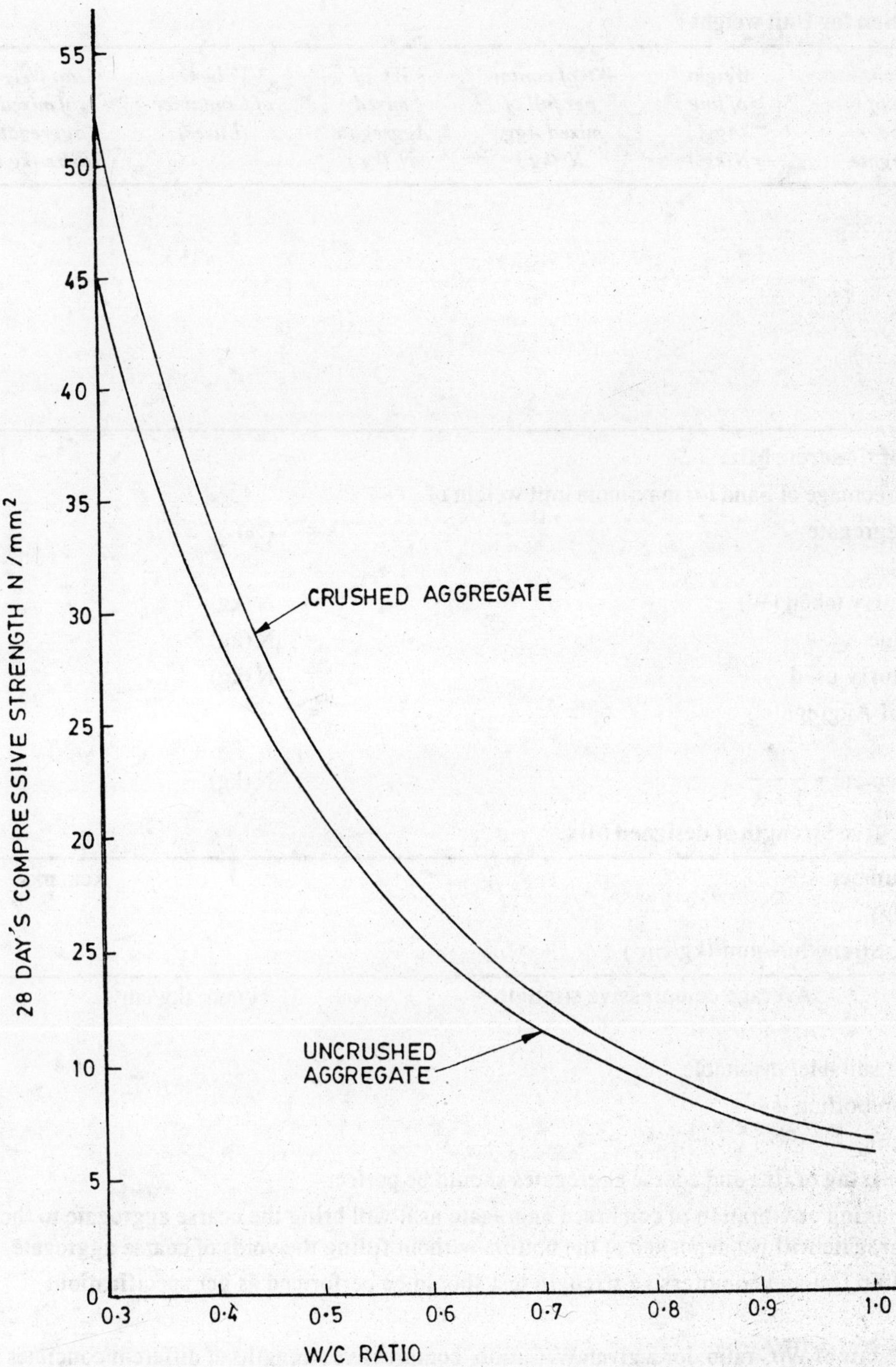

Fig. 3.1 Relation between W/C Ratio and Compressive Strength.

Weight of water in container = N (kg.)

Volume of container = Litres.

(b) Observation for Unit weight :

Sl. No.	*Percentage of Fine Aggregate*	*Weight of fine Agg. N(kg.)*	*Wt. of container full of mixed Agg. N (kg.)*	*Wt. of mixed Aggregate N (kg.)*	*Volume of Container (Litres)*	*Unit Weight of mixed aggregate N/litre (kg.lit.)*
1.						
2.						
3.						
4.						
5.						
6.						
7.						

(c) Proportion of Concrete Mix:

Optimum percentage of Sand for maximum unit weight of combined aggregate = (%)

W/C ratio (X) =

Weight of slurry taken (W) = N (kg)

Slurry Residue = N (kg)

Weight of slurry used = N (kg)

Proportion of Aggregate =

Weight of Cement= $\frac{W}{1+X}$ = N (kg)

(d) Compressive Strength of designed Mix:

Specimen Number	1	2	3	Remarks
Load in N (kg)				
Compressive Strength N/mm^2(kg/cm^2)				

Average compressive strength = N/mm^2 (kg/cm^2)

6. Result :

1. The mix is suitable/unsuitable
2. The mix proportion is

7. Precautions :

(*i*) The dry mixing of fine and coarse aggregates should be perfect.

(*ii*) Avoid shaking or vibration of combined aggregate as it will bring the coarse aggregate to the top and fine aggregate will get deposited at the bottom without filling the voids of coarse aggregate.

(iii) The slump test and compressive strength test should be performed as per specifications.

8. Comments :

According to law of W/C ratio, for a given W/C ratio, compressive strengths of different concretes will be same provided they are compacted to the same extent. By merely increasing the quantity of cement, the strength will not get increased, unless W/C ratio is reduced. Therefore the proportioning of concrete

mix is to fix a certain water-cement ratio giving desired strength and then to so select the proportions of fine and coarse aggregates such that combined aggregate needs the least amount of water-cement paste for full compaction. The concrete obtained in this way will be most economical for a given strength. Full compaction means that all voids get filled with cement paste and there is no air entrapped.

9. Questions :

(a) How do you specify the proportions of a concrete mix.

(b) State the relationship between compressive strength at 28 days and water cement ratio.

(c) State the importance of trial method of proportioning.

(d) Explain the meaning of complete compaction.

(e) Is the relation between unit weight of combined aggregate and percentage of sand linear.

(f) Can we increase the strength of concrete mix by increasing the quantity of cement?

EXPERIMENT NO.3/2

DESIGN OF A CONCRETE MIX BY FINENESS MODULUS METHOD

1. **Object**–To design a concrete mix by Fineness Modulus method.

   (*i*) 28 day's cube compressive strength = 15 N/mm^2 (150 kg/cm^2)

   (*ii*) Slump = 40 mm (4 cm)

2. **Theory**–Fineness modulus of an aggregate gives an indication of the probable behaviour of a concrete mix prepared from aggregate having certain gradings. Thus it is only an index of fineness and gives an idea of the mean size of particles in the entire body of the aggregate.

3. **Apparatus**–Weighing machine, cylinderical measure, graduated cylinder, Sieve sets for determining fineness modulus of fine aggregate and coarse aggregate, slumps cone apparatus.

4. **Procedure :**

   (a) Find the maximum size of given coarse aggregate.

   (b) Determine the fineness modulus of given fine aggregate.

   (c) Determine the fineness modulus of given coarse aggregate.

   (d) Obtain a combined aggregate of a certain fineness modulus from the given materials. The proportions of fine to combined aggregate by weight is given by:

$$P = \frac{F_c - F_m}{F_c - F_f} \times 100$$

Where,

P = Percentage of fine aggregate by weight to combined or mixed aggregate

F_c = Fineness modulus of the coarse aggregate.

F_f = Fineness modulus of fine aggregate.

F_m = Fineness modulus of mixed or combined aggregate.

The fineness modulii of combined aggregates for different maximum sizes of aggregates are:

Table 3.1 Limits of Fineness Modulii

Sr.No.	*Maximum size of aggregate*		*Fineness Modulus*	
			Min	*Max.*
1.	Fine Aggregate		2.00	3.50
2.	Coarse Aggregate	20 mm	6.00	6.90
		40 mm	6.90	7.50
		75 mm	7.50	8.00
		150 mm	8.00	8.50
3.	Mixed Aggregate	20 mm	4.70	5.10
		25 mm	5.00	5.50
		32 mm	5.20	5.70
		40 mm	5.40	5.90
		75 mm	5.80	6.30
		150 mm	6.50	7.20

(e) Fix the proportion of fine aggregate to coarse aggregate to obtain the desired mixed or combined aggregate.

(f) Select a W/C ratio for the required strength of concrete from tables or graphs.

(g) Determine workability in terms of slump for a particular job (40 mm given for the present case).

(h) Prepare the slurry of cement and water for the above W/C ratio.

(i) Calculate the weights of fine and coarse aggregate and cement and water to prepare necessary concrete.

(j) Add water-cement slurry (gradually increasing) till a slump of 40 mm is obtained.

(k) Weight the slurry residue.

(l) Fix the proportions of the materials.

(m) Prepare three cubes of 150 mm (15 cm) size and test them wet after 28 days of curing and check for the desired compressive strength.

5. **Observations and Calculations:**

(a) Proportions of Concrete Mix.

$$P = \frac{F_c - F_m}{F_c - F_f} \times 100$$

W/C ratio (x) =

Weight of Slurry taken = N(Kg.)

Slurry residue = N(Kg.)

Weight of Slurry used = W = N(Kg.)

Weight of cement used = $\frac{W}{1+x}$ = N(Kg.)

Proportions of Aggregate = ...

Mix proportions =

(b) Compressive Strength of designed Mix.

Specimen Number	*1*	*2*	*3*	*Remarks*
Load in N(Kg.)				
Compressive Strength (N/mm^2) (Kg/cm^2)				

Average compressive strength = N/mm^2 (Kg/cm^2)

6. **Results :**

(a) The mix is suitable/unsuitable

(b) The mix proportions is......

7. **Precautions :**

(a) The dry mixing of fine and coarse aggregate should be perfect. Avoid shaking or vibration of combined aggregate.

(b) The slump test and compressive strength tests should be performed as per specifications.

8. **Comments :**

Combined aggregate should be well graded so that the voids in them in the fully compacted state are the minimum. Sometimes the coarse aggregate is not uniformly graded i.e. particles of certain sizes are

absent. Fineness modulus value above a specified value will result in a harsh mix and a value below the specified value will give an uneconomical mix.

9. Questions :

(a) Define fineness modulus of an aggregate

(b) Define grading of an aggregate

(c) What is gap grading

(d) Discuss the importance of grading curve

(e) State the factors affecting the requirement of paste for an aggregate

(f) State Abrahms water cement ratio law

(g) State the formula relating water cement ratio and compressive strength at 28 days

(h) Show graphically the relation between compressive strength and water-cement ratio and comment on this relation.

EXPERIMENT NO. 3/3

CONSISTENCY OF FRESHLY MIXED CONCRETE BY SLUMP TEST

1. **Object:–To determine the consistency of fresh concrete of given proportions by slump test where the nominal maximum size of the aggregate does not exceed 38 mm.**
2. **Theory:–This is a test used extensively at construction site all over the world. The slump test does not measure the workability of concrete, however it is very useful in detecting the variations in the uniformity of a mix of given nominal proportions. It also gives an idea of W/C ration needed for concrete to be used for different works.**

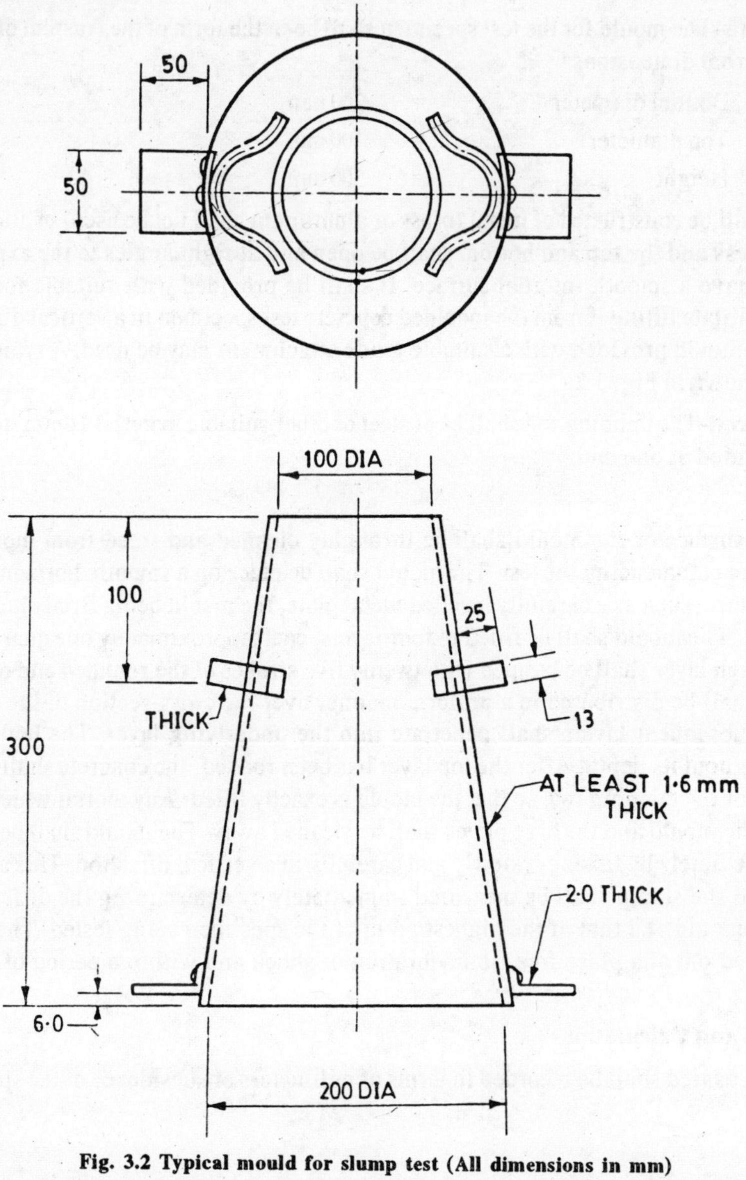

Fig. 3.2 Typical mould for slump test (All dimensions in mm)

Fresh un-supported concrete flows to the sides and a sinking in the height takes place. This vertical settlement is known as slump. In the slump test fresh concrete is filled in a mould of specified shape and dimensions and settlement or slump is measured when the supporting mould is removed.

Concrete is said to be workable if it can be easily mixed, placed, compacted and easily finished. A workable concrete should not show any segregation or bleeding. Segregation is said to occur when coarse aggregate tries to separate out from the finer material and we get concentration of coarse aggregate at one place. This results in large voids, less durability and less strength. Bleeding of concrete is said to occur when excess water comes up at the surface of the concrete. This causes small pores in the mass of the concrete and is undesirable.

3. **Apparatus:**

(a) **Slump cone**–The mould for the test specimen shall be in the form of the frustum of a cone having the following internal dimensions:

Bottom diameter	=	200 mm
Top diameter	=	100 mm
Height	=	300 mm

The mould shall be constructed of metal (brass or aluminium shall not be used) of atleast 1.6 mm (or 16 SWG) thickness and the top and bottom shall be open and at right angles to the axis of the cone. The mould shall have a smooth internal surface. It shall be provided with suitable foot pieces and also handles to facilitate lifting if from the moulded concrete test specimen in a vertical direction as required by the test. A mould provided with a suitable guide attachment may be used. A typical mould without the guide is shown in Fig. 3.2.

(b) **Tamping rod**-The tamping rod shall be of steel or other suitable material 16mm in diameter, 600mm long and rounded at one end.

4. **Procedure:**

The internal surface of the mould shall be throughly cleaned and freed from moisture and any set concrete before commencing the test. The mould shall be place on a smooth, horizontal, rigid and non-absorbent surface, such as a carefully levelled metal plate, the mould being firmly held in place while it is being filled. The mould shall be filled in four layers, each approximately one quarter of the height of the mould. Each layer shall be tamped with twenty five strokes of the rounded end of the tamping rod. The strokes shall be distributed in a uniform manner over the cross-section of the mould and for the second and subsequent layers shall penetrate into the underlying layer. The bottom layer shall be tamped throughout its depth. After the top layer has been rodded, the concrete shall be struck off level with a trowel or the tamping rod, so that the mould is exactly filled. Any mortar which may have leaked out between the mould and the base plates shall be cleaned away. The mould shall be removed from the concrete immediately by raising it slowly and carefully in a vertical direction. This allows the concrete to subside and the slump shall be measured immediately by determining the difference between the height of the mould and that of the highest point of the specimen being tested. The above operations shall be carried out at a place free from vibration or shock and within a period of two minutes after sampling.

5. **Observations and Calculations**

The slump measured shall be recorded in terms of milimeters of subsidence of the specimen during the test.

Sl. No.	*W/C Ratio*	*Slump (mm)*
1.		
2.		
3.		
4.		

Study the plot between W/c ratio and slump.

6. Precautions :

(a) Apply the strokes with the tamping rod uniformly through the full depth of the concrete of previous layer.

(b) Remove the mould very slowly by lifting it upwards so that concrete within mould does not get disturbed.

(c) The base plate used in the experiment should be clean and smooth so that there is complete contact between base plate and bottom of the mould.

(d) Test should be performed away from the ground vibrations produced due to machinery or some other sources.

(e) Test should be completed in a minimum time say 2 to 3 minutes.

7. Comments:

This test does not given a true picture of workability. For example, harsh course mix cannot be said to have same workability as one with a large proportion of sand even though they have the same slump.

Any slump specimen which collapses or shears off laterally gives incorrect result and if this occurs, the test shall be repeated with another sample. If in the repeat test also the specimen should shear, the slump shall be measured and the fact that the specimen sheared shall be recorded.

Some indication of the cohensiveness and workability of the mix can be obtained, if after the slump measurement has been completed, the side of the concrete is tapped gently with the tamping rod. A well proportioned concrete mix which has a appreciable slump, will gradually slump further, but if the mix has been badly proportioned, it is likely to fall apart.

By slump test, we can determine the water-cement ratio to give the specified slump value. In this test W/C is varied and every time slump value is measured till we arrive at W/C ratio giving the required slump value.

8. Questions :

(a) Define slump of concrete.

(b) State the significance of slump test.

(c) State the slump range for concrete used for:

   (a) Concrete for reinforced concrete beams and slabs.

   (b) Concrete for roads.

   (c) Columns and retaining walls.

   (d) Mass concrete in foundations.

(d) Differentiate by sketches the terms true slump, shear and collapse type of slumps.

(e) Define workability and consistency of freshly mixed concrete.

(f) How does W/c ratio effects the workability?

EXPERIMENT NO. 3/4

WORKABILITY OF FRESHLY MIXED CONCRETE BY COMPACTION FACTOR TEST

1. **Object :**–To determine the workability of freshly mixed concrete by the compaction factor test.
2. **Theory** :–Compaction factor test specifies the procedure for determining the workability of concrete, where the nominal maximum size of the aggregate does not exceed 38 mm. The test is designed primerely for use in the laboratory, but if circumstances permit, it may also be used in the field. It is more precise and sensitive than the slump test and is particularly useful for concrete mixes of very low workability as are normally used when concrete is to be compacted by vibration, such concrete may consistently fail to slump. This test is based upon the definition, that workability is that property of the concrete which determines the amount of work required to produce full compaction. These test therefore consists essentially of applying a standard amount of work to standard quantity of concrete and measuring the resulting compaction.
3. **Apparatus :**

(a) Compaction factor apparatus : A diagram of the apparatus is shown in Fig. 3.3. It consists of two conical hoppers (A and B) mounted above a cylindrical mould (C). The essential dimensions of the hoppers and mould and the distances between them shall be as shows in table 3.2.

TABLE 3.2 Essential dimensions of the Compaction Factor Apparatus for use with Aggregate Not exceeding 38 mm Nominal Max. size.

		Dimensions (mm)
Upper Hopper 'A'		
Top internal dia	...	25.4
Bottom internal dia	...	12.7
Internal height	...	27.9
Lower Hopper 'B'		
Top internal dia	...	22.9
Bottom internal dia	...	12.7
Internal height	...	22.9
Cylinder 'C'		
Internal diameter	...	15.2
Internal height	...	30.5
Distance between bottom of Upper hopper and top of lower hopper	...	20.3
Distance between bottom of lower hopper and top of cylinder	...	20.3

(b) Trowels, graduated cylinder of 100 ml capacity, balance to weigh upto 30 N (3kg) and sensitive nearest to 0.1 N (10gms) tamping rod.

4. **Procedure :**

The sample of concrete to be tested shall be placed gently in the upper hopper. The hopper shall be filled level with its brim and the trap door shall be opened so that the concrete falls into the lower hopper. Certain mixes have a tendency to stick in one or both the hoppers. If this occurs, the concrete may be helped through by pushing the rod gently into the concrete from the top. During this process,

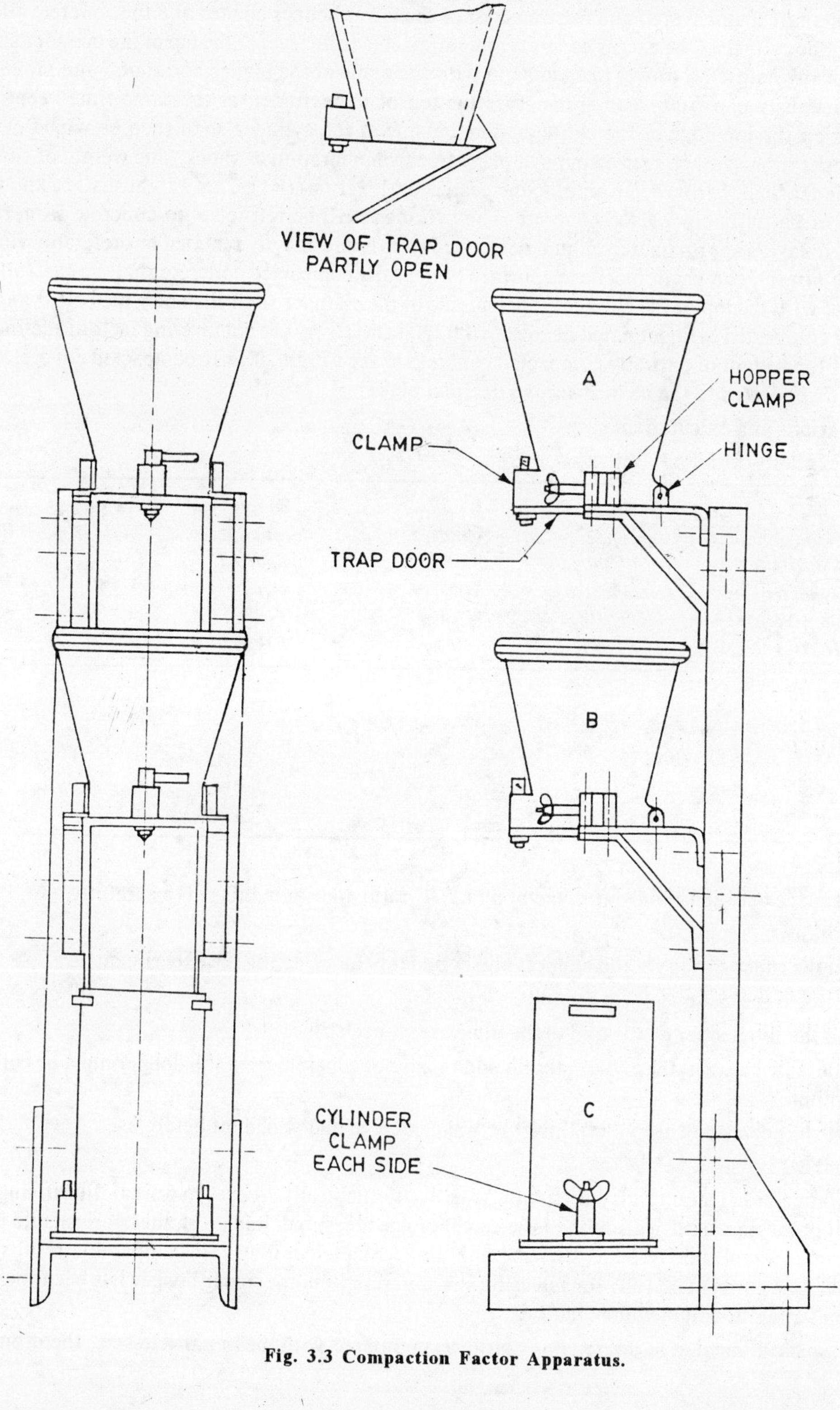

Fig. 3.3 Compaction Factor Apparatus.

the cylinder shall be covered by the trowels. Immediately after the concrete has come to rest, the cylinder shall be uncovered and the trap door of the lower hopper opened and the concrete allowed to fall into the cylinder. The excess concrete remaining above the level of the top of the cylinder shall then be cut off by holding a trowel in each hand with the plane of the blades horizontal and moving them simultaneously one from each side across the top of the cylinder, at the same time keeping them pressed on the top edge of the cylinder. The outside of the cylinder shall then be wiped clear. The above operation shall be carried out at a place free from vibration or shock. The weight of concrete in the cylinder shall then be determined to the nearest 0.01 N(1gm) (W_2). This weight shall be known as the weight of partially compacted concrete. The cylinder shall be refilled with concrete from the same sample to layers approximately 50mm deep, the layers being heavily rammed or preferably vibrated so as to obtain full compaction. The top surface of the fully compacted concrete shall be carefully struck off level with the top of the cylinder. The outside of the cylinder shall then be wiped clear and weight of fully compacted cylinder noted nearest to 0.0 IN(1gm) (W_3). The compacting factor is defined as the ratio of the weight of partially compacted concrete to the weight of fully compacted concrete. It shall normally be stated to the nearest second decimal place.

5. **Observations and calculations :**

Weight of empty cylinder = W_1........................= N (kg)

Sr. No	W/C ratio	Wt. of cylinder with partially compacted conc. (W_2) N (kg.)	Wt. of cylinder with fully compacted conc. (W_3) N(kg.)	Wt. of partially compacted conc. (W_2-W_1) N (kg.)	Wt. of fully compacted conc. (W_3-W_1) N (kg.)	C.F. = $\frac{W_2-W_1}{W_3-W_1}$
1.	0.50					
2.	0.55					
3.	0.60					
4.	0.65					
5.	0.70					

6. **Results :**

Plot a curve between compaction factor and W/C ratio and study this curve carefully.

7. **Precautions:**

(a) Oil the inner surface of the hoppers and cylinder before starting the experiment.

(b) Perform the test on a level ground.

(c) Fill the top hopper gently and to the same extent each time.

(d) The time between the end of mixing and release of concrete from top hopper must be constant say two minutes.

(e) The hoppers and the cylinder must be washed clean and wiped off before use.

8. **Comments :**

The compaction factor test is sufficiently sensitive to enable differences in workability arising from the initial processes in the hydration of the cement to be measured. Each test, therefore should be carried out at a constant time interval after the mixing is completed, if strictly comparable results are to be obtained. A convenient time for releasing the concrete from the upper hopper has been found to be 2 minutes after the completion of mixing.

When maximum size of aggregate is large as compared with mean particle size, the drop in to the cylinder will produced segregation and give unreliable comparisons with other mixes of smaller maximum aggregate. This test clearly indicates that with increase in the size of coarse aggregate the workability will decrease.

9. Questions:

(a) Define compaction factor. (C.F.)

(b) How do you compare slump test with compaction factor test?

(c) Will the workability increase or decrease with increase in compaction factor and why?

(d) Does compaction factor test gives a better measure of workability than slump test?

(e) Differentiate between workability and consistency.

(f) Can we use this test in the field also?

(g) Write a note on the importance of compaction factor in concrete mix design.

EXPERIMENT NO. 3/5

WORKABILITY OF FRESHLY MIXED CONCRETE BY THE USE OF FLOW TABLE

1. **Object**–To determine the workability of freshly mixed concrete by the use of flow table, when the nominal size of the aggregate does not exceed 38 mm.

2. **Theory** –This method specifies the procedure for the use of the flow table to determine the fluidity of concrete. It also gives an indication of consistency of the concrete and its tendency to segregation by measuring the spread of a pile of concrete subjected to jolting. It is with regard to segregation that the flow test is of greatest value but it also gives a good assessment of consistence of stiff, rich and rather cohesive mixes. It should be noted that the flow test does not measure workability as concretes having the same flow, may differ considerably in their workability.

3. **Apparatus :**

(a) Mould—The mould shall made of a smooth metal casting as shown in the Fig.3.4(a) in the form of

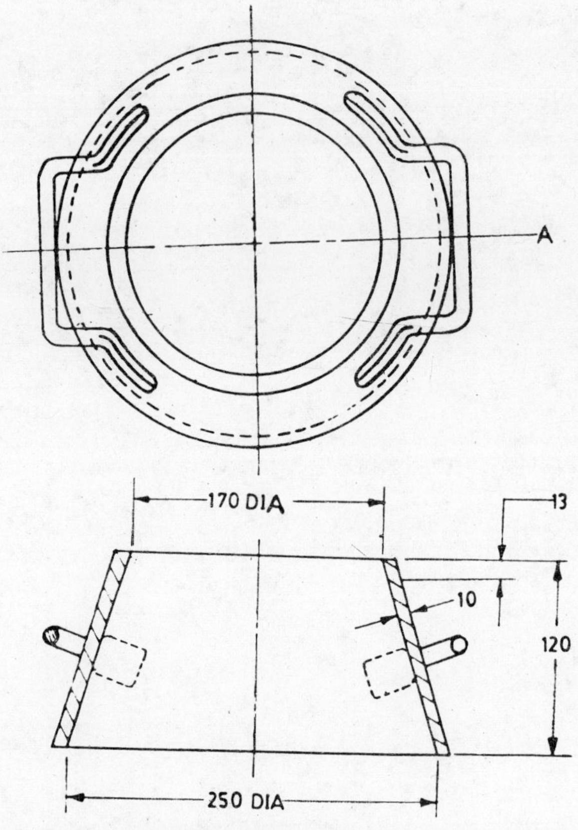

Fig. 3.4 (a)—Details of Flow Table

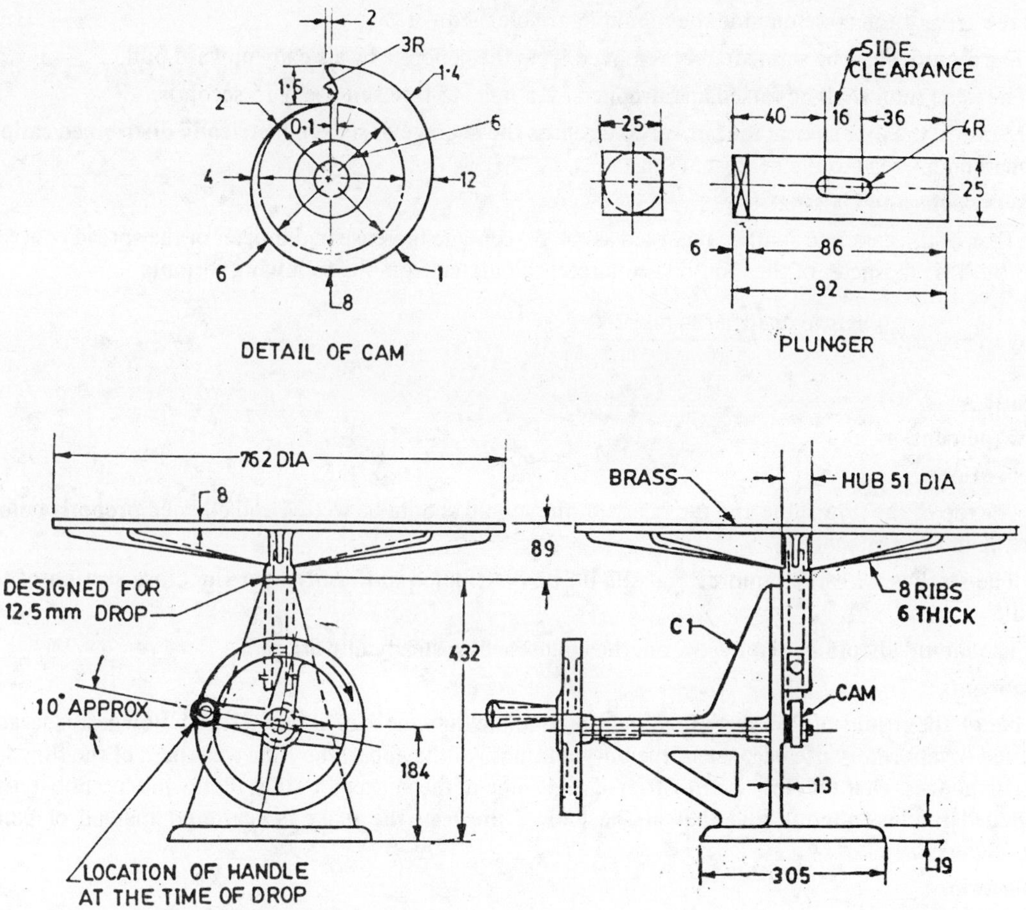

Fig. 3.4(b) Details of Flow Table

the frustum of a cone with the following internal dimensions. A base 250 mm in diameter, upper surface 170 mm in diameter, and height 120 mm, the base and the top shall be open and at right angles to the axis of the cone. The mould shall be provided with handles.

(b) Flow table—Flow table shall conform to the design shown in Fig. 3.4 (b) and shall be mounted on and bolted to a concrete base having a height of 400 to 500 mm and weighing not less than 1400 N (140 kg)

4. **Procedure :**

(a) Wet and clean the table top and inside of the mould of all the grilling material and remove all excess water with a wet cloth.

(b) Centre the mould on the table and hold it firmely in place.

(c) Fill the mould in two layers, each approximately, one half the volume of the mould. Each layer shall be rodded with 25 strokes of a straight round metal rod 16 mm in diameter and 600 mm long, rounded at the lower tamping end. The strokes shall be distributed in a uniform manner, over the cross section of the mould and shall penetrate into the underlying layer. The bottom layer shall be rodded throughout its depth.

(d) After the top layer has been rodded, the surface of the concrete shall be struck off with a trowel so that the mould is exactly filled. The excess concrete which has over flowed the mould shall be removed and the area of the table outside the mould again cleaned.

(e) The mould, shall be immediately removed from the concrete by a steady upward pull.

(f) The table then shall be raised and dropped 12.5 mm, 15 times in about 15 seconds.

(g) Measure the diameter of the spread concrete as the average of six symmetrically distributed caliper measurements read to the nearest 5mm.

5. **Observations and Calculations :**

The flow of the concrete shall be recorded as the percentage increase in diameter of the spread concrete over the base diameter of the moulded concrete, calculated from the following formula :

$$\text{Flow (percent)} = \frac{\text{Spread diameter in mm } 250}{250} \times 100$$

6. **Result**

Flow (percent) =

7. **Precautions :**

(a) The top of the flow table and the inside of the mould should be wetted and cleaned properly before starting the experiment.

(b) The strokes with the tamping rod should be distributed uniformly over the cross section of the mould.

(c) The mould should be removed from the concrete by a steady upward pull.

8. **Comments :**

Although the results of flow test are more reproducible than those of slump test, the flow test is largely limited to laboratory use because of the un-wieldiness of the apparatus. The weakness of the flow test lies in the facts that the flow is unrestricted and some of the aggregate rides along and are only partly embeded in the concrete and that at the end of the test, the mass is scattered instead of being homogeneous.

9. **Questions :**

(a) Define segregation in concrete.

(b) Differentiate between segregation and bleeding.

(c) Can we use this test in the field?

(d) Comment on the statement, 'Concrete having the same flow may differ considerablyin their workability'.

(e) What do you understand by consistency of concrete?

EXPERIMENT NO.3/6

WORKABILITY OF FRESHLY MIXED CONCRETE BY REMOULDING TEST

1. **Object :**—To determine the workability of freshly mixed concrete by remoulding test.
2. **Theory :**—This test measure the relative effort required to change a mass of concrete from one definite shape to another by means of jiging. The amount of effort, called 'remoulding effort' is taken as the number of jigs required to complete the change. The results of remoulding test are of value in studying the mobility of masses of concrete made with varying amounts of water and cement and with various types and gradations of aggregates.
3. **Apparatus :**

   (a) The power remoulding apparatus (Fig. 3.5) consists essentially of a base plate and an outer shell 300 mm in dia and 200 mm high, which is mounted centrally on flow table set for a 6 mm drop. Inside the outer shell is an inner ring 206 mm in diameter and 125 mm in height, mounted with its bottom 70 mm above the top of the base plate.

   (b) Trowels, graduated cylinder of 1000 ml capacity, balance to weight upto 300N (30kg) (nearest to 0.1N (10gms).
4. **Procedure :**

   (a) To perform the test, set a standard slump cone on the base plate in the centre of the inner ring.

   (b) Fill the slump cone and remove it vertically.

   (c) Place the 83 mm diameter horizontal disk of the remoulding apparatus on top of the slumped concrete and jig the flow table at the rate of one drop per second until the mix settles down to 34.7 mm above the base plate, which is indicated when mark on the vertical rod reaches at top of the guide. During the jigging operations, the concrete moves down-ward in the inner ring and up-ward into the annular space between the inner and outer ring.
5. **Observations and Calculations :**

   The effort required to achieve the remoulding is expressed as the number of jolts required to change the shape of concrete from a frustrum of a cone to a cylinder.

Sr. No.	*W/C ratio*	*Mix used*	*Remoulding Effort (No. of jigs)*
1.	0.45		
2.	0.50		
3.	0.55		
4.	0.60		
5.	0.65		

6. **Result** :

   Remoulding effort (No. of Jigs) =
7. **Comments :**

   The test is purely a laboratory one, but is valuable as the remoulding effort appears to be closely related to workability. For dry mixtures, a considerable effort may be necessary.

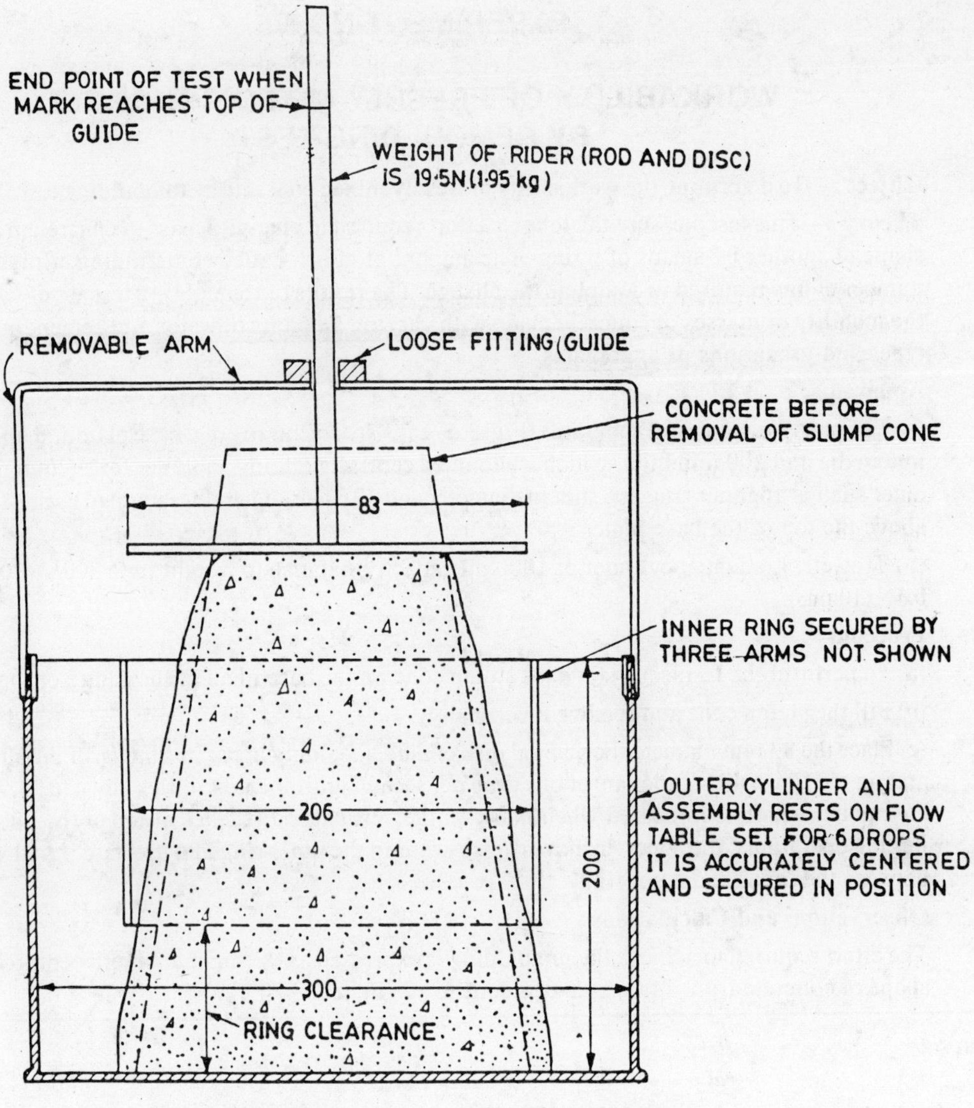

Fig. 3.5 Remoulding Apparatus. (All dimension in mm.)

8. Precautions :

(a) Slump cone should be filled in the standard manner as outlined in slump test.

(b) Jolt the flow table at the rate of one jolt per second and see that the shape of the concrete has changed from a frustrum of a cone to a cylinder.

(c) Before using remoulding apparatus, check height of drop of table to see that it is 6mm.

9. Questions :

(a) Define remoulding effort.

(b) State the importance of this test.

(c) Compare the remoulding effort of dry and wet mixes.

(d) Define mobility of concrete.

EXPERIMENT NO.3/7

WORKABILITY OF FRESHLY MIXED CONCRETE BY VEE-BEE CONSISTOMETER METHOD

1. **Object :**—To determine the workability of freshly mixed concrete by Vee-Bee consistometer method.
2. **Theory :**—Vee-Bee consistometer is used to determine the consistency and indirectly the workability of a freshly prepared concrete mix. The time required to transform by vibration a concrete specimen in the shape of a conical frustrum into a cylinder is a measure of consistency or workability of the mix.
3. **Apparatus :**

The Vee-Bee consistometer (Fig. 3.6) consists of

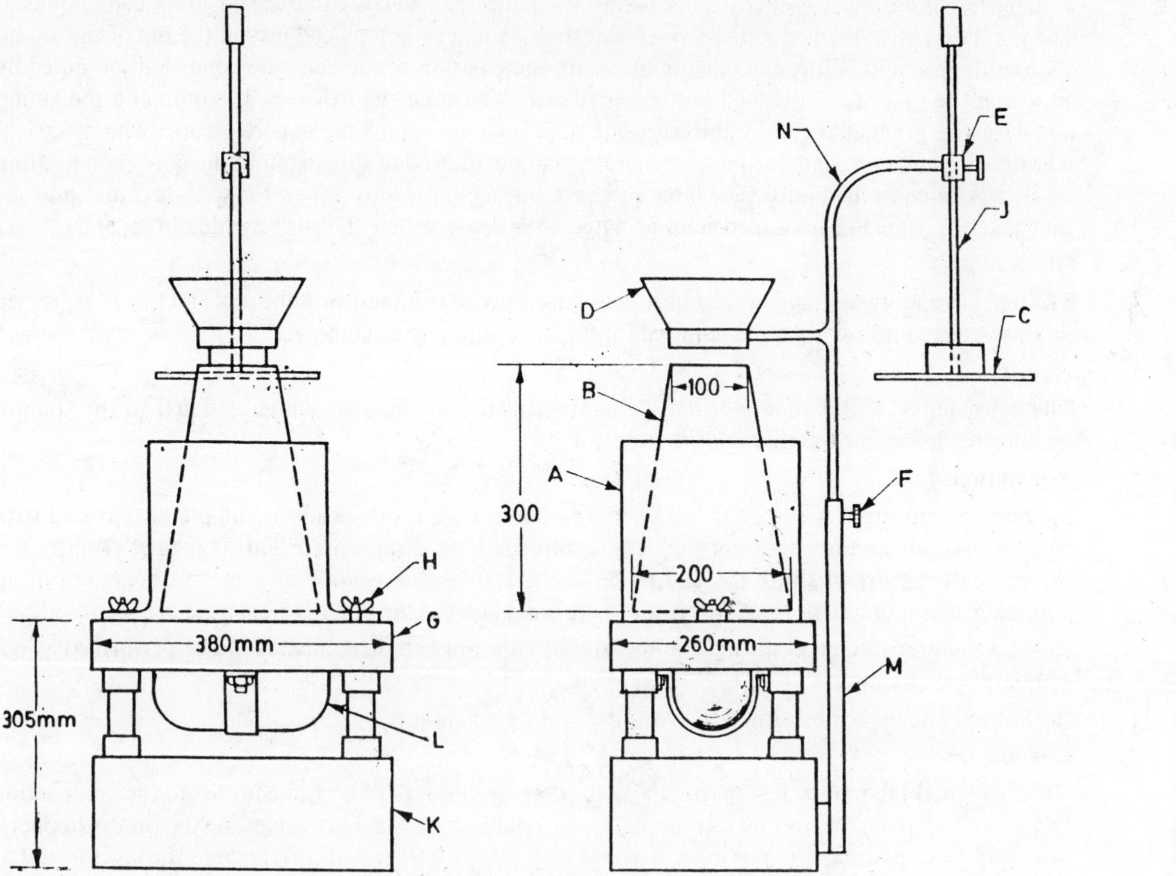

Fig. 3.6 Vee-Bee consistometer

(a) a vibrating table resting upon elastic supports

(b) a metal pot

(c) a sheet metal cone, open at both ends and

(d) a standard iron rod.

The vibrating table (G) is 380 mm long and 260 mm wide and is supported on rubber shock absorbers at a height of about 305 mm above floor level. The table is mounted on base (k) which rests on three rubber feet and is equipped with an electriclly operated vibrometer mounted under it operating on 220 volts, three phase 50 cycles alternating current.

The sheet metal cone (B) open at both ends is place d in the metal pot (A) and the metal pot is fixed on the vibrator table by means of two wingnuts. The sheet metal cone is 300mm high and its bottom diameter is 200mm and top diameter 100mm. A swivel arm holder (M) is fixed to the base and into this is telescoped another swivel arm (N) with funnel (D) and guide sleeve (E). The swivel arm can be detached from the vibrating table. The graduated rod (J) is fixed on to the swivel arm and at the end of the graduated arm a glass disc (C) is screwed. The divisions of the scale on the rod records the slump of the concrete cone in the pot. The standard iron rod is 20mm in diameter and 500mm in length.

4. Procedure:

A slump test as described earlier shall be performed in the sheet metal cylindrical pot of the consistometer. The glass disc (C) attached to the swivel arm shall be moved and placed just on the top of the slump cone in the pot and before the cone is lifted up, the position of the concrete cone shall be noted by adjusting the glass disc attached to the swivel arm. The cone shall then be lifted up and the slump noted on the graduated rod by lowering the glass disc on top of the concrete cone. The electrical vibrator shall be switched on and the concrete shall be allowed to spread out in the pot. The vibration shall then be continued until the whole concrete surface uniformly adheres to the glass disc and the time taken for this to be attained shall be noted with a stop watch. This is recorded in seconds.

5. Observations:

The input of energy required for compaction is a measure of workability of the mix and this is expressed in Vee-Bee seconds i.e. the time required for the remoulding to be complete.

6. Results:

The consistency of the concrete shall be expressed in V-be degrees which is equal to the time in seconds recorded, for the remoulding to bc complete.

7. Precautions:

(a) The remoulding is assumed to be complete when the glass plate rider is completely covered with concrete and all cavities in the surface of the concrete have disappeared. This is judged visually and the difficulty of establishing the end point of the test may be source of error. To overcome it an automatically operated device for recording the movement of the plate against time may be fitted.

(b) The slump test to be performed before giving vibrations to the table, should be performed as per standard specifications.

(c) The test should be performed away from vibrating machinery.

8. Comments:

Vebe is a good laboratory test, particularly for very dry mixes. This is in contrast to the compaction factor test, where error may be introduced by the tendency of some dry mixes to stick in the hoppers. The Vebe test also has the additional advantages that the treatment of concrete during the test is comparatively closely related to the method of placing in practice.

9. Questions:

(a) How do you measure the workability of the mix in this test?

(b) Why the name Vebe has been given to this test?

(c) This test is a development of the remoulding test. Explain.

(d) State the number of Vebe degrees for the following types of mixes: (a) Very dry (b) Dry (c) Plastic (d) Semi fluid (e) Fluid.

EXPERIMENT NO.3/8

WORKABILITY OF FRESHLY MIXED CONCRETE BY KELLY BALL PENETRATION TEST

1. **Object:**— To determine the workability of freshly mixed concrete by kelly ball penetration test.
2. **Theory** :— This is a simple field test consisting of the determination of the depth to which a 152mm diameter metal hemisphere weighing 136 N(13.6 kg) will sink under its own weight into fresh concrete.
3. **Apparatus** :— The apparatus is very simple and consists of a hemispherical ball having diameter equal to 152 mm and weighing 136 N (13.6 kg.). The ball is attached to a handle marked with a scale to note down the dpeth of penetration. The handle passes through a metallic base called the stirrup feet.
4. **Procedure** :— Level the surface of the concrete, working it as little as possible. Set the base of the apparatus on the concrete, lower the weight to the concrete surface and release slowly. Read the penetration to the nearest mm. Take a minimum of three readings from a batch or location. These readings shall not be taken with feet of the stirrup within 150 mm of a point where the feet rested in a previous test. No correction shal be made for any slight settlement of the feet of the stirrup.
5. **Observations :**

   Penetration in mm =
6. **Precautions :**

   (a) Place the stirrup feet over the sample of concrete gently.

   (b) Leave the ball on the concrete surface very slowly.

   (c) Take sufficient readings at spacings of atleast 150 mm between the feet of metal stirrup.
7. **Comments :**

   The use of this test is similar to that of the slump test, that is routine checking of consistency for control purposes. Kellyball test is an alternative to the slump test, over which it has some advantages. In particular, the ball test is simpler and quicker to perform and, what is more important, it can be applied to concrete in a wheel barrow or actually in the form. In order to avoid the effects of a boundary, the depth of concrete, being tested, should be not less than 200 mm and the least lateral dimension 460 mm. The ball test is relatively free from personel errors whereas the slump test is subject to personel errors. A disadvantage of the ball test for use in the laboratory, where test batches are usually small, is that the minimum sample required (to avoid boundary conditions) is several times that required for a slump test.
8. **Questions :**

   (a) State the relation between penetration and slump.

   (b) State the minimum depth of the concrete sample for this test.

   (c) State the minimum horizontal distance from the centre line of the handle to the nearest edge of the level surface.

   (d) Compare slump test and ball penetration test.

   (e) Can we use this test at a construction site?

EXPERIMENT NO. 3/9

COMPRESSIVE STRENGTH OF CEMENT CONCRETE

1. **Object:**

To determine the cube strength and cylinder strength of concrete of given proportions say 1:2:4 by weight and W/C = 0.6 by weight.

2. **Theory:**

The compressive strength of concrete is one of its most important and useful properties and most easily determined. In most structural applications, concrete is employed primarily to resist compressive stresses. In those case where strength in tension or in shear is of primary importance, the compressive strength is used as a measure of overall quality of the concerte and thus as an indication of other properties relating to the deformations or durability. Finally concrete making properties of the various gradients of the mix are usually measured in terms of compressive strength.

3. **Apparatus:**

Cube moulds 150 mm is size, Cylinder moulds 150 mm diameter and 300 mm in height, weighing machine, mixer, tamping rods, capping appratus, compression testing machine.

(a) Moulds for Cube Test : These should be of steel or cast iron. The internal faces should be machined flat to a tolerance of ±0.025 mm. All interior angles between internal faces should be 90 ± 0.5°. A base plate with machined plane surface, large enough to prevent leakage of cement slurry during filling of the mould should be provided. Spring clips or screws should be supplied to assist in holding the mould the mould on the base plate.

(b) Moulds for cylinder test : The standard size of test cylinder is 300 mm in height at 150 mm in diameter. These moulds are of cast iron.

(c) Tamping Rod : It is 16 mm diameter steeo rod, 600 mm in length and bullct nosed at one end.

4. **Procedure:**

(a) Weigh 110 N (11.0 kg) of cement, 220N (22.0 kg) of fine aggregate and 440N (44.0 kg) of coarse aggregate and 66 N (6.6 kg) of water. Mix them thoroughly in the mechanical mixer until uniform colour of concrete is obtained. This material will be suffient for casting of 3 cubes and 3 cylinder of the size 150 mm × 150 mm × 150 mm and 150 mm × 300 mm respectively.

The concrete may also be mixed by hand in such a manner as to avid loss of water. In mixing by hand the cement and fine aggregate shall be first mixed dry to uniform colour and then the coarse aggregate is added and mixed until the coarse aggregate is uniformly distributed throughout the batch. Now the water shall be added and whole is mixed until the resulting concrete is uniform in colour (mix atleast for two minutes).

(b) Pour the concrete so prepared in the moulds which have been oiled with a medium viscosity oil. Fill concrete in cube moulds in three layers and cylinder moulds in six layers each of approximately 50 mm and ramming each layer as follows:

(a) **150 mm cube**:

Each layer to be ramed more than 35 times.

(b) **150 × 300 mm cylinder**:

Each layer to be ramed more than 30 times over the surface, the blows shall be evently distributed on the layer.

(c) In place of hand ramming suitable vibrators may be used.

(c) Trowel off surplus concrete from the top of moulds.

(d) Cover the moulds with wet mats and mark them after about 3 to 4 hours.

(e) **Curing of Specimens** :

(a) Specimens are removed from the moulds after 24 hours and cubes specimens cured in water for another 27 days.

(b) After 24 hours of casting, cylinderical speciments are capped by neat cement paste of 33% water content, on the capping apparatus and the after another 24 hours immersed in water for final curing of 26 days.

Testing of Specimens:

Compression test of cube and cylindrical specimens are made as soon as practicable after removing from curing tank. Test specimens during the period of their removal from the curing pit and testing are kept moist by a wet mat nearest to 0.2 mm by averaging the particular dimensions, atleast at two places. The length of the cylinder including caps is measured to the nearest 0.2 mm. The weight of each specimen is also recorded.

Place central the specimen in the compression testing machine and load is applied continuously, uniformly and without shock. The rate of loading should be 14 N/mm^2 (140kg/cm^2)/minute or 300 KN/minute, for cube and 250 KN/minute for cylinder. The load is increased until the specimen fails. Record the maximum load taken by each specimen during test. Also note the type of the failure and appearance of cracks.

5. Observations and Calculations:

The following information is normally included in t.e report of each compression test.

Table 3.3

(a)	Identification mark	—
(b)	Date of casting	—
(c)	Date of testing	—
(d)	Age of specimen	—
(e)	Curing condition	—
(f)	Dimensions of specimen	—
(g)	Weight of specimen	—
(h)	Cross sectional area	—
(i)	Maximum load	—
(j)	Compressive strength	—
(k)	Appearance of factured faces of concrete and type of fracture.	—

Table 3.4

Specimen No.	1	2	3	Average
Load in Newtons on cube	—	—	—	—
Load in Newtons on cylinders	—	—	—	—

(a) Cube strength $= \dfrac{\text{Average Load}}{\text{Area of Cross - section of Cube specimen}} = (\text{N/mm}^2) \text{ or } (\text{Kg/cm}^2)$

(b) Cylinder strength $= \dfrac{\text{Average Load}}{\text{Area of cross - section of cylinder specimen}} = (\text{N/mm}^2) \text{ or } (\text{Kg/cm}^2)$

6. Precautions :

(a) All the materials should be weighed to an accuracy of 1 in 1000.

(b) The mould and the base plate must be oiled lightly before use to prevent the concrete from sticking to the moulds.

(c) During compaction the blows should be evenly distributed over the surface of each layer.

(d) Excess vibration should be avoided when compaction is done by vibration to avoid segregation and loss of water from the spaces between moulds and their base plates.

(e) The cubes and cylinders should not be allowed to dry and they must be tested wet.

(f) Atleast three specimens should be tested for each test and mean crushing strength of three should be taken as crushing strength of concrete. While calculating the average load, if any individual variation from the average is more than 15% the test results should be rejected and the test is repeated.

(g) Cubes should be placed in the testing machine centrally on plattens.

(h) In cylinderical specimens, the caping should be plane and parallel with bottom surface of cylinder.

7. Comments :

Compressive strength test affords the most reliable means of judging the quality of concrete. There are various factors which affect the compressive strength. Larger specimens give a lower crushing strength. The height of the specimen in relation to its lateral dimensions greatly influence the strength. The more slender is the test piece, lower will be crushing strength. The strength of concrete obtained with ratio of $\frac{\text{height}}{\text{lateral dimensions}}$ as $\frac{1}{2}$, 2 and 4, is about 125, 75, 70 percent respectively of the strength when this ratio is unity. A quicker rate of loading will give an apparent increase in strength of test specimens. A rate of loading 14N/mm^2 (140 kg/cm^2) minute should always be used.

The cubes are better in the sense because they offer plane and parallel faces of testing. In case of cylinder, its top surface has to be specially prepared to ensure good contact with testing machine. Cubes should remain in water right upto the moment of test, even an hour's drying may have an appreciable effect upon the crushing strength.

This test is adopted due to its simplicity and importance of crushing strength in structural work. Specimens are easy and unexpensive to prepare. It gives very good indication of general quality of concrete. concretes which have high crushing strengths are likely to give good durability and impermeability and high flexural and tensile strengths. They are also likely to give high modulus of elasticity.

8. Questions :

(a) State the importance of compressive strength test.

(b) What are different types of standard test specimens ?

(c) State the minimum number of tests to be conducted for each batch.

(d) State the sequence of mixing ingredients of concrete by (a) hand mixing (b) mechanical mixer ?

(e) Why the moulds are oiled before use ?

(f) State the methods of compacting concrete in the cube and cylinder moulds.

(g) Why capping is necessary for cylindrical specimens ?

(h) State the rate of applying load on compression specimens.

(i) State the nature of compression failures observed by you during testing.

(j) What is permissible variation in strength of a specimen while taking the average ?

(k) The cubes should be tested on sides and not along the direction of casting. Comment on this statement

(l) In what respect cubes are better than cylinderical specimens ?

(m) State the effect on compressive strength of (a) Size of specimen (b) Slenderness (c) rate of loading.

(n) Does the friction between the plattens of compression testing machine and specimen affect the strength ?

(o) State the relationship between cube strength and cylinder strength.

EXPERIMENTS NO. 3/10

FLEXURAL STRENGTH OF CONCRETE

1. **Object:**—To determine the flexural strength (modulus of rupture) of concrete of given proportions.
2. **Theory:**—When concrete is subjected to bending, tensile and bending compressive stresses and in many cases, direct shear stresses are developed. The most common plain concrete structure subjected to flexure is a highway pavement and the strength of concrete for pavements in commonly evaluated by means of bending test. Flexure test is intended to give the flexural strength of concrete in tension. The flexure test is also more easily carried out and may even be more convenient than the crushing test for use in field, since in this test much smaller loads are required.
3. **Apparatus:**—Steel prism moulds of the following sizes will be used :
   (a) 100 mm × 100 mm × 500 mm when maximum size of aggregate is less than 20 mm.
   (b) 150 mm × 150 mm × 700 mm, when maximum size of aggregates is upto 30 mm.
   The testing machine may be of any reliable type of sufficient capacity for the tests and capable of applying the load at 4kN (400 kg)/minute for the 150 mm specimens and at a rate of 1.8 kn (180 kg,)/ minute for the 100 mm specimens. The bed of the testing machine shall be provided with two steel rollers, 38 mm in diameter, on which the specimen is to be supported and these rollers shall be so mounted that the distance from centre to centre is 600 mm for 150 mm specimens or 400 mm for 100 mm specimens. The load shall be applied through two similar rollers mounted at the third points of the supporting span, that is spaced at 200 or 133 mm. centre to centre. The load shall be divided equally between the two loading rollers and all rollers shall be mounted in such a manner that the load is applied axially and without subjecting the specimen to any torsion or restraints. One suitably arrangement which complies with these requirements is indicated in Fig. 3.7.

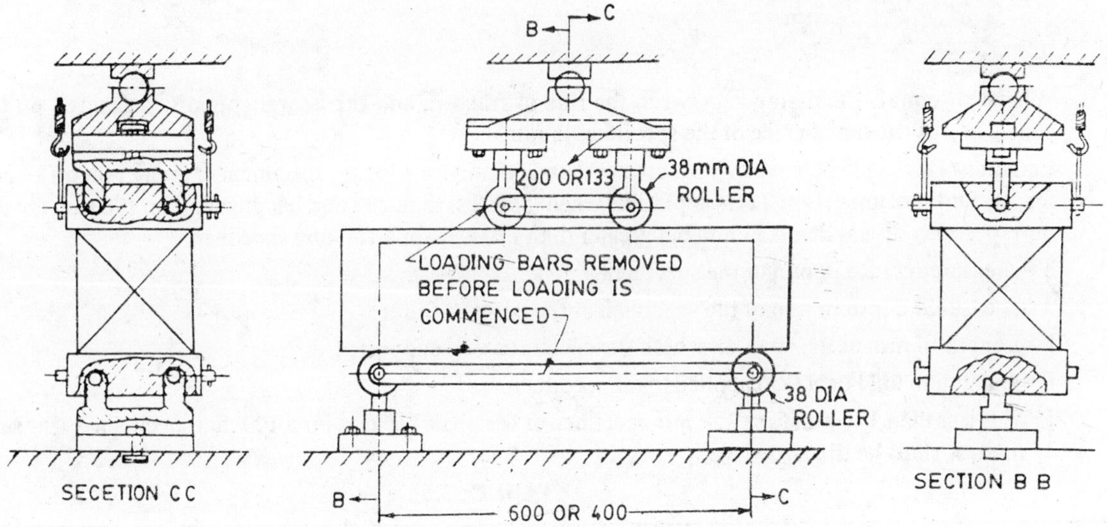

Fig. 3.7—Arrangement for loading of Flexure Test specimens.

4. **Procedure :**

   (a) With 20 mm maximum size aggregate cast three prism of size 100 × 100 × 500 mm. Take mix proportions as 1:2:4. W/C ratio = 0.6. For this take coarse aggregate = 260 N (26.0 kg.) Fine aggregate = 130 N(13.0

kg), Cement = 65 N (6.5 kg) and water 39 N (3.9 kg).

(b) The mould shall be filled in two layers each layer to be rammed more than 100 times by a standard steel ramming rod 25 mm square at one end and 400 mm long having a weight of 20 N (2.0 kg.). Ramming of each layer may also be done by suitable vibrators.

(c) After casting, the moulds shall be covered with wet cloths or gunny bags, Demoulded after 24 hours and wet cured for 27 days. Specimens shall be tested immediately on removal from the water whilst they are still in wet condition. The dimensions of each specimen shall be noted before testing.

(d) The bearing surfaces of the supporting and loading rollers shall be wiped clean and any loose sand or other material removed from the surface of the specimens where they are to make contact with the rollers. The specimen shall then be placed in the machine in such a manner that the load shall be applied to the upper most surface as cast in the mould, along two lines spaced 200 mm or 133 mm apart. The axis of the specimen shall be carefully aligned with the axis of the loading device. No packing shall be used between the bearing surfaces of the specimen and the rollers. The load shall be applied without shock and increasing continuously at a rate such that the extreme fibre stress increases at approximately 0.7 N/mm^2 (7kg/cm^2)/mint that is at a rate of loading of 4 kN (400 kg)/mint for the 150 mm specimen and at a rate of 1.8 kN (180 kg.)/mint for the 100 mm specimens. The load shall be increased until the specimen fails and maximum load applied to the specimen during the test shall be recorded. The appearance of the fractured faces of concrete and any unique features in the type of failure shall be noted.

5. Observations and Calculations :

The flexural strength of the specimen shall be expressed as the modulus of rupture and shall be calculated to the nearest 0.05N/mm^2(0.5 kg/cm^2) as follows:

$$\sigma_r = \frac{P.a.}{bd^2} \quad \ldots \quad (1)$$

and

$$\sigma_r = \frac{3\,P.a.}{bd^2} \quad \ldots \quad (2)$$

Where 'a' equals the distance between the line of fracture and the nearer support, measured on the centre line of the tensile side of the specimen in mm.

Equation (1) is applicable when 'a' is greater than 200 mm for 150 mm specimen, or greater than 133 mm for 100 mm specimen. Eqn. (2) is applicable when 'a' is less than 200 mm but greater than 170 mm for 150 mm specimen or less than 133 mm but greater than 110 mm for a 100 mm specimen.

b = measured width in mm of the specimen

d = measured depth in mm of the specimen at the point of failure.

l = Length in mm of the span on which the specimen was supported.

P = maximum load in N (kg) applied to the specimen.

If 'a' is less than 170 mm for a 150 mm specimen or less than 110 mm for a 100 mm specimen, the results of the test shall be discarded.

TABLE : 3.5

Sr. No.	*Mix Proportions*	*W/C Ratio*	*Size of Specimens*	*Max. Load N (kg.)*	*Modulus of Rupture*
1.					
2.					
3.					

6. **Report:**

The following information shall be included in the result report on each specimen:

(a) identification mark.

(b) date of test

(c) age of specimen

(d) curing conditions

(e) size of specimen

(f) span length

(g) maximum load

(h) position of fracture (value 'a')

(i) modules of rupture [N/mm^2 (kg./cm.^{2})]

(j) appearance of concrete and type of fracture.

7. **Precautions :**

(a) The loading should be applied axially and without subjecting the specimen to any torsional stresses or restrants.

(b) The axis of the specimen shall be carefully aligned with the axis of the loading device.

(c) No packing shall be used between the bearing surfaces of the specimen and the rollers.

(d) The load shall be applied without shock and increasing continuously at the specified rate.

8. **Comments :**

Flexural tension tests maybe made in several ways and the most common being the ASTM (American Society for Testing Materials) standard method of Test for flexrual strength of concrete using simple beam with third point loading and ASTM tentative method of test for Flexural Strength of concrete using beam with centre point loading. The second method is for small specimens and is not alternate to the first which is normally for beams 150 mm × 150 mm or larger sections. The flexural strength is expressed in terms of (modulus of rupture) which is the maximum tensile stress at rupture computed from the well known flexural 'formula'.

$$\sigma_r = \frac{M.y}{I} \quad (10.3)$$

where,

σ_r = modulus of rupture or the stress in the fibre farthest from the neutral axis.

M = bending moment at the section

Y = distance from netural axis to the farthest fibre.

I = moment of interia of the section.

The modulus of rupture ranges from 10 to 23% of the compressure strength.

9. **Questions :**

(a) What do you want to find from flexure test results ?

(b) What are the size requirements of flexure test specimens ?

(c) State the rate of loading of a flexural test specimen.

(d) What type of loading is used in laboratory for flexure test ?

(e) Sketch the first crack pattern of a flexure test specimen.

(f) State the formulate for calculation of flexural strength.

(g) State the approximate relation between flexural strength and compressive strength of concrete.

(h) How does flexure specimen fail ?

(i) What does the following abbreviations stand for (i) ASTM (ii)B.I.S. (iii) A.C.I. (iv) B.S.I. (v) I.R.C. (vi) I.C.I.

EXPERIMENT NO. 3/11

SPLIT TENSILE STRENGTH OF CONCRETE

1. **Object :**—To determine the split tensile strength of concrete of given proportions.

2. **Theory :**—Concrete is not usually expected to resist direct tensile forces because of its low tensile strength and brittle nature. However, tension is of importance with regard to cracking, which is a tensile failure. Most cracking arise from that due to load or due to settlement of parts of the structure or due to the restrant of contraction induced by drying or by lowering of temperature.

   Direct tension tests of concrete are seldom made because of difficulties in mounting the specimens and uncertainties as to the secondary stresses induced by the holding devices. An indirect test for tensile strength of concrete developed originally in Brazil has recently come rather in general use and has been standardised by ASTM, with diameters not less than four times the maximum size of the coarse aggregate and not less than 15cm. The length of the specimens shall not be less than the diameter and not more than twice the diameter. For routine testing and comparison of results unless otherwise specified the specimens shall be cylinders 15 cm in diameter and 30 cm long.for concrete having maximum nominal size of the aggregate not greater than 38 mm, the sample of aggregate shall be screened to exclude aggregate of size larger than 38 mm.

3. **Apparatus :**

   Any compression testing machine of reliable type of sufficient capacity for the tests and capable of applying the load at the rate specified. The bearing faces of both plattens shall provide a minimum loading area of 12 times the length of the cylinder in mm so that the load is applied over the entire length of the specimen. If necessary a supplementary bearing bar or plate of machined steel may be used.

   Two packing strips of plywood conforming to IS 303-1960 and 12 mm wide and 3 mm thick shall be provided for specimen and shall be used once only.

4. **Procedure :**

   (a) Cast 150 × 300 mm cylinder of mix ratio 1:2:4, W/C = 0.6. Take total material for one cylinder = 140 N(14.0 kg). The casting shall be done as described earlier.

   (b) Tests shall be made at the recognised ages of the test specimens, the most usual being 7 and 28 days. The ages shall be calculated from the time of the addition of water to the dry ingredients. At least three specimens shall be tested for each type of test.

   (c) Specimens shall be tested immediately on removal from the water whilst they are still wet. Surface water and grit shall be wiped off the specimens and any projecting fins removed from the surface, which are to be in contact with the packing strips.

   (d) Diameteral lines shall be drawn on the two ends of the specimen using any reliable procedure and device that will ensure that they are in the same axial plane.

   The diameter and the dimensions of the specimen shall be noted before testing. The diameters of the specimen, lying in the plane of the premarked lines, shall be ensured near the ends and the middle of the specimen and the average taken to the nearest 0.2mm. The length of the specimen shall be taken to the nearest 0.2 mm by averaging the two lengths measured in the plane containing the premarked lines.

   The bearing surface of the testing machine and of the packing strips shall be wiped clean. One of the plywood strips shall be centred along the centre of the lower platen. The specimen shall be placed on the plywood strip and aligned so that the lines marked on the ends of the specimen are vertical and centered over the plywood strip. The second plywood strip shall be placed lengthwise on the cylinders, centered on the lines marked on the ends of the cylinder. The rate of loading will be 1.4 to 2.1N/mm^2

(14 to 21 kg/cm^2) or 99KN/mint to 148.5KN/mint for 150mm × 300mm cylinders.

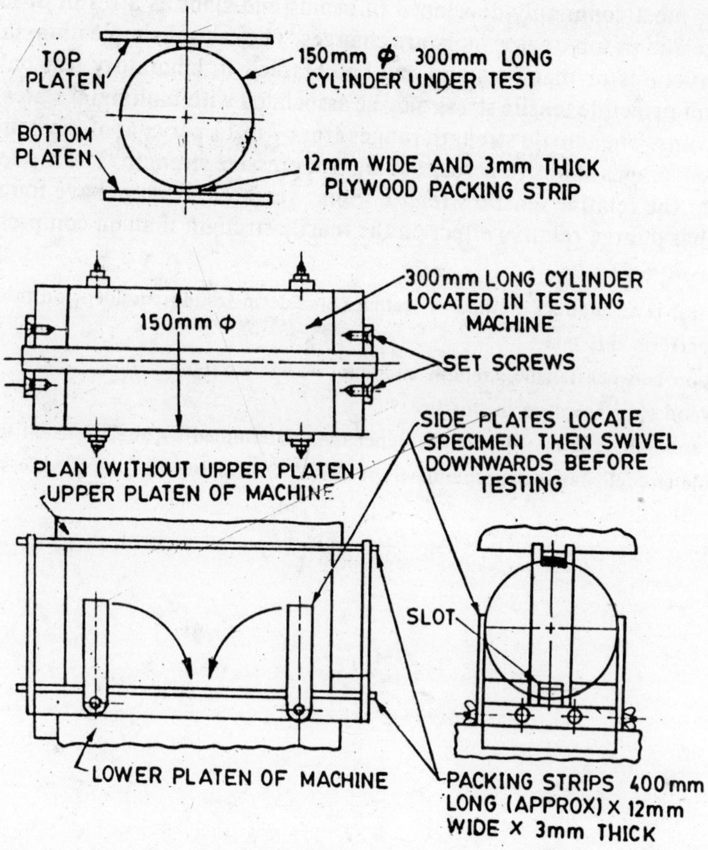

Fig. 3.8—Typical Jig for locating 150mm diameter and 300mm long concrete cylinder for split tensile strength of concrete.

5. Observations and Calculations :

The split tensile strength shall be calculated from the following formula:

$$\sigma_{sp} = \frac{2P}{dl}$$

Where σ_{SP} = measured splitting tensile strength calculated to 0.05N/mm^2(0.5 kg/cm^2)

P = max load in N(kg)

d = diameter in mm of the specimen

l = measured length of the specimen in mm.

6. Result :

Split tensile strength = N/mm^2(kg/cm^2)

7. Precautions :

(a) All the materials should be weighed to an accuracy of 1 in 1000.

(b) The mould and the base plate must be oiled lightly before use.

(c) The cylinders should not be allowed to dry and they must be tested in wet.

(d) The cylinders should be placed in the testing machine centrally.

(e) The load shall be applied without jerks.

8. Comments :

Flexural tension is most commonly developed in beams and slabs as a result of loads, temperature changes, shrinkage and in some cases moisture changes. The case of simple uniaxial tension is rarely encountered in structures or members and can be obtained in laboratory test only with difficulty. However significant principle tensile stress may be associated with multiaxial states of stress in walls, shells and deep beams. The tensile strength ranges from 7 to 11 per cent of the compressive strength and at usual levels averages about 10 percent of the compressive strength. The higher the compressive strength the higher the relative tensile strength. Some research workers have found that the type of coarse aggregate has a large relative effect on the tensile strength than on compressive strength.

9. Questions :

(a) Split cylinder test is an indirect method of testing concrete in testing comment on this statement.

(b) Why do you perform this test?

(c) State the relation between tensile strength and compressive strength.

(d) Why the plywood strip are used in this test ?

(e) Split cylinder strength is about 15 percent higher than determined by direct tension tests comment.

(f) The split tensile strength ranges approximately from 50 to 75 percent of the flexure strength. Comment.

EXPERIMENT NO. 3/12

MODULUS OF ELASTICITY OF CEMENT CONCRETE

1. **Object :**—To plot the stress strain curve of concrete for the given mix and to determine the modulus of elasticity by means of an extensometer.

2. **Theory :**—The modulus of elasticity is defined as the change of stress with respect to elastic strain (deformation) and may be computed from the equation :

$$\text{Modulus of elasticity} = \frac{\text{Unit stress}}{\text{Unit strain}}$$

Modulus of elasticity is a measure of the stiffness or of the resistance of the material to deformation. Concrete exhibits creep under substained loading, within elastic limits it may be definitely considered an elastic material and its modulus of elasticity is used in practically all calculations of structural deformation. It is used in the analysis of reinforced structures to determine the stresses developed in simple elements and to determine the moments, stresses and deflections in more complicated structures.

3. **Apparatus :**

The test specimens shall consist of concrete cylinders 150 mm in diameter and 300 mm long. alternatively, other sizes of cylinders or square prism maybe used provided that the height/diameter or height/width ratio is atleast 2. The test specimens shall be prepared in accordance with the procedure laid for compressive strength testing. Normally test shall be made when the specimens reach the age of 28 days. Atleast three specimens shall be made and tested.

In order to determine the compressive strength of the concrete, three test cubes for compressive strength shall be made together with each set of cylinders or prisms. The test specimens for compressive strength shall be made from the same sample of concrete as the cylinders or prisms and shall be covered and stored under identical conditions.

Two extensometers are required each having a gauge length of not less than 103 mm and not more than half the length of the specimen. They shall be capable of measuring strains to an accuracy of 2×10^{-6}. Mirror extensometers of the roller and rocker type are suitable.

4. **Procedure :**

(a) Cast three cylinders of size 150 × 300 mm and three cubes of size 150 × 150 × 150 mm with a mix ratio of 1:2:4, W/C ratio = 0.6.

(b) Take 105 N (10.5 kg) of cement, 210 N (21.0 kg) of Sand, 420 N (42.0 kg) coarse aggregate and 63 N (6.3 kg) of water for the above casting.

(c) The casting and curing of the above specimens shall be done as described earlier.

(d) The three test specimens for compressive strength shall first be tested and the average compressive strength shall be recorded. Immediately on removing the cylinder from the water and while it is still in a wet condition the extensometres shall be attached at the ends or on opposite sides of the specimen and parallel to its axis, in such a way that the gauge points are symmetrical about the centre of the specimen and in no case are nearest to either end of the specimen than a distance equal to half the diameter or half the width of the specimen. The extensometer shall be fixed with the recording points at the same end. The specimen shall be immediately placed in the testing machine and accurately centered. The load shall be applied continuously and without shock at a rate of 14 N/mm^2 (140 kg./cm.^{2})/mint until an average stress of (C + 0.5) N/mm^2 [(c + 5)kg/cm.^{2}] is reached, where C is one third of the average compressive strength of the cubes calculated to the nearest 0.5 N/mm^2 (5 kg./cm^2). The load shall be maintained at this stress for atleast one minute and shall then be reduced gradually to an average stress of 0.15 N/mm^2 (1.5 kg.cm.^{2}) when extensometer readings will be taken. The load shall be applied a second time at the same rate until an average stress of (C = 0.15) N/mm^2 [C + 1.5) kg./cm.^{2}] is reached. The load shall be maintained at this figure while extensometer readings are taken. The load shall again be reduced gradually and readings again taken at 0.15 N/mm^2 (1.5 kg./cm^2). The load shall be applied a third time and extensometer readings taken at ten approximately equal increments of stress upto an average stress of (C + 0.15) N/mm^2 [(C + 1.5) kg/cm^2]. Readings shall be taken at each stage of loading with as little delay as possible. If the overall strains observed on the second and third readings differ by more than 5 percent, the loading cycle shall be repeated until the difference in strain between consecutive readings at [(C + 0.15) N/mm^2 (C + 1.5) kg./cm^2] does not exceed 5 percent.

5. Observations and Calculations :

The strains at the various loads in the last two cycles shall be calculated separately for each extensometer and the results shall be plotted graphically against the stress. Straight lines shall be drawn through the points for each extensometer, the slopes of these two lines shall be determined and from them the average value shall be found. If the difference between the individual values is less than 15 percent, of average value, this average value expressed in N/mm^2 (kg./cm^2) to the nearest 100 N/mm^2 (1000 kg./cm^2) shall be recorded as the modulus of elasticity of the concrete. If the difference is greater than 15 percent, the specimen shall be recentered in the testing machine and the test repeated. If the difference after recentering and testing is still greater than 15 percent of the average value, the results of the test shall be discarded.

TABLE 3.6 Compressive Strength

Cube No.	*Load in N(kg)*	*Strength N/mm^2(kg/cm^2)*	*Average Strength N/mm^2(kg/cm^2)*
1.			
2.			
3.			

Data Record :

(a) Date of casting =

(b) Date of testing =

(c) Age of specimen =

TABLE : 3.7 Strain Record

Sr. No.	*Cylinder 1*			*Cylinder 2*			*Cylinder 3*		
	Load N(kg)	*E.R. (Δ)*	*Defor-mation*	*Load N(kg)*	*E.R. (Δ)*	*Defor-mation*	*Load N(kg)*	*E.R. Δ*	*Defor-mation*
1.									
2.									
3.									
4.									
5.									
6.									
7.									
8.									
9.									
10.									

* E.R. stands for Extensometer reading.

(d) Sectional area of cylinder – $mm^2(cm^2)$

(e) Stress due to load $P = \frac{P}{area}$ – $N/mm^2(kg/cm^2)$

(f) Gauge length – mm(cm)

(g) $Strain = \frac{Deformation}{Gauge\ length}$ – Percent

TABLE : 3.8 Stress-Strain Record

Sr. No.	*Load N(kg)*	*Stress $N/mm^2(kg/cm^2)$*	*Number of specimens I*	*II*	*III*
1.					
2.					
3.					
4.					
5.					
6.					
7.					
8.					
9.					
10.					

SECANT MODULUS :

1.	Compressive Strength of concrete				$N/mm^2(Kg/cm^2)$
2.	33% of Compressive Strength				$N/mm^2(Kg/cm^2)$
3.	Specimen No.	I	II	III	
4.	Strain at 33% of Compressive strength				
5.	Secant modulus at 33% of compressive strength				
6.	Average secant modulus				$N/mm^2(Kg/cm^2)$

6. **Results :** Modulus of Elasticity of concrete is ......N/mm^2 (Kg/cm^2)

7. **Comments :**

The value of the modulus of elasticity of concrete ranges from $0.15 \times 10^5 N/mm^2$ $(1.5 \times 10^5 Kg/cm^2)$ for low quality concrete at early ages to 0.4×10^5 N/mm^2 $(4.0 \times 10^5$ $Kg/cm^2)$ for high quality concrete at longer ages. It increases with age. It also increase with the reduction of w/c ratio as does the compressive strength. Type of aggregate also affects the elastic modulus of the concrete.

8. **Questions :**

(a) Define secant modulus of elasticity.

(b) Why do you need secant modulus?

(c) Differentiate between tangent modulus and secant modulus.

(d) State the loading rate in this experiment.

(e) Why two extensometers are used for reading the compressive strains?

(f) Why the specimen is loaded and reloaded a number of times before actually taking the readings?

(g) State the stress level to which the specimen is loaded.

(h) State the range of values of modulus of elasticity of concrete.

(i) State the factors on which modulus of elasticity depends.

(j) Define creep of concrete.

EXPERIMENT NO. 3/13

CEMENT CONTENT OF HARDENED CEMENT CONCRETE

1. **Object**—To determine cement content of hardened portland cement concrete.

2. **Theory**—Cement is the most important ingredient in concrete as well as in mortar. It is much costly as compared to sand or fine aggregates and coarse aggregates. It is very essential to have quality control but some times it may not be taken into consideration by the people at site. So, to have check over the quality control, this experiment helps to find out the cement content even after the concrete or mortar has hardened. On the one hand it determins whether the mix conforms to the specifications laid down for a particular job, on the other hand it has a big drawback also. This method can not be used for concretes which contain aggregates of admixtures which liberate soluble silica.

3. **Apparatus**—A weighing machine, Gooch crucible, ball mill disc-pulveriser, crushing machine, burners, filter papers (ashless), vacuum filtering arrangement, wash bottle, three 250 ml beakers, glass rod, a set of sieves and reagents.

Reagents :

(a) $H_2\ So_4$ of specific gravity 1.84

(b) Hcl of specific gravity 1.9 and normality 3.3N

(c) Hydrofluoric Acid (Hfl) - 40%

(d) Sodium Hydroxide (NaoH) of normality 1.0N.

Note: Hcl of 3.3N can be obtained by adding 20 ml of Hcl of sp.gr. 1.19 to 600 ml of distilled water while NaoH of normality 1N can be obtained by dissolving 40 gm of NaoH in 500 ml of distilled water and then diluted to make a volume of one litre.

4. **Procedure :**

1. Collect a few samples from the site, each weighing around 20 N (2kg) and crush them in a crushing machine.

2. Further pulverise them in a ball mill disc pulveriser to a fineness of about 100 μm. Sieve through 80 μm sieve and mix thoroughly. Take a sample of 100 gm by the method of quartering.

3. Using a strong magnet make this sample (100 gm) free from any metallic iron particles.

4. Put the sample in oven at 105°C for 2 hours. Weight out into each of three 250 ml beakers about 3 gm of this sample.

5. Taking care that there is no lump formation, moisten the samples with a steam of hot water. Keep on stirring along.

6. Add 100 ml of Hcl very slowly while stirring it thoroughly. All lumps should be reduced with the help of glass rod or stirrer.

7. After Co_2 gas has ceased to come out, heat the specimen for a few minutes and then allow it to settle.

8. Take Gooch crucible and decant through this ignited crucible. Regulate the suction so as to maintain a rapid rate of dropping during greater part of filtration.

9. Try to retain as much residue in beaker as possible and wash it by decantation twice with hot water from a wash bottle.

10. Add and stir about 75 ml of NaoH and heat to about 75°C. Again wash by decantation twice with hot water.

11. Now transfer the whole residue from beaker to the crucible and wash the residue with about 60 ml of hot water.

12. After washing, add about 10 ml of Hcl to the filtrate.

13. Carefully transfer the filtrate to the clean beaker.

14. Put it in over for evaporation. Then further heat to bake it at not over 120°C for one hour.

15. Moisten with little Hcl and follow the step no 14 again.

16. Dissolve this in 75 ml of Hcl of normality 3 N and heat to boiling.

17. Filter through ashless filter paper and wash the residue with 50 ml of hot Hcl (normality 1N) and then with distilled water until the washings are free from chloride (cl^-) ions.

18. Repeat the evaporation and filtering processes to recover the small amount of silica dissolved and add these to first residue.

19. Titrate the sample with hydrofluoric acid and sulphuric acid to obtain the amount of silica.

20. Determine the percentage of the cement in the sample by dividing the percentage of silica by silica content of the cement (usually this factor is 0.214).

Note: The step No.12 is carried out only when aggregate in original sample are largely clacareous and dolomitic.

5. Observations and Calculations

Mass of original dry sample (gm) 1. =

2. =

Mass of silica in sample (gm) 1. =

2. =

Percentage of silica in sample 1. =

2. =

Percentage of cement in sample 1. =

2. =

6. Results

The total percentage of cement in the sample is = --------------

7. Precautions

1. Take truly represented sample at the start of the experiment.
2. Use only distilled water for washing the sample.
3. Take the required quantity of reagenets as specified.
4. Don't heat the standard volumetric apparatus.

8. Comments

Comment on the amount of cement actually specified by the designer and the amount of cement determined by this experiment.

9. Questions

1. What is the significance of performing this experiment?
2. What are the short-comings of this experiments?
3. How will you take out truly represented sample from the site?
4. What is the process of quatering?
5. What is meant by decantation?
6. What does normality of an acid mean?

EXPERIMENT NO. 3/14

COEFFICIENT OF SHRINKAGE AND EXPANSION

1. **Object**:—To determine the (i) co-efficient of drying shrinkage (ii) Moisture movement and (iii) co-efficient of expansion of cement concrete with w/c ratios 0.5 and 0.7.

2. **Theory:**—When the concrete member is restrained, the shrinkage results. Importance of the shrinkage is more in case of pre-stressed concrete members as this shrinkage has the effect of reducing the force expected by tensioned reinforcement. High shrinkage of concrete members may give rise to tensile stresses which may ultimately cause cracks. These tensile stresses may be as high as 3.5 N/mm^2 (35 kg/cm^2)

When the concrete dries after curing under wet conditions, it shrinks during the drying process. This is called the drying shrinkage or initial drying shrinkage. If the same concrete gets saturated then there is a expansion of concrete and this phenomena is called moisture movement. The **Fig.**3.9 gives an idea about the drying shrinkage and moisture movements with alternate drying and wetting.

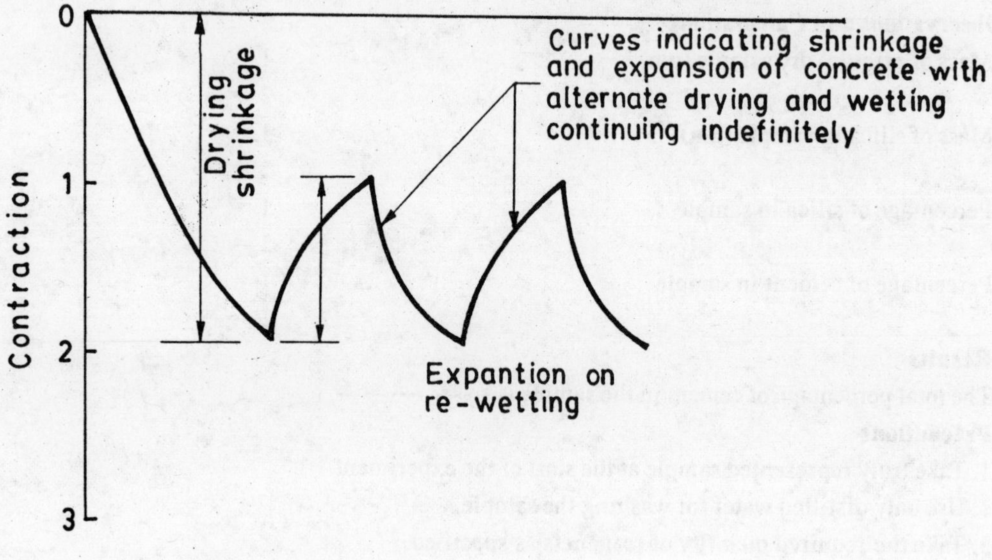

Fig.3.9 Drying Shrinkage and Moisture Movement.

3. **Apparatus**:—Weighing machine, Prism moulds, shrinkage tester, graduated cylinder, trowels, tamping rod, mixing pan, oven for drying.

(a) Prism Moulds–It consists of a wooden base and cast iron sides. It has a standard length equal to the length of a standard rod. The standard rod is made of invar steel which is exactly 340 mm in length and is used as a comparison bar.

(b) Shrinkage Tester–It consists of a horizontal but rectangular steel frame which can move along its length on rollers. The specimen is mounted in this frame and standard pressure is exerted on the specimen. Details of the apparatus is shown in Figure 3.10·

4. **Procedure :–**

(A) Initial Drying shrinkage and moisture movement-

1. With 240 N(24 kg) of coarse aggregate,. prepare the concrete of the mix proportion 1:2:4.

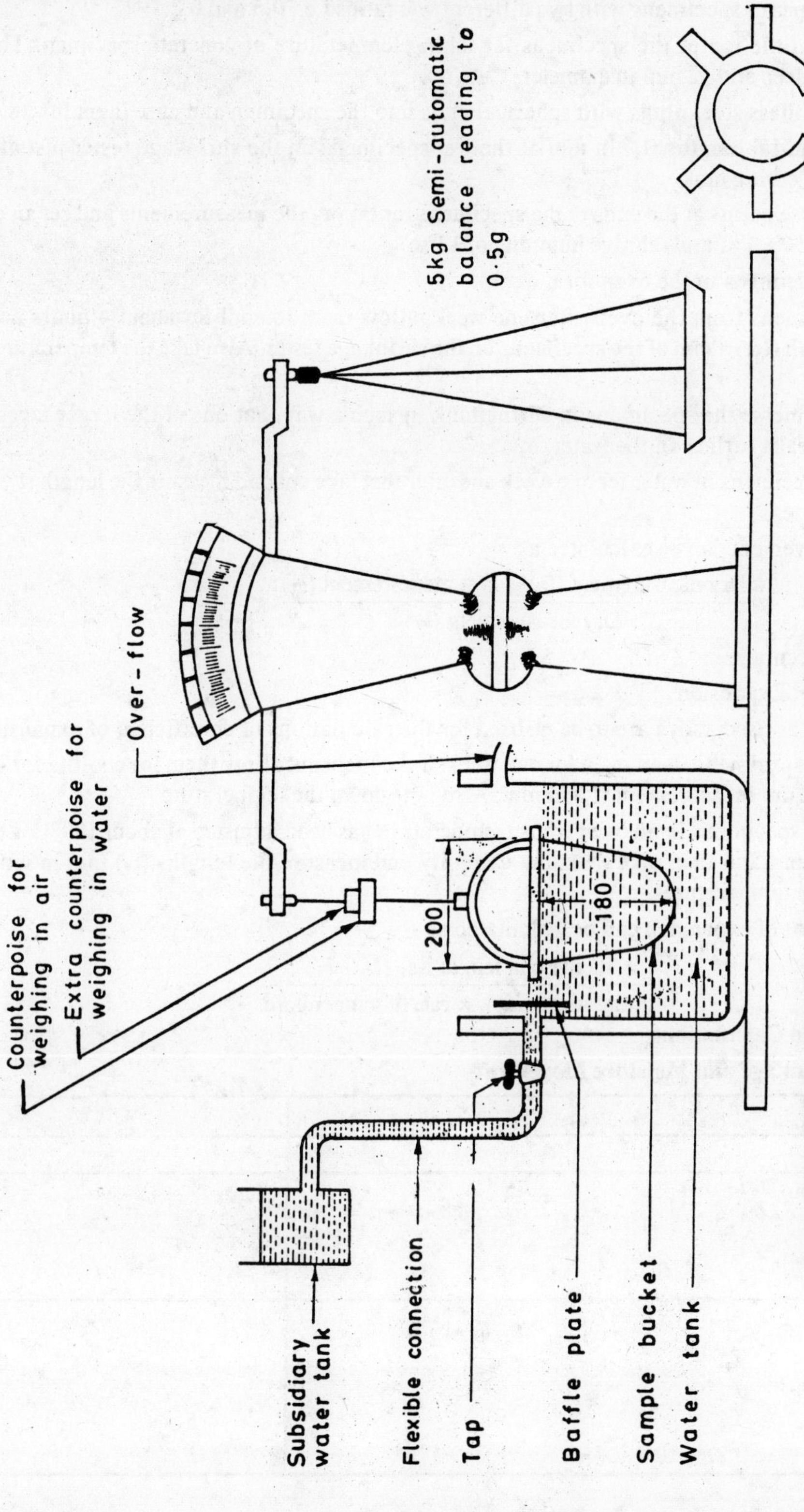

FIG. 3.10. APPARATUS FOR THE DETERMINATION OF DRYING SHRINKAGE AND MOISTURE MOVEMENT.

2. Prepare two types of specimens with two different w/c ratios i.e., 0.5 and 0.7.

3. Make a hole at the top of the specimens for taking temperature of concrete specimen. The hole should be 25mm deep and 12 mm in diameter.

4. Mount the stainless steel plugs with spherical ends into the specimen and cure them for 28 days.

5. Measure the initial lengths (l_1) in mm of the wet specimens on the shrinkage tester just after the removal from the curing tank.

6. Fix the reference points at the ends of the specimens for taking the measurements and set an oven at a temperature of 50 ± 1⁰C and relative humidity of 17%.

7. Keep these specimens in the oven for a week.

8. Remove specimens from the oven after one week, allow them to cool for about 4 hours and then measure the length (l_2) in mm of the specimens on the shrinkage tester. Also take the temperature of the specimens.

9. Now again immerse the specimens in curing tank in such a way that one of the larger faces of the specimen just breaks surface in the water.

10. Keep these specimens in water for one week and after that take out and measure the length (l_3) in mm of the wet specimens.

11. Moisture movement can be calculated as

$$= \frac{\text{Dry measurement } (l_2) - \text{Wet measurement } (l_3)}{\text{Dry measurement } (l_2)}$$

expressed in percentage.

(B) Co-efficient of Expansion

Same specimens as used above are to be utilised for the calculations of co-efficient of expansion.

1. Dry the above specimens in an oven for one week. Take them out allow them for çooling for 4 hours and then take the dry measurement (l_4) in mm. Also note down the temperature.

2. Now put these specimens in an oven whose temperature has been adjusted at about 180⁰C. Let them be there for an hour and then take them out carefully and measure the lengths (l_5) in mm with their increased surface temperatures.

3. The co-efficient of expansion can be calculated as -

$$= \frac{\text{increase in length i.e. } (l_4 - l_5)}{\text{initial length } (l_4) \times \text{rise of temperature}}$$

5. Observations and Calculations

(A) Drying shrinkage and Moisture Movement-

W/C ratio		0.5		0.7	
specimen		1	2	1	2
Length (in mm)	l_1				
	l_2				
	l_3				
	l_4				
Temperature (in °c)					
	T_1				
	T_2				
	T_3				
	T_4				

Drying shrinkage at 0.5 w/c ratio = 1. = 2. } average =

Drying shrinkage at 0.7 w/c ratio = 1. = 2. } average =

Moisture movement at 0.5 w/c ratio = 1. = 2. } average =

Moisture movement at 0.7 w/c ratio = 1. = 2. } average =

(B) Co-efficient of Expansion

W/c ratio		0.5		0.7		Co-efficient of expansion
specimen		1	2	1	2	
Length in mm	l_4 l_5 l_5					For 0.5 w/c ratio = For 0.7 w/c ratio =
Temperature in ^0C	T_4 T_5					

6 **Results**

Average drying shrinkage at 0.5 w/c ratio = ------------------

Average drying shrinkage at 0.7 w/c ratio = ------------------

Average moisture movement at 0.5 w/c ratio = -----------------

Average moisture movement at 0.7 w/c ratio = -----------------

Average co-efficient of expansion at 0.5 w/c ratio = -----------------

Average co-efficient of expansion at 0.7 w/c ratio = -----------------

7. **Precautions**

1. Prism Moulds should be cleaned before casting
2. While casting the concrete should be rammed properly into the prism moulds.
3. Plugs should be taken out soon after the setting starts.
4. It is important to note that while taking measurements, the temperature should be standard temperature of the specimen. In the standard test all the measurements are taken at 24°C. If the temperature, while taking measurement is not 24°C then suitable temperature correction should be applied while calculating drying shrinkage and moisture movement.
5. It is very essential to make comparison measurement with standard rod, every time, because a small change in length of frame carrying micrometer will influence the readings a lot.

8. **Comments**

Compare your results with the standard values and give a brief commentry on your results.

9. Questions

1. What is drying shrinkage? What is its effect on the concrete members?
2. Why do we regard contraction more significant than expansion?
3. What is moisture movement? Clarify with the help of a graph.
4. What is the effect of w/c ratio over drying shrinkage and moisture movement?
5. How is the shrinkage affected by the curing period?
6. What is the effect of relative humidity on the shrinkage of concrete?
7. What is the effect of fineness of cement and richness of mix on the shrinkage of concrete?

EXPERIMENT NO. 3/15

ANALYSIS OF FRESHLY MIXED CONCRETE

1. **Object**—To determine the mix proportions of freshly mixed concrete.
2. **Theory**—Whenever there is need for spot checking or surprise checking of concrete job, this test is the best. This method quite precisely gives the proportions of the ingredients of freshly mixed concrete. The methodology adopted for the analysis is actually the removal of cement from aggregate and weighing the different quantities so recovered.
3. **Apparatus**—A fine quality balance with least count of 0.5 gm or less, Eight standard bucket shaped non-ferrous containers, large water tank, a connecting subsidiary water tank for raising or lowering water level in the main tank, Baffle plate to minimise disturbance due to water current, Two nesting sieves with IS: 480 mesh and IS: 15 mesh (as shown in Fig. 3.11). A funnel, a hose fitted with fine nozzle, a metallic stirring rod.

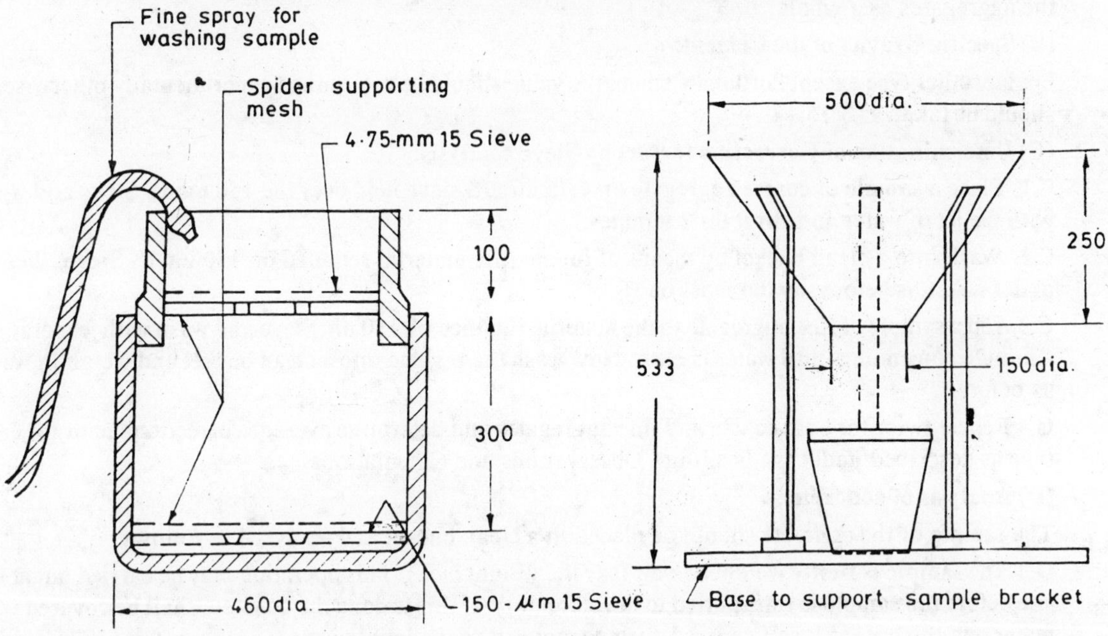

Fig. 3.11

4. **Procedure**—There are three major steps evolved in the analysis of the fresh concrete, namely, determination of specific gravity of Aggregates, determination of correction factors by sieve analysis and analysis of concrete. The description of these steps is as follows:

(A) Determination of Specific Gravity of Aggregates:–

A.1 Take four samples of each coarse and fine aggregates obtained by quatering as specified in IS: 383-1970 and reduce the main samples to the required size.

Note:-The mass of these samples should be in same ratio as nominal proportions of the concrete and total weight should be about 35 N (3.5 kg).

A.2 Dry out each sample of coarse and fine aggregate in ventilated oven at 100°C to 110°C for 24 hours. Then cool it and weight. Weights recorded may be A_c for the coarse aggregates or A_f for the fine aggregates.

A.3. Each sample is placed in a clean bucket and the bucket filled with water to within 25 mm of the lip. The sample should be stirred for one minute to remove any trapped air and the level of the tank should be raise steadily by raising the subsidiary tank untill the water starts to run from the overflow spout.

A.4 The sample is then weighed in water. During weighing, the maximum movement of the bucket shall be limited to 6.5 mm to avoid any inaccuracy caused by variations in its displacement or by agitation of the contents.

A.5 The sample is now left under water for 20 minutes, stirred, re-immersed and re-weighed. This procedure shall be repeated until the change in weight between consecutive weighings is less than 0.5 gm but in any case the period of immersion shall not exceed 8 hours.

A.6 The final weights may be recorded as B_c for the coarse aggregate of B_f for the fine aggregate. The time required to attain constant weight shall be recorded. The maximum time required for any of the samples to attain constant weight shall be regarded as the time required for the absorption of water by the aggregates as a whole.

(B) Specific Gravity of the Cement:-

For any other type except Portland Cement the value should be determined experimentally otherwise its should be taken as 3.15.

(C) Determination of Correction factors by Sieve Analysis:-

C.1 Place a sample of coarse aggregate on 4.75 mm IS sieve held over the 150 um IS Sieve and wash with the jet of water and stir it for 2 minutes.

C.2 Wash into a clean bucket by means of funnel, the material retained on 150 um IS Sieve. Weight under water as before say the mass be D_c.

C.3 Add a sample of fine aggregate to the material retained on 150 um Sieve and wash with jet spray for a minute continuing until water is clear. Now wash the residue into a clean bucket and weigh in water as before.

C.4 Repeat twice for both coarse and fine aggregates and determine average correction factor for each type as described under the heading - Observations and Calculations.

(D) Analysis of concrete :-

The sample of the concrete should be placed in a clean bucket and analysed as follows:

D.1 The sample is firstly weighed in air (say the weight is *W*). This operation may be carried out at the site before the sample is transported to the laboratory. If this is done the concrete shall be covered with water and the bucket it self covered during transport to the laboratory.

D.2 The bucket shall be filled with water to within 25 mm of the lip and the contents stirred throughly for one minute to remove any trapped air.

D.3 The sample shall be left immersed in water for a period of time not less than that required for the absorption of water by the aggregate, but in any case not longer than 8 hours. After this period of immension, the concrete shall again be throughly stirred for one minute to remove any air expelled from the aggregates.

D.4 The bucket shall be hung in the water tank from the balance with the water level in the tank below the lip of the bucket, namely with the subsidiary tank below the main tank and the top open. The bucket shall then be carefully filled with water upto the lip and the sample left to settle for five minutes.

D.5 The water level in the tank shall then be raised steadily by raising the subsidiary tank. When water overflows from the spout in the main tank, the top shall be turned off and the sample weighed in water (weight w). During this process, care shall be taken to avoid shaking the sample and the maximum movement of the bucket shall be limited to that specified under A.4. If the water level is raised steadily, little of the water containing fine particles of cement will spill out of the bucket. If the water in tank becomes discoloured, it shall be changed between weighings to avoid any change in its specific gravity.

D.6 The concrete shall be washed from the bucket on to the IS sieve 480 placed over IS sieve 15, care being taken to wash the bucket clean. The sample shall then be washed under the spray of water for at least two minutes continuously until the coarse aggregate is clean, the material being stirred during the washing.

D.7 The clean coarse aggregate retained on the IS sieve 480 shall then be washed into a clean bucket by means of the funnel and spray of water. The spray shall be used to remove any small particles from the mesh. Unless the water at this stage is clear, the washing specified above shall be repeated before the aggregate is placed in the bucket.

D.8 The coarse aggregate in the bucket shall be covered with water and stirred throughly for one minute. The bucket shall then be immersed in water in the tank and the aggregate weighed as before (weight w_c)

D.9 The fine aggregate remaining on the IS sieve 15 shall be washed under the spray of water.

D.10 The clean fine aggregate shall be washed into a clean bucket, stirred immersed in water and weighed as before (weight w_f).

5. Observations and Calculations

Average specific gravity :

1. Coarse aggregate $= \dfrac{Ac}{Ac - Bf}$

2. Fine aggregate $= \dfrac{Af}{Af - Bf}$

3. Cement = 3.15

$S_c = \dfrac{\text{Specific gravity}}{\text{specific gravity - 1}}$ for the corase aggregate

$S_f = \dfrac{\text{Specific gravity}}{\text{specific gravity - 1}}$ for the fine aggregate

$\text{Scement} = \dfrac{\text{Specific gravity}}{\text{specific gravity - 1}}$ for the cement

Average correction factors:

For the coarse aggregate $C_{ca} = \dfrac{B_c}{D_c}$

For the fine aggregate $C_f = \dfrac{B_c}{D_f}$

The proportion of each constituent in the concrete shall be calculated as follows:

Weight of coarse aggregate in the sample, $W_c = w_{c'} \times C_{ca} \times S_c$

Weight of fine aggregate in the sample, $W_f = w_f \times C_f \times S_f$

Weight of cement in the sample,

$W_{cement} = (W - (W_c \cdot C_c + W_f\, C_f))$ Scement

Weight of water in the sample,

$W_w = W - (W_c + W_f + W_{cement})$

where

W = Weight of concrete in air,

w = weight of concrete in water,

w_c = weight of coarse aggregate in water,

w_f = weight of fine aggregate in water.

6. **Results**

Mix proportion -

Cement	=
Fine aggregate	=
Coarse Aggregate	=

7. **Precautions**

(1) Before weighing any material in water, remove any entrapped air by stirring the water.

(2) Care should be taken while stirring so that not a fraction of material is lost.

(3) If water in the main tank becomes turbid, it should be changed between weighings to avoid any change in specific gravity.

(4) Weighing should be accurate upto 0.5 gm.

8. **Comments**

In considering the ingredients of a concrete mix we usually assume that the actual proportions corrospond to those specified in the mix. If these were invariably so, there would be little need for testing the strength of hardened concrete. However in practice, mistakes, errors and even delibrate actions can lead to incorrect mix proportions and it is sometimes useful to determine the composition of concrete at an early stage. The two values of greatest interest are the cement content and water/cement ratio.

9. **Questions**

(i) What is the significance of performing this experiment?

(2) Can the replacement of cement by a mineral additive such as pozzolana and as fine as cement be detected by this test?

(3) What could be the other methods of quality control at the construction site?

(4) What are the possible sources of errors in this test?

EXPERIMENT NO. 3/16

NON-DESTRUCTIVE TESTING OF CONCRETE

1. **Object**—To test the concrete specimens by the non-destructive test methods i.e., Ultra sonic pulse and Rebound hammer.

2. **Theory**—In actual structure, at a construction site, it is not possible to estimate the strength directly. Some estimate of the quality of concrete as well as of the uniformity of casting of a structure can, however, be obtained by non-destructive techniques such as ultra sonic pulse (USP) and Rebound Hammer tests. Ultra sonic pulse is introduced by an electro-accoustic transducer on one side of the concrete specimen. It travels through the material at a velocity which is dependent on the nature of the material. The velocity V of pulse for an elastic homogenous material is given by

$$V = \frac{E}{\rho} \frac{(1 - \nu)}{(1 + \nu)(1 - 2\nu)}$$

where

E - Young's modulus of elasticity

ρ - density

ν - Poisson's ratio.

The elastic constants E and ν are affected by the nature, continuity of solid phase, porosity and presence of micro cracks. The same parameters affect the strength of concrete. So the pulse velocity can give an estimate of modulus of elasticity and the compressive strength of concrete. Available data obeys the following relationship approximately, provided the same aggregates have been used. Compressive strength (S) of concrete varies with pulse velocity V, as

$$S = A + B \cdot V^n$$

where

V – Ultrasonic pulse velocity

A, B - constants, the exponent n may have values ranging from 3 to 4.

Rebound hammer, also called Schmidt Hammer, Impact Hammer or sclerometer (Fig. 3.12) measures the hardness of a material surface by the rebound of a standard ball after an elastic impact against the surface, the mass being released from a standard precompressed spring, thus having a fixed amount of energy. The distance travelled by the mass after this elastic impact expressed as a percentage of the original distance is termed as rebound number. This rebound number as an index of the hardness of the surface, can give a resonable estimate of the concrete strength if a good lot of data giving empirical relationship between the rebound number and concrete strength is available.

3. **Apparatus**—Universal–Testing Machine, Balance, Scale, cement paste with water cement ratio of 0.33, Ultrasonic pulse velocity equipment, schmidt hammer etc.

4. **Procedure**

(A) Ultrasonic Pulse Velocity

(a) Make standard cylinders with capping at the top (cast-face). Weight each cylinder and measure its dimensions accurately.

(b) Grease shall be applied to the transducer surface of the ultrasonic probes and the sides of the specimen so as to ensure complete contact as the interface, without any air voids.

(c) The equipment shall be kept on for about 10 minutes before taking the actual measurement.

(d) The transducers shall be held against the greased surfaces, under gentle manual pressure. The

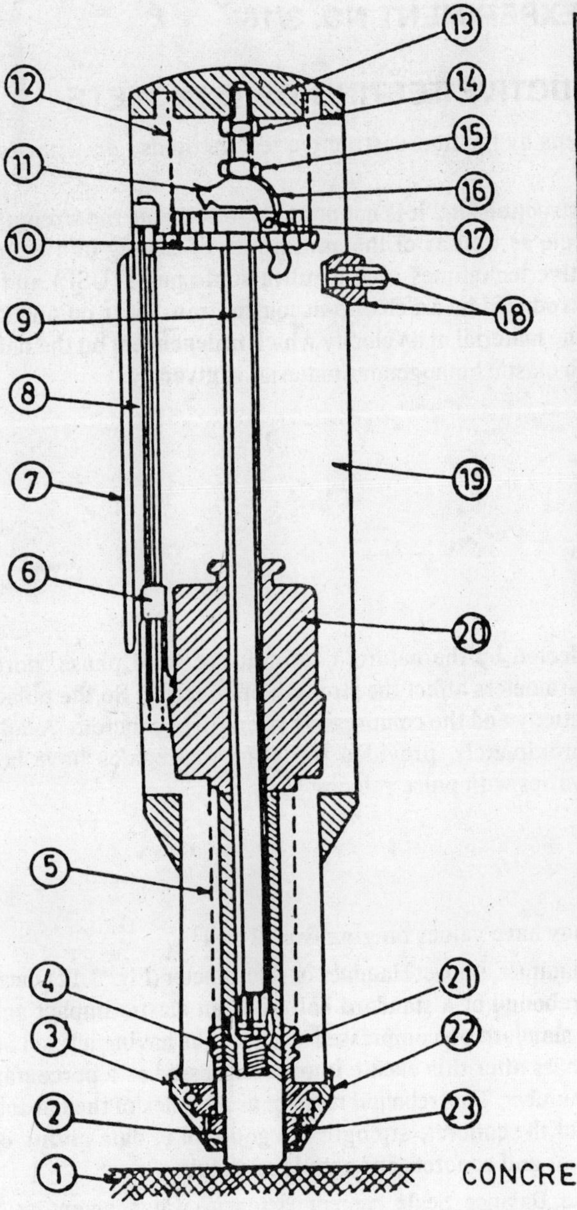

NO.	DESCRIPTION
1	TESTING SURFACE
2	IMPACT PLUNGER
3	CAP
4	RATAINING SPRING
5	IMPACT SPRING
6	RIDER WITH GUIDE ROD
7	PLEXI GLASS WINDOW
8	SCALE
9	HAMMER GUIDE BAR
10	DISK
11	PAWL SPRING
12	COMPRESSION SPRING
13	REAR COVER
14	LOCK NUT
15	TRIP SCREW
16	PAWL
17	PIN
18	PUSH BUTTON COMPL
19	HOUSING COMPL
20	HAMMER MASS
21	GUIDE SLEEVE
22	TWO-PART RING
23	FELT WASHER

CONCRETE TEST HAMMER

Fig 3.12

transducers shall be applied near the centre of the surface and never near the edge or corner of the specimen.

(e) The time taken by the pulse to travel through the specimen is measured in micro seconds in the apparatus. The reading may, generally, be varying within very small range. The most probable or most consistent reading shall be assumed to be the actual reading.

(f) The cubical specimens, at least one reading shall be taken on each face and for cylinders at least three readings shall be taken between the same surfaces.

(B) Rebound Hammer

(a) The specimen to be tested shall be kept and cured in such a way that the softening or hardening of

the surface due to leaching of calcium hydroxide, corrosion or carbonation is avoided.

(b) The specimen surface shall be cleaned of dust or any loose material.

(c) The specimen shall be held or fixed in such a way that is does not yield under the impact of hammer.

(d) The plunger of the hammer shall always be kept prependicular to the surface.

(e) About ten to twelve readings shall be taken and then their average value calculated to get a representative index of hardness.

(f) All the readings which are to be compared shall be taken while keeping the hammer in a specified inclination with the vertical, with the hammer pointing always in the same direction. For the same surface, the readings taken vertically are likely to be different from those taken by keeping the hammer in the horizontal position.

5. Observations and Calculations :

1. Concrete mix used.
2. Type of cement and aggregate used.
3. Curing conditions.
4. Age of concrete.
5. Wheather wet or dry.

5.1 Ultra Sonic Pulse Test :

Equipment employed:

	Repetitions			
	1	2	3	Ave. Velocity
Velocity time				
Cubes				
1				
2				
3				
Cylinders				
1				
2				
3				

5.2 Rebound Hammer Test

Sr. No.	1	2	3	4	5	6	7	8	9	10
Rebound No.										
Compressive Strength										

6. Results

Average velocity =

Average Index of hardness =

Compressive strength by ultrasonic pulse velocity method =

Compressive strength by Rebound Hammer =

7. **Precautions**

1. Don't forget to cap the cylinders before testing.
2. Apply grease to the transducer surface of the ultrasonic probes and the sides of the specimen.
3. Most stable reading should be taken as the actual reading of the time.
4. Before, rebound hammer test is conducted on the surface, all loose material should be removed.
5. Plunger of the hammer should always be kept perpendicular to the surface.

8. **Comments**—Tests can be made for different purposes. The main two objectives of the tests are the control of quality and compliance with specifications. Additional tests can be made for specific purpose e.g. compressive strength tests to determine the strength of concrete at transfer of prestress or at the time of striking the form work. It should be remembered that tests are not an end in themselves. In the case of concrete they seldom lend themselves to a neat, concise interpretation, so that in order to be of real value, tests should always be used against the background of experience.

9. **Questions**

1. What is the significance of performing the ultrasonic pulse velocity test.
2. Compare ultrasonic pulse velocity test with Rebound hammer test.
3. Out of these two tests, which one is more useful in estimating the strength of walls or old monuments and why?
4. What are the drawbacks of these tests?
5. Are these tests quite reliable?

EXPERIMENT NO. 3/17

CONCRETE MIX DESIGN AS PER IS RECOMMENDATIONS

1. **Object**—To determine the quantities of aggregates and water for a concrete mix in accordance with Indian standard recommended guide-lines.

2. **Theory**—Design of concrete mixes involves determination of the proportions of the given constituents, namely, cement, fine aggregates, coarse aggregates, water and admixture, if any, which would produce concrete possessing specified proportions both in the fresh and hardened states with the maximum overall economy. Workability is specified as the important property of concrete in the fresh state and for hardened state compressive strength and durability are important. The mix design is therefore, generally carried out for a particular compressive strength of concrete with adequate workability so that fresh concrete can be properly placed and compacted to achieve the required durability.

   The proportioning of concrete mixes is accomplished by the use of certain relationships established from experimental data, which afford reasonably accurate guide to select the best combination of ingredients so as to achieve the desirable properties.

3. **Apparatus**—Weighing balance, measuring cylinder, trowels, moulds, tamping rod, vibration table and universal testing machine.

4. **Procedure**—The target mean strength is first determined as follows:

(a) $f_t = f_{ck} + K.S = f_{ck} + 1.65S$ ... (17.1)

where K = a statistical value depending upon the accepted proportion of low results and the numberof tests. K is taken equal to 1.65

f_{ck} = characteristic compressive strength at 28 days S is the standard deviation depending upon the level of quality control. The value of standard deviations is chosen from Table *17.1*.

(b) The water cement ratio for the target mean strength is chosen from Fig. 3.13. The water cement ratio so chosen is checked against the limiting water cement ratio for the requirements of durability (Table *17.2*) and the lower of the two values is adopted.

(c) The air content (amount of entrapped air) is estimated from table *17.3* for the maximum size of aggregate used.

(d) The water content and percentage of sand in total aggregate by absolute volume are next selected from tables *17.4 and 17.5* and for medium and high strength concretes respectively, for the following standard references conditions:

(*i*) Crushed (angular) coarse aggregates

(*ii*) Fine aggregates consisting of natural sand confirming to grade zone II of table (4) of IS: 383-1970 in saturated surface dry conditions.

(*iii*) Water-cement ratio of 0.60 and 0.35 for medium and high strength concretes respectively.

(*iv*) Workability corresponding to compaction factor of 0.80.

(e) For other conditions of workability, water-cement ratio, grading of fine aggregate and for rounded aggregates, adjustment in water content and percentage of sand in total aggregate are made as per table *17.6*.

(f) The cement content is calculated from the water cement ratio and the final water content arrived after adjustment. The cement content so calculated is checked against the minimum cement content from the requirements of durability (Table *17.2*) and the greater of the two values adopted.

(g) With quantities of water and cement per unit volume of concrete and the percentage of sand in the total aggregate already determined, the coarse and fine aggregate content per unit volume of concrete are calculated from the following equations:

$$V = \left(W + \frac{c}{s_c} + \frac{1}{p}\ \frac{fa}{S_{fa}}\right) \times \left(\frac{1}{1000}\right)$$

$$V = \left(W + \frac{c}{s_c} + \frac{1}{1-p}\ \frac{Ca}{S_{ca}}\right)\left(\frac{1}{1000}\right)$$

Where V = Absolute volume of fresh concrete

= Gross volume ($1m^3$) minus the volume of entrapped air.

W = Absolute volumc of water.

Sc = Sp gravity of cement

c = Mass of cement (Kg/m^3) of concrete

p = ratio of fine aggregate to total aggregate by absolute volume

f_a, Ca = Total masses of fine aggregates and coarse aggregates (Kg/m^3) of concrete respectively.

S_{fa}, S_{ca} = Specific gravity of saturated surface dry fine aggregate and coarse aggregates respectively.

(h) Calculate the concrete mix proportions for the first trial mix.

(i) Prepare the concrete mix from the calculated proportions got from the step (h) and cast three cubes of 150 mm size and after 28 days of curing test them wet for compressive strength.

(j) Conduct trial mixes with appropriate adjustments till the final mix proportions are arrived at.

5. **Observations and Calculations**

Characteristic strength, (f_{cK}) =

Level of quality control (Refer table (17.7) =

Value of standard deviation adopted, S =

Mean target value, f_t (using equation 17.1) =

Water cement ratio (i) For mean target strength =

(ii) For durability requirements =

Water cement ratio adopted (lower value from (i) and (ii) =

Type of cement =

Grading of fine aggregate =

Type of coarse aggregate =

Nominal size of coarse aggregate, (mm) =

Specific gravity of cement, (s_c) =

Specific gravity of saturated surface dry fine aggregates, (S_{fa}) =

Specific gravity of saturated surface dry coarse aggregates, (S_{ca}) =

Percentage of entrapped air =

Water content per cubic metre of concrete, *W(kg)*

Before adjustment =

After adjustment =

Ratio of fine aggregate in total aggregate by absolute volume, (p)

Before adjustment =

After adjustment =

Cement content per cubic meter of concrete, *c (kg)*

From W/c ratio =
From durability requirements =
Total fine aggregates per cubic metre of concrete, fa (kg) =
Total coarse aggregates per cubic metre of concrete, Ca (kg) =
Mix proportions (by weight) =

Designation of specimen	1	2	3	Average
Load in kg after 28 days				
Strength in kg/cm^2				
Strength in N/mm^2				

Compressive strength of concrete = N/mm^2

6. Results

The mix proportions is --------------------

The designed mix is unsuitable/suitable

7. Precautions

1. Special care should be taken for the adjustment of water content and percentage of fine aggregate.
2. Proper testing should be done for the determining the grading of fine aggregates and nominal size of coarse aggregates.
3. All tests like slump test, cube casting, curing and testing for compressive strength should be done according to the IS specifications.

8. Comments

Apart from Indian Standard method for the concrete mix design, other methods which are commonly used are:

(a) The USBR Mix Design Method.

(b) The A.C.I. Mix Design Method.

(c) The British Mix Design Method.

In all these methods, water-cement ratio is chosen for the target mean strength from empirical compressive strength.

Comment on the different methods of mix design by taking into consideration various steps involves in the design of a particular mix.

9. Questions

1. What do you understand by proportioning of a concrete mix?
2. What is the characteristic strength of concrete?
3. What do you mean by workability of a concrete mix?
4. Explain target mean strength and how is it calculated?
5. What is standard deviation?
6. Does the type of cement affect the mix design?
7. Describe the factors which influence the choice of nominal maximum size of coarse aggregates.
8. How does this method differs from ACI mix design method and the British mix design method and the British mix design method.
9. What do you understand by degree of control on a construction site and in a testing laboratory.

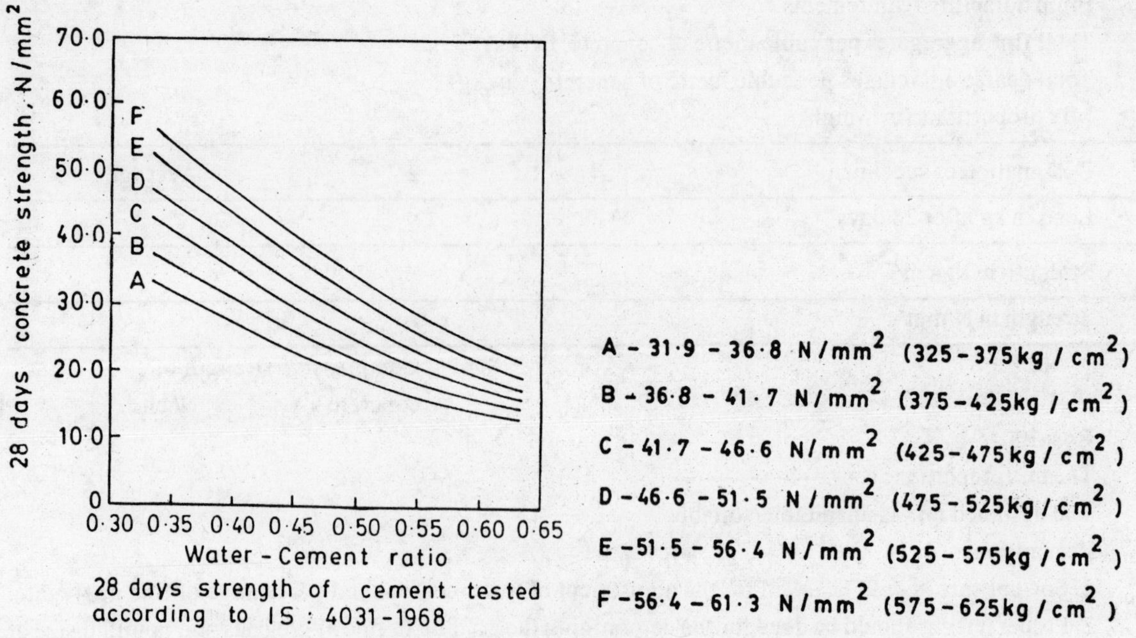

Fig. 3.13

TABLE 17.1 SUGGESTED VALUES OF STANDARD DEVIATION

Grade of concrete	Standard deviation for different degress of control (N/mm^2)		
	Very Good	Good	Fair
(1)	(2)	(3)	(4)
M 10	2.0	2.3	3.3
M 15	2.5	3.5	4.5
M 20	3.6	4.6	5.6
M 25	4.3	5.3	6.3
M 30	5.0	6.0	7.0
M 35	5.3	6.3	7.3
M 40	5.6	6.6	7.6
M 45	6.0	7.0	8.0
M 50	6.4	7.4	8.4
(1)	(2)	(3)	(4)
M 55	6.7	7.7	8.7
M 60	6.8	7.8	8.8

TABLE 17.2 MINIMUM CEMENT CONTENT REQUIRED IN CEMENT CONCRETE TO ENSURE DURABILITY UNDER SPECIFIED CONDITIONS OF EXPOSURE

EXPOSURE		PLAIN CONCRETE		REINFORCED CONCRETE	
		Minimum Cement Content	Maximum Water Cement Ratio	Minimum Cement Content	Maximum Water Cement Ratio
(1)		(2)	(3)	(4)	(5)
		kg/m^3		kg/m^3	
Mild –	For example, completely protected against weather, or aggressive conditions except for a brief period of exposure to normal weather conditions during construction	220	0.7	250	0.65
Moderate –	For example, sheltered from heavy and wind driven rain and against freezing, whilst saturated with water; buried concrete in soil and concrete continuously under water	250	0.6	290	0.55
Severe –	For example, exposed to sea water, alternate wetting and drying and to freezing whilst wet, subject to heavy condensation of water or corrosive fumes	310	0.5	360	0.45

Note:– (1) When the maximum water-cement ratio can be strictly controlled, the cement content may be reduced by 10 percent.

(2) The minimum cement content is based on 20 mm aggregate. For 40 mm aggregate, it should be reduced by about 10 percent; for 12.5 mm aggregate, it should be increased by about 10 percent.

TABLE 17.3 APPROXIMATE ENTRAPPED AIR CONTENT

Nominal Maximum size of Aggregate (mm)	Entrapped Air, as percent of volume of concrete
(1)	(2)
10	3.0
20	2.0
40	1.0

NOTE:– Table 17.3 is from 'Hardened Concrete; Mechanical Aspects; ACI Monograph No.6 (1971) by A.M. Neville with the permission of the American Concrete Institute, USA.

Table 17.4 APPROXIMATE SAND AND WATER CONTENTS PER CUBIC METRE OF CONCRETE

W/C = 0.60

Workability = 0.80 CF

(Applicable for concrete upto grade M 35)

Maximum size of Aggregate (mm)	Water content* Per cubic metre of concrete (kg)	Sand as Percent of Total Aggregate by Absolute Volume
(1)	(2)	(3)
10	208	62
20	186	45
40	165	40

* Water content corresponding to saturated surface dry aggregate.

TABLE 17.5 APPROXIMATE SAND AND WATER CONTENTS PER CUBIC METRE OF CONCRETE

W/C = 0.35

Workability = 0.80 CF

(Applicable for concrete above grade M 35)

Maximum size of Aggregate (mm)	Water content* per cubic metre of concrete (kg)	Sand as percent of Total Aggregate of Absolute volume
(1)	(2)	(3)
10	200	26
20	180	23

* Water content corresponding to saturated surface dry aggregate.

TABLE 17.6 ADJUSTMENT OF VALUES IN WATER CONTENT AND SAND PERCENTAGE FOR OTHER CONDITIONS

Change in conditions stipulated for tables 17.4 and 17.5	**Adjustment required in** Water Content	Percent Sand in Total Aggregate
(1)	(2)	(3)
For sand conforming to grading Zone I, Zone III or Zone IV	0	+ 1.5 percent for -Zone I

of Table 4, IS: 383-1970		– 1.5 percent for Zone III – 3.0 percent for Zone IV
Increase or decrease in the value of compacting factor by 0.1	± 3 percent	0
Each 0.05 increase or decrease in water-cement ratio	0	± 1 percent
For rounded aggregate	-15 kg/m^3	-7 percent

TABLE 17.7 DEGREE OF QUALITY CONTROL, EXPECTED UNDER DIFFERENT SITE CONDITIONS

Degree of Control	Conditions of Production
Very Good	Fresh cement from single source and regular tests, weighbatching of all materials, aggregates supplied in single sizes, control of aggregate grading and moisture content, control of water added, frequent supervision, regular workability and strength tests, field laboratory facilities.
Good	Carefully stored cement and periodic tests, weighbatching of all materials, controlled water graded aggregate supplied, occasional grading and moisture tests, periodic check of workability and strength, intermittent supervision, experienced workers.
Fair	Proper storage of cement, volume batching of all aggregate allowing for bulking of sand, weighbatching of cement, water content controlled by inspection of mix, occasional supervision and tests.

REFERENCES:

1. IS 1199-1959, 'Methods of Sampling and Analysis of Concrete'.
2. IS 516-1959, 'Methods for strength of concrete'.
3. IS 5816-1976, 'Method of Test for Splitting Tensile Strength of Concrete cylinders.
4. IS 456-1978, 'Code of Practice for plain and reinforced concrete'.
5. Gambhir M.L., Laboratory Mannual on Concrete Testing (Part-I). Dhanpat Rai and Sons. Jallandhar.
6. Neville, A.M.-Properties of concrete. The English language Book Society, Pitman Publishing.
7. Troxell G.E., Davis. H.E. and Kelly J.W.-Composition and Properties of concrete. Second Edition, M.C. Graw Hill Book Company, New York.
8. Baver, E.E., Plain concrete, Mc. Graw Hill Book Company, New York.
9. A basis for Designing laboratory Experiment in Civil Engineering. A curriculum development seminar 1977. Curriculum Development group, Department of Civil Engineering, University of Roorkee.
10. Kaushal Kishore-Design of concrete mixes with high strength ordinary Portland Cement. The Indian Concrete Journal Vol. 53. April, 1979, pp. 103-104.
11. Design of normal concrete mixes, Department of Environmental, B.R.H. Transport and Road Research Laboratory, H.M.S.O. London.
12. Concrete Hand book-Published by Concrete Association of India, Bombay.
13. BS 1881 Part - 2, 1970
14. Laboratory Manual for Building Materials Published by Indian Society For Technical Education, New Delhi.

PART IV

REINFORCED CONCRETE

EXPERIMENT NO.4/1

ULTIMATE STRENGTH OF BEAMS

1. **Object**-To determine the flexural ultimate strength of:

   (a) an under reinforced beam of size 100 mm × 150 mm × 1830 mm.

   (b) an over reinforced beam of the same size.

   And to compare the results with those advocated by Indian Standard code based on limit strength theory.

2. **Apparatus**-Graduated cylinder, concrete mixer, platform, weighing machine, trowels, tamping rods, table vibrator, beam mould (100 mm × 150 × 1830 mm), transverse testing machine or a loading reaction frame.

3. **Theory**- Structures may be designed either by the methods based on working stress consideration or by the methods based on ultimate load considerations. The working stress method assumes a linear relationship between load and stresses upto failure of the structure which is justified if material i.e. concrete and steel are fully elastic upto their failure. To calculate the collapse load, it is necessary to take into account the inelastic or the plastic strains that occur in the material before it fails. The method of calculations, taking into account these plastic strains near failure is called ultimate load theory.

   As per IS: 456-1978 code the ultimate moment of resistance of an under reinforced section is given by

$$M_u = 0.87 \text{ ssy. Ast. d} \left(1 - \frac{\text{Ast } \sigma \text{sy}}{\text{b.d.fck}}\right) \quad \dots (1)$$

Similarly the ultimate moment of resistance of a balanced section to given by

$$M_u \text{lim} = 0.36. \frac{Xu, \max}{d}\left(1 - 0.42\frac{Xu, \max}{d}\right)bd^2 \text{ fck} \quad \dots (2)$$

where,

M_u = Ultimate moment of resistance

b = width of the section

d = effective depth of the section

Ast = Area of X-Section of steel in the section = p.bd

σsy = yield strength of reinforcing steel used.

fck = cube characteristic strength of concrete mix used

Xumax = limiting value of Xu and is given by

$$\frac{Xu}{d} = \frac{0.87\sigma_{sy}.\ Ast}{036 fck.b.d.} = 0.53 \text{ for } \sigma sy = 250 \text{ N/mm}^2 (2500 \text{ kg./cm}^2) \quad \dots (3)$$

4. **Procedure**:

   (a) Prepare a 1:2:4 concrete mix by weight with w/c ratio equal to 0.6, taking 300N (30 kg) of cement, 600N (60 kg.) of sand 1200N (120 kg) of coarse aggregate.

   (b) Mix the above dry ingredients to uniform colour in a concrete mixer and add 18 litres of water and get a homogeneous mix.

   (c) Cast the following speciments on a table vibrator.

   (i) One 100 mm × 150 mm × 1830 mm beam reinforced with two 6 mm diameter bars at the bottom with

an effective cover of 12.5 mm (1.25 cm) and provide two legged vertical stirrups at lever arms spacing.

(ii) One 100 mm × 150 mm × 1830 mm beam reinforced with four 10 mm diameter bars at the bottom in two layers of two bars each and shear stirrups. The bars to be used should have hooks at both the ends in case plain bars are used and no hooks when deformed bars are used.

(iii) Three or more 150 mm (15 cm) cubes.

(d) Remove the beams and cubes from moulds after 24 hours and immerse them in fresh water.

(e) Test speciments after 27 days of wet curing on the 50 KN (5 tons) transverse testing machine or on a loading reaction frame under gradually increasing two concentrated loads spaced at 567 mm (56.7 cm) apart in the middle. Effective span of the beam may be kept equal to 1700 mm (170 cm).

(f) Test the cubes on the compression testing machine also after 27 days of wet curing.

(g) Sketch the crack patterns of the under-reinforced and over reinforced beams.

(h) Measure the effective depth of reinforcement.

(i) Draw the load. Deflection curve for the central section.

5. Observations and Calculations:

TABLE-4.1. Cube Strength of Concrete

Sl. No.	*Failure load N(kg.)*	*Cube Strength $N/mm^2 (kg/cm^2)$*	*Average*	*Remarks*
1.				
2.				
3.				

TABLE-4.2. Strength of Beams

Sl. No.	Mix Propo-rtion	Type of Beam	Age	Observed load at failure N (kg.)	Percentage of Steel	Actual effective depth	Ultimate moment of resis-tance	Calculated or theore-tical failure load
1.	1:2:4 W/c = 0.6	Under rein-forced	28 days					
2.	1:2:4 W/c = 0.6	Over rein-forced	28 days					

6. Results:

(a) Under-Reinforced Beam

1. Observed failure load, P_{obs} =
2. Calculated failure load, P_{th} =
3. Ratio of P_{obs}/P_{th} =

(b) Over-Reinforced Beam

1. Observed failure load P'_{obs} =
2. Calculated failure load, P'_{tk} =

3. Ratio of P'_{obs}/P'_{th} =

7. Precautions:

1. The ingredients should be thoroughly mixed dry before adding water.
2. The interior surface of the mixer should be absolutely clean before use.
3. The moulds should be filled in three equal layers and the moulds should be properly oiled.
4. The cubes and beams stored in water should be tested immediately after they are removed from water and any surface water, grit and projections should be removed.
5. The cubes should be tested on sides.
6. No packing should be used between the cube and platens of the testing machine.

8. Comments:

The beams in which failure is initiated by yielding of tensile steel are called under reinforced. If the percentage of steel is sufficient to ensure that steel yield does not take place, such beams are called over reinforced.

The behaviour of a beam subjected to increasing load can be discussed in the following three stages.

1. Before the development of first crack.
2. After first crack is developed and both concrete and steel are within their elastic limits.
3. Materials have crossed their elastic limits. The stage can be discussed under two sub-heads:-

(a) Tension failure for under reinforced beams.

(b) Primary compression failure for over reinforced beams.

9. Questions :

(a) Why is a concrete section reinforced with steel ?

(b) Why steel alone is used in R.C. members and not cast iron, aluminium etc.?

(c) What are the assumptions made in the bending theory of reinforced concrete design ?

(d) What is limit state theory and how does it over come the deficiencies of working stress theory ?

(e) Differenciate between an under reinforced and an over reinforced section ?

(f) What is the nature of cracks developed in an under-reinforced and over reinforced beam ?

(g) Explain tension failure and compression failure of beams.

(h) What is the effect of shrinkage and temperature on the tensile strength of concrete ?

(i) In under reinforced and over reinforced sections, failure occurs by crushing of concrete, what is the difference in the behaviour at failure ?

(j) List the various types of reinforcing materials used in reinforced concrete.

EXPERIMENT NO. 4/2

ULTIMATE STRENGTH IN DIAGONAL TENSION AND BOND

1. **Object**-To determine the ultimate strength of Reinforced Concrete beam (100mm × 150mm × 1220mm).

   (a) In diagonal tension

   (b) in bond.

   Compute the ultimate shear and bond stresses in concrete.

2. **Apparatus**-Graduated cylinder, concrete mixer, platform weighing machine, balance, moulds, trowels, tamping rods, transverse testing machine or a loading reaction frame.

3. **Theory** - The diagonal tensile stresses require special attention in reinforced concrete design. A reinforced concrete section properly designed in all respects should normally be safe in shear, which is measure of diagonal tension.

   The knowledge of bond is very essential in reinforced concrete design. The resistance of steel to tension can be utilised only through the bond between concrete and steel. When the bond between concrete and steel is broken the reinforcing bar will slip instead of resisting tensile stresses and the beam will thus fail even if it is reinforced with sufficient amount of tensile reinforcement.

4. **Procedure :**

   (a) Prepare 1:2:4 concrete mix (by weight) with W/C ratio equal to 0.6, taking 200N(20Kg.) of cement, 400N(40 Kg.) of sand and 800N(80Kg.) of coarse aggregate.

   (b) Mix the dry aggregates to uniform colour, in a concrete mixer, than add 12 litres of water and get a homogeneous mix.

   (c) Cast the following specimens on a table vibrator :

   (i) One beam of 100 mm × 150mm × 1220mm reinforced with 4 bars of 10mm diameter with hooks at the bottom in two layers, with an effective cover of 25mm to be tested in shear.

   (ii) One other beam of the same size but reinforced with only two bars of 10mm diameter without any books at the ends with an effective cover is 25mm.

   (iii) Three or more 150 mm cubes.

   (d) Remove the specimens from the moulds after 24 hours and immerse them in fresh water.

   (e) Test the specimens after 27 days of wet curing. For testing the beams in shear and bond, place the beams on supports with an effective span of 1050mm on the 50 KN(5t) transverse testing machine or on a loading reaction frame and apply a gradually increasing concentrated load at 230mm from the support.

   (f) Note the load when first crack appears and when the complete failure takes place in each case.

   (g) Test the cubes in compression.

   (h) Sketch the crack pattern at first crack and at failure of the beams. Ascertain the actual effective depth of the reinforcement by measuring the same.

5. **Observations and Calculations**

TABLE-4.3. Cube Strength of Concrete

S.No.	*Failure Load KN(tonnes)*	*Cube Strength N/mm²(Kg./Cm²)*	*Average (σcu) N/mm²(Kg./cm²)*	*Remarks*
1.				
2.				
3.				

TABLE-4.4. Shear Strength of Concrete

1. Load at first crack ... ... N(Kg.)
2. Ultimate Load ... ... N(Kg.)
3. Actual effective depth ... ... mm
4. Shear stress when first crack appears

$$\sigma sh = \frac{Vf}{b \times jd} \quad N/mm^2(Kg/cm^2)$$

5. Ultimate shear stress

$$\sigma sh = \frac{Vu}{b \times d} \quad N/mm^2\,(Kg/cm^2)$$

6. Theoretical Shear Stress = 0.1 × σcb

TABLE-4.5. Bond Strength of Concrete

1. Load at first crack ... ... N(Kg.)
2. Ultimate Load ... ... (N(Kg.)
3. Actual effective depth ... ... mm
4. Bond stress when first crack appears

$$\sigma_{bf} = \frac{Vf}{j\,d\,S_o} \quad N/mm^2(Kg/cm^2)$$

5. Ultimate bond stress (Kg/Cm²) $= \sigma_{bu} = \frac{Vu}{d\,S_o}$ N/mm²(Kg/cm²)

6. Results :

1. Shear stress at first crack =
2. Ultimate shear stress =
3. Bond stress at first crack =
4. Ultimate bond stress =
5. Ultimate cube strength =

7. Precautions:

1. All normal precautions while casting, curing and testing shall be observed.

8. Comments :

The difference between the first crack load and ultimate load depends upon the strength of the concrete. Concrete is quite strong is shear but a combination of horizontal and vertical shear stresses along with the tensile stresses due to bending produces tension in concrete in a diagonal direction, which has to be closely examined in view of the weakness of concrete in tension. Diagonal cracks join the supports and the load section. Their inclination with the horizontal is nearly 45°. Bar bent at about 45° from the bottom and vertical stirrups are provided in berms to prevent diagonal tension failure.

9. Questions :

(a) What is the importance of diagonal tension in reinforced concrete design ?

(b) Discuss the significance of bond ?

(c) How does inadequacy in bond between steel and concrete affect the strength of a beam?

(d) Discuss the difference in behaviour of beams with lean and rich mixes ?

(e) Why are hooks provided at the ends of plain bars where-as they are not provided in case of deformed bars?

(f) What is length of embedment in case of a plain bar ?

(g) What measures are adopted to prevent diagonal tension failure ?

(h) What is the theoretical ratio of diagonal tensile stress and bending stress ?

(i) What is the difference between local bond and average bond stress ?

(j) Elaborate the statement "Bond is an agency through which tensile force is transferred from concrete to steel" ?

EXPERIMENT NO. 4/3

BOND STRENGTH BETWEEN STEEL AND CONCRETE

1. **Object**-To determine the bond strength between ordinary mild steel bars and cement concrete.
   (a) in a reinforced concrete beam with overlapping reinforcement.
   (b) by pullout test.
2. **Apparatus**-Beam mould (100mm × 150mm × 1830mm), cylinder mould (150mm × 300mm), aligning stand, 50KN (5 tons) transverse testing machine or a loading reaction frame, 100KN (10 tons) universal testing machine with pull out test attachment, dial gauges, tamping bar, trowels, graduated,jar, platform weighing balance, concrete mixer, table vibrator.
3. **Theory**-The bond strength is the measure of the effectiveness of the grip between concrete and steel and has no standard quantitative definition. In pull out tests on plain bars, the maximum load generally represents the bond strength that can be developed between concrete and steel. With plain bars the maximum load is not very different from the load at the first visible slip, but in the case of deformed bar, the maximum load may correspond to a large slip which may not in fact be obtained in practice before other types of failure occur. It is preferable, therefore, when comparing plain and deformed bars to determine not only the maximum load but also the load at the arbitrary amount of slip and also plot the complete load slip curves for the plain and deformed bars under comparison. One such basis of comparison is the load at a relative movement (slip) between steel and concrete of 0.125 mm at the free end of the bar in a pull out test.

Comparison of bond characteristics between concrete and different types of steel reinforcing bars may be made for any purpose, from routine acceptance tests to research testing, in so far as applicable to a particular project.

4. **Procedure:**

   (a) Prepare 1:2:4 concrete mix by weight taking water cement ratio equal to 0.6. For this take 170N(17 Kg.) cement, 340N (34 Kg.) Sand 680N (68 Kg.) coarse aggregate and 102N (10.200 Kg.) of water.

   (b) Cast the concrete beam 100mm × 150mm × 1830mm. Using two, 10mm bars having an effective cover of 12.5mm and overlapping of 200mm in the middle. The four pieces of bars will have hooks at one end only. Cast three cubes alongwith the beams for crushing strength of concrete.

   (c) Cast three cylinders upto a height of 200mm with a 10mm dia rod placed at the centre of cylinder.

   (d) Remove the specimens from moulds after 24 hours and put them in water. Test the beam after 27 days of wet curing applying the load gradually on 50 KN (5 tons) transverse testing machine or on a loading reactions frame. Test the three cubes in compression.

   (e) Perform the pull out test on 100 KN (10 tons) universal testing machine using pull out test attachment at 28 days age.

   (f) Attach a dial gauge for finding out the slip between steel and concrete and plot the curve between load and slip.

   (g) Note the load at 0.125mm slip and at bond failure.

5. **Observations and Calculations :**

TABLE-4.6. R.C. Beam Test

1.	Load at first crack	... ...	N(tonnes)
2.	Ultimate load at bond failure (P)	... ...	N(tonnes)
3.	Maximum B.M. at first crack	... ...	Nm(Kg cm)
4.	Maximum B.M. at failure	... ...	Nm(Kg cm)

5. actual effective depth ... ... mm
6. Crushing strength of concrete ... ... N/mm²(Kg/cm²)
7. Ultimate bond stress

$$\sigma bu = \frac{P_b}{\pi \times d \times 1}$$

Where σbu	=	Ultimate bond stress
Pb	=	Bond failure load
d	=	dia of bar
l	=	length of bar (200mm in this case)

TABLE-4.7. Pull Out Test

1. Load at 0.125mm slip (P_1)
2. Load at bond failure (P_2)
3. Average bond strength at 0.125mm

   slip $= \dfrac{P_1}{\pi \times d \times 1}$
4. Average bond strength at failure

   $= \dfrac{P_2}{\pi \times d \times 1}$

6. Precautions:

(1) Use an aligning stand while casting the cylinderical specimens, to keep the bars in vertical positions.

(2) The beam and cylinder specimens would be tested just after removing from curing tank.

7. Results :

(1) Ultimate bond stress at failure in beam test. =

(2) Average bond strength at 0.125mm slip in pull out test = N/mm²(Kg/cm²)

(3) Average bond strength at failure in pull out test = N/mm²(Kg/cm²)

8. Discussions:

The average bond stress is taken as the value obtained for such specimen, by dividing the applied load at the slip specified, by the surface areas of the embedded length of the bar and then taking the average value for the groups of each types of bar in the test series.

9. Questions :

(a) State the significance of pull out test?

(b) What is the minimum overlap for tensile bars in R.C. beams ?

(c) Why the slip is specified as 0.125mm in a pull out test ?

(d) Why is bond stress increased in case of deformed bars as compared to plain bars?

(e) What are the different methods of increasing the bond in R.C. beams?

(f) Why hooks are not provided at ends in case of deformed bars whereas they are provided in case of plain bars?

(g) Define the nominal size of a deformed bar ?

(h) How does the rusting affect the strength of steel bar ?

(i) Why is it necessary to provide a concrete cover for the reinforcement?

EXPERIMENT NO.4/4

TESTING OF REINFORCED CONCRETE COLUMNS

1. **Object**

To determine ultimate compressive strength of the columns when the cross-section is (i) circular (ii) Rectangular or Square.

2. **Theory**

Columns form the most important part of a structure. The failure of any other part (beam or slab) of a structure may not cause no serious a damage as that caused by the failure of a column. It can endanger even the whole structure. All vertical members may not be termed as columns. Only those members whose effective length is more than three times the least lateral dimensions are called columns and those members whose effective length is less than 3 times the least lateral dimension are called "pedastals." Though column is a member in compressive yet the possibility of tension is some part of it cannot be ruled out. This tension may occur due to two main reasons:

(i) Accidental eccentricity of loading

(ii) bending in columns.

To take care of the tension, some amount of steel has to be provided on tension face in the longitudinal direction. The amount of steel should be just sufficient to take care of the tensile stresses only. The longitudinal steel is kept in its position with the help of binders (Steel bars of small diameter) or ties which also prevent the buckling of vertical bars.

A compressive member may be considered as short when both the slenderness ratio $\frac{Lex}{d}$ and $\frac{Ley}{b}$ are less than 12

where lex, ley = effective length in respect of the major axis and minor axis respectively.

D = Depth in respect of the major axis

b = Width of the member.

If the above slenderness ratios are greater than 12, then it shall be considered as slender compression member or a long column.

When the designer wants to reduce the section of the column, he will like to reinforce it with steel bars which will help in compression.

3. **Apparatus**

UTM or Reaction frame, moulds, steel, cement, aggregates, measuring jar, mixer, vibrator etc.

4. **Procedure**

(a) Three types of columns may be cast, namely, circular columns with Helical reinforcement, circular columns with circular ties and rectangular columns with rectangular ties. Select the dimensions of the column depending upon the fixed value of the slenderness ratio choosen.

(b) Design the column taking the cross-section as circular and rectangular by selecting any allowable axial load (say 400 KN (40 t)

(c) For longitudinal reinforcement design the columns in accordance with the specifications of IS: 456-1978 Code.

(d) For transverse reinforcement the steel provided should also be as per the above code.

(e) Cast the columns using any choosen grade of concrete (say M 20).

(f) Keep the cast columns in wet condition for 28 days.

(g) Load the columns on the reaction frame and apply axial load at constant rate.

(h) Observe the cracks which propagates over the whole length of column.

(i) Take the final reading of load carrying capacity when the column fails.

5. Observations and Calculations

Slenderness ratio of column =

Dimensions of rectangular column =

Dimensions of circular column =

Concrete grade used = M20

W/c ratio used

TABLE 4.8. Ultimate loads

Specimen No.	1	2	3	Average
Ultimate axial load noted for circular columns with Helical reinforcement				
Ultimate axial load noted for circular columns with circular ties				
Ultimate axial load noted for rectangular columns with rectangular ties				

6. Results

Axial load taken by circular column with
Helical reinforcement = (Kg) = (kN)

Axial load taken by circular column with
Circular ties = (Kg) = (kN)

Axial load taken by Rectangular column
with rectangular ties = (Kg) = (Kg)

7. Precautions

1. Don't forget to cap the columns
2. Compaction should be done using needle vibrator.
3. While loading there should be minimum possible eccentricity in the column.
4. Load should be released in increments.

8. Comments

Comment on the difference of axial load between the designed axial load and ultimate axial load achieved. Also comment on the load carrying capacity of different types of columns tested by you.

9. Questions

(a) What is the slenderness ratio?

(b) How do you differentiate between a short column and a long column?

(c) What is difference between a pedestal and a column?

(d) What is a composite column?

(e) What do you understand by effective length of the column

(f) How can we achieve fixed end and hinged end conditions in a column on a construction site and in the laboratory.

REFERENCES

(1) I.S. 2770-1970 Part I Methods of Testing Bond in Reinforced concrete Pull out Test.

(2) I.S. 456-1978 Indian Standard code of Practice for Plain and Reinforced concrete.

(3) A Basis for Designing Laboratory Experiments in Civil engineering. A curriculum Development Seminar. March 1977. Curriculum Development Group. Department of Civil Engg. University of Roorkee, Roorkee (U.P.) India.

(4) Gambhir M L, 'Laboratory mannual on concrete Testing, Published by Dhanpat Rai and Sons. Delhi.

(5) Concrete Hand Book Published by Concrete Association of India Bombay.

(6) V. Rama Krishnan and P.D. Arthor, Ultimate Strength Design for structural concrete. The Africa and Asia Edition.

(7) Proceedings of Summer School on Limit State Design of Concrete Structures. May 1973,. University of Roorkee, Roorkee (U.P.) India.

(8) Reinforced Concrete-Limit State Design by A.K. Jain Published by M/s Nem Chand and Brothers, Roorkee.

PART V

BRICKS

EXPERIMENT NO.5/1

EFFLORESCENCE OF BURNT CLAY BUILDING BRICKS

1. **Object**-To determine Efflorescence of Burnt Clay Building Bricks.

2. **Theory:**

   Bricks made from clay containing a relatively large proportions of soluble salts particularly calcium sulphate are liable to become discoloured by the formation of a whitish deposits. While this effloresence or salting is particularly common to new brick work, it may also form on the face of old external wall which are subjected to excessive dampness.

3. **Apparatus:**

   A shallow flat bottom dish containing sufficient distilled water to completely saturate the specimen. The dish shall be made of glass, porcelain or glazed stone work and of size not less than 150 mm in diameter and 30 mm in depth.

4. **Procedure:**

   Take 3 bricks, place the end of the bricks in the dish, the depth of immersion in water being 25 mm. Place the whole arrangement in a warm (for example 20 to 30°C) well-ventilated room until all the water in the dish is absorbed by the specimen and the surplus water evaporated. when the water has been absorbed and bricks appear to be dry, placed a similar quantity of water in the dish and allow it to evaporate as before. Examine the bricks for efflorescence after the second evaporation and report the results.

5. **Report:**

   The liability of efflorescence shall be reported as nil, slight, moderate, heavy or serious in accordance with the following definitions:

   (a) Nil-when there is no perceptible deposit of efflorescence.

   (b) Slight-When not more than 10 percent of the exposed area of the bricks is covered with a thin deposit of salts.

   (c) Moderate-When there is a heavier deposit than under slight and covering upto 50 percent of the exposed area of the brick surface but un-accompanied by powdering or flaking of the surface.

   (d) Heavy-When there is a heavy deposit of salts convering 50 percent or more of the exposed area of the brick surface but unaccompanied by powdering or flaking of the surface.

   (e) Serious-When there is a heavy deposit of salts accompanies by powdering and/or flaking of the exposed surface.

6. **Results :**

   Sample No.

   1. Nil/Slight/moderate/heavy/serious.
   2. Nil/Slight/moderate/heavy/serious.
   3. Nil/Slight/moderate/heavy/serious.

   Remark ; The efflorescence shall not be more than slight for higher class brick.

7. **Questions :**

   (a) Define a brick.

   (b) What are the different classification of bricks ?

   (c) What are ingredients of a good brick earth ?

   (d) Name the harmful constituents of brick earth ?

   (e) Define Efflorescence.

   (f) Why this test is performed ?

EXPERIMENT NO.5/2

WATER ABSORPTION OF BURNT CLAY BUILDING BRICKS

1. **Object**-To determine Water absorption of burnt clay building bricks.
2. **Theory:**

Bricks for external use must be capable of preventing rain water from passing through them to the inside of walls of reasonable thickness. A good brick should absorb water maximum $\frac{1}{7}$ th of the weight of the brick.

3. **Apparatus:**

A sensitive balance capable of weighing within 0.1 percent of the mass of the specimen and a ventilated oven.

4. **Preconditioning:**

Take 5 bricks and dry in a ventilated oven at a temperature of 105 to 115°C till it attains substantially constant mass. Cool the specimen to room temperature and obtain its weight (M_1). Specimen warm to touch shall not be used for the purpose.

5. **Procedure:**

Immerse completely dried specimen in clean water at a temperature of 27 ± 2°C for 24 hours. Remove the specimen and wipe out any traces of water with a damp cloth. Weigh the specimen. Complete the weighing within three minutes after the specimen has been removed from water (M_2).

Water absorption, percent by mass, after 24 hours immersion in cold water is given by the formula :

$$\frac{M_2 - M_1}{M_1} \times 100$$

6. **Results :**

Water Absorption (percent by weight after 24 hours immersion in cold water).

Simple No.

1.
2.
3.
4.
5.

Remark-For higher class bricks the water absorption after immersion in cold water for 24 hours shall not be more than 15 percent.

7. **Comments:**

After immersion in cold water for 24 hours, the average water absorption shall not be more than 20 percent by weight upto class 125 and 15 percent by weight for higher classes.

8. **Questions**

(a) Discuss the importance of this test ?

(b) Name the characteristics of good bricks ?

(c) State the maximum limit on water absorption of building bricks ?

(d) What is the standard size and weight of a building brick ?

(e) What are the standard sizes of building tiles ?

(f) What is a modular brick ?

EXPERIMENT NO. 5/3

COMPRESSIVE STRENGTH OF BURNT CLAY BUILDING BRICKS

1. **Object**—To determine Compressive Strength of burnt clay building bricks.
2. **Theory :**

Bricks are mostly subjected to compression and rarely to tension. The usual crushing strength of common hand moulded well burnt bricks is about 5 to 10 N/mm² (50 to 100/Kg/cm²) varying according to the nature of preparation of the clay. Pressed and machine moulded bricks made of thorougly pugged clay are much stronger than common hand moulded bricks made from carelessely prepared clay.

3. **Apparatus :**

A compression testing machine having a compression plate with a ball seating in the form of portion of sphere the centre of which coincides with the centre of the plate.

Preconditioning of Samples :

Take 5 bricks, remove unevenness observed in the bed faces to provide two smooth and parallel faces by grinding. Immerse the bricks in water at room temperature for 24 hours. Remove the specimen and drain out any surplus moisture at room temperature. Fill the frog (where provided) and all voids in the bed face flush with cement mortar (1 cement, 1 clean coarse sand of grade 3 mm and down). Store under the damp Jute bags for 24 hours followed by immersion in clean water for 3 days. Remove, and wipe out any traces of moisture.

4. **Procedure :**

Place the specimen with flat faces horizontal and mortar filled face facing upwards between two 3-plywood sheet each of 3 mm thickness and carefully centered between plats of the testing machine. Apply load axially at a uniform rate of 14N/mm² (140 Kg/cm²) per minute till failure occurs and note the maximum load at failure. The load at failure shall be the maximum load at which the specimen fails to produce any further increase in the indicator reading on the testing machine.

NOTE-In place of plywood sheets plaster of pairs may be used to ensure a uniform surface for application of load.

5. **Report :**

The test result shall be reported as below :

$$\text{Compressive strength} = \frac{\text{Maximum load at failure N (Kg)}}{\text{Average area of the bed faces mm}^2\ (\text{cm})^2}$$

6. **Observations :**

Sr.	*Brick No.*	*Identification No.*	*Date of testing*	*Size (Cm)*	*Load N(Kg)*	*Compressive strength N/mm² (Kg/Cm²)*	*Remarks*
1.							
2.							
3.							
4.							
5.							

7. Comments :

Specification of Burnt Clay Building Bricks as per IS: 1077-1976.

The Compressive strength of various classes of bricks shall be as follows:

Table 5.1-Class of common burnt clay bricks

Class designation	*Average compressive strength*			
	Not less than		*Less than*	
	Kg/cm² (N/mm²)		*Kg/cm² (N/mm²)*	
350	350	(35)	400	(40)
300	300	(30)	350	(35)
250	250	(25)	300	(30)
200	200	(20)	250	(25)
175	175	(17.5)	200	(20)
150	150	(15)	175	(17.5)
125	125	(12.5)	150	(15)
100	100	(10)	125	(12.5)
75	75	(7.5)	100	(10)
35	35	(3.5)	50	(5)

9. Questions :

(a) Why bricks are tested for compressive strength ?

(b) State I.S. specifications for compressive strength for the bricks.

(c) What are tiles and name some of their types used in India ?

(d) Why do you sprinkle water on bricks before actual use?

(e) Compare hand moulded and machine moulded bricks.

(f) Should we test the bricks in tension ?

EXPERIMENT NO. 5/4

WARPAGE OF BRICKS

1. **Object**

To determine Warpage of bricks.

2. **Theory**

Water is added to dry ground clay to make it plastic so that bricks can be cast out of it. The cast bricks are dried by keeping them in air (natural drying) or in the kilns (artificial drying). When water content of the wet clay decreases, shrinkage takes place. It is not the total shrinkage that is important because that gives only proportional change in dimension but it is the differential shrinkage which can also result in the change of shape or distortion of bricks as characterised by warpage. This happens when one side of the brick dries more than the other, consequently resulting in differential shrinkage, thus warping the brick i.e. distorting the shape of brick.

Also if the firing is non-uniform and the temperatures are such that a greater fraction of material is produced due to viscous fusion, a distortion of the shape of bricks may take place.

Bricks are used in the construction of masonry structures such as wall, piers etc. by laying them in courses and binding them my mortar. If the bricks are warped to a greater degree, the mortar demand will be more, the structural performance will not be satisfactory and from the aesthetic point of view, the work will not be of proper quality.

3. **Apparatus**

A steel rule graduated from one end in 0.5 mm division. Alternately, a steel measuring wedge 60 mm in length, 15 mm in width and 15 mm in thickness at one end and tapered, starting at line 15 mm at one end to zero thickness at the other end. The wedge shall be graduated in 0.5 mm divisions and numbered to show the thickness of the wedge's between base AB and the slope AC (Fig. 5.1)

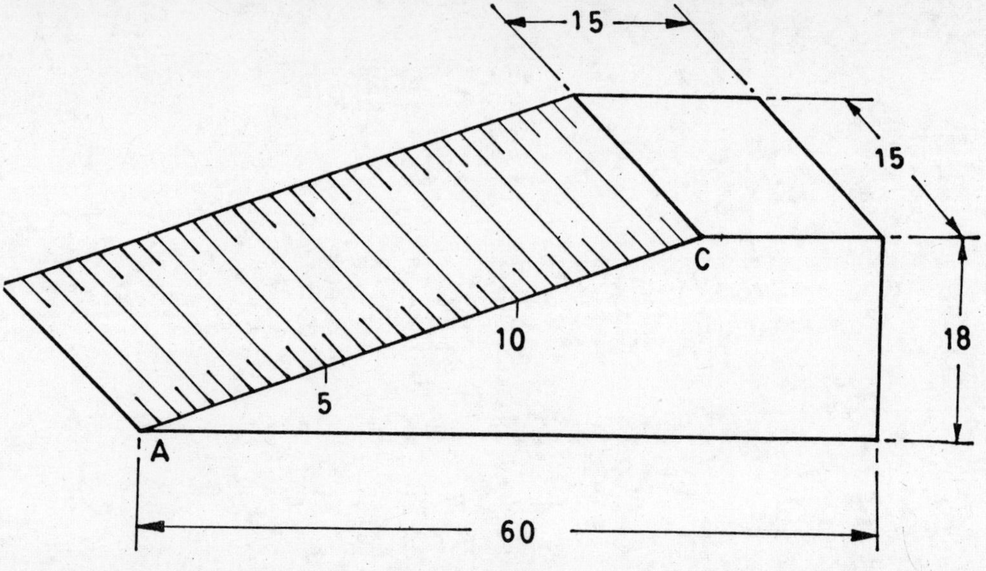

Fig. 5.1

4. Procedure

(a) For concave warpage:-Place the brick on any plane surface with the concave surface of the brick in contact with it. Measured the greatest distance of the brick surface from the plane surface by a steel rule or wedge.

(b) For convex warpage:-Place the brick on any plane surface with the convex surface of the brick in contact with it. Measure the distance from the flat surface to the four corners of the brick and take the maximum of the four measurements.

5. Observations & Calculations

Convex warpage = (mm)

Concave warpage = (mm)

The higher of the convex and concave warpage shall be reported as warpage.

Warpage of brick = (mm)

6. Precautions

(1) The plane surface used in this test should be truely plane.

(2) The measurements in the concave warpage and convex warpage should be taken sincerely and carefully.

7. Questions

(a) Why warpage test is carried out ?

(b) Explain differential shrinkage.

(c) Differentiate between convex warpage and concave warpage.

REFERENCES

1. I.S. 1077-1976-Specification for common burnt clay building bricks.
2. I.S. 3495-1976-Methods of tests of burnt clay building bricks. (Part I to IV)
3. Building Materials-by N. Chawdhuri Bani Book Co., Calcutta.
4. Engineering Materials-by Sushil Kumar, Metropolitan Book Co., Pvt. Ltd, Delhi.
5. Building Construction-by Sharma and Kaul.

PART VI

TIMBER

EXPERIMENT NO. 6/1

MOISTURE CONTENT AND SPECIFIC GRAVITY

1. **Object** : To determine the Moisture content and specific gravity of timber.
2. **Theory** : Almost all the mechanical properties of seasoned timber vary with moisture content and it is, therefore, necessary that moisture content of timber and its specific gravity be determined at the time of tests, preferably immediately after the test.

   It is essential that timber used for the manufacture of wooden structural elements should have attained a moisture content as near as possible to the value that will be attained in equilibrium with the average atmospheric conditions in service.
3. **Apparatus** : Weighing balance with accuracy of 0.001 gm., electric Oven.
4. **Test Piece**: Immediately after each mechanical test a disc approximately 25 mm in length and full section as test piece, shall be taken normally at the place of failure, failing which at the central portion of the test specimen. In the case of shear test, the detached portion of the section approximately 50 × 50 mm shall be taken for determination of moisture content.

   Prior to test the dimension of each specimen shall be measure to 0.1mm and the specimen shall be weighed correct to 0.001 gm.
5. **Procedure:** The sample shall be weighed and then dried in an oven at a temperature of 103°C ± 2°C. The weight shall be recorded at each interval. The drying shall be considered to be complete when the variation between last two weighings shall not exceed 0.002 gm. The final weight shall be taken as oven dry weight. The loss in weight expressed as percentage of oven dry weight, shall be taken as the moisture content of the test specimen. The formula for calculation shall be as given below :

$$\text{Percentage of moisture content} = m = \frac{W_1 - W_o}{W_o} \times 100$$

Where,

W_1 = Weight of sample at test in gm, and

W_o = Oven dry weight of sample in gm.

The specific gravity of parallelopiped, specimen shall be calculated as given below:

$$\text{(a) Specific gravity at test} = \frac{W_1}{V_1} \quad \text{... (a)}$$

$$\text{(b) Adjusted specific gravity} = \frac{W_1}{V_1} \times \frac{100}{100 + m}$$

Where,

W_1 = Weight in gm of test specimen originally taken.

V_i = Volume in cm³ of specimen measured before test.

m = Percentage moisture content of test specimen as determined.

NOTE : 1. If initial condition of the specimen is green, (that is, well above the fibre saturation point) adjusted specific gravity calculated by formula (b) is known as standard specific gravity, and if the specimen is dry, the specific gravity is called dry specific gravity.

2. Great care shall be taken to prevent any change in moisture content between the cutting of the disc and the first weighing and between the removal from the oven and subsequent weighings.

3. The moisture content of the disc shall be taken a representing the moisture content of the test specimen as a whole.

6. Observations and Calculations :

TABLE 6.1

Specimen of Wood	*Size l × B × H*	*Weight w_1 (gm)*	*Weight w_o (gm)*	*Moisture content % (m)* $\frac{W_1 - W_o}{W_o} \times 100$	*Specific gravity at test* $\frac{W_1}{V_1}$	*Adjusted specific gravity* $\frac{W_1}{V_1} \times \frac{100}{100+m}$	*Weight in kg/m³ at test = Sp. gravity at test × 100*
1	2	3	4	5	6	7	8
Teak	1						
	2						
	3						
Shisham	1						
	2						
	3						
Deodar	1						
	2						
	3						
Rose wood	1						
	2						
	3						
Chir	1						
	2						
	3						
Kail	1						
	2						
	3						
Mango	1						
	2						
	3						
Haldu	1						
	2						
	3						
Babul	1						
	2						
	3						

Maximum permissible moisture content of timber for different uses (as per I.S. 87-1973)

Sl. No.	*Use*	*Moisture content percent Max.* Zone I	Zone II	Zone III	Zone IV
1	2	3	4	5	6
1.	Aircraft		12	12	14 15
2.	Agricultural implements	12	14	16	16
3.	Amunition boxes	10	12	14	14
4.	Artificial limbs	8	10	12	12
5.	Automobile bodies:				
	(a) 50 mm and above in thickness	10	12	14	16
	(b) Thinner than 50 mm	8	10	12	14
6.	Beams and rafters	12	14	17	20
7.	Boot lasts	10	12	14	16
8.	Box shooks	12	14	16	18
9.	Carts and vehicles (not motor driven)	10	12	14	16
10	Cooperage	10	12	12	14
11.	Doors and Windows :				
	(a) 50 mm and above in thickness	10	12	14	16
	(b) Thinner than 50 mm	8	10	12	14
12.	Electrical industry	10	12	14	15
13.	Flooring strips for general purposes	8	10	10	12
14.	Flooring strips for the tea gardens	12	12	14	16
15.	Furniture and cabinet making	10	12	14	15
16.	Handles	12	12	14	15
17.	Pattern making	8	10	12	14
18.	Railway carriage building :				
	(a) 50 mm and above in thickness	10	12	14	14
	(b) thinner than 50 mm	8	10	12	12
19	Rifle parts and gun stocks	8	10	12	12
20	Shuttles and bobbins	8	10	12	12
21.	Sports goods, umbrellas and walking sticks	10	12	14	16
22.	Ship and boat building Deck	10	12	12	14
	Frame	12	14	16	18
	Planking	12	14	14	16
23.	Timber meant for further conversion posts and poles	20 percent in all zones, moisture content being determined within a depth of 12 mm from the surface and excluding 30 cm from each end.			
24.	Toys, turnery, carving, clocks, brushes, picture frames, brooms, cigar, boxes, pens pencils, mathematical and musical instruments and house hold goods.	8	10	12	12.

NOTE: Uttar Pradesh, Madhya Pradesh, Himachal Pradesh, Delhi and Jammu & Kashmir come into zone II for details refer Survey of India map reproduced in I.S. 287-1973 on page 13.

7. **Precautions:**

(a) All the weighing should be accurate to the nearest 0.1 gm.

(b) Dry the sample very carefully.

8. **Comments:**

Comment on the result obtained by you and recommend the appropriate use of this timber in building industry.

9. **Questions:**

(a) What is the importance of this test ?

(b) Name the common defects in timber ?

(c) What do you mean by seasoning of timber ?

(d) What are the characteristics of a good timber ?

(e) What do you mean by decay of timber ?

(f) What is the effect on the strength of timber with decreases of moisture content ?

(g) List a few important uses of timber in building industry.

EXPERIMENT NO. 6/2

COMPRESSIVE STRENGTH

1. **Object—To dedtermine th ecompressive strength of timber parallel to grain and prependicular to grain.**

A—Compression Parallel to Grain

A1. Theory:

The compressive strength characteristic of the timber parellel to grain shall be determined by the following formula.

Sr. No.	*Characteristics*	*Unit*	*Formula*
I.	Compressive stress at limit of proportionality	N/mm^2 (Kg/cm^2)	$\frac{P}{A}$
II.	Compressive Stress at maximum load	N/mm^2 (Kg/cm^2)	$\frac{P'}{A}$
III.	Modulus of elasticity in compression parallel to grain	N/mm^2 (Kg/cm^3)	$\frac{L.P.}{\Delta.A}$

Where,

P = Load at the limit of proportionality in N (Kg)

A = Cross-sectional area in mm^2 (cm^2)

P′ = Maximum crushing load in N (kg)

L = Gauge length between compressometer points in mm (cm)

Δ = deformation at the limit of proportionality in mm (cm)

A.2. Apparatus:

The tests shall be carried out on a suitable testing machine and with a suitable ecopressometer. At least one platen of the testing machine shall be equipped with a hemispherical bearing to obtain uniform distribution of load over the ends of the specimen.

A.3. Test Specimen:

Compression-parallel to grain test shall be made on specimen 50 × 50 × 200 mm in size. The specimen shall be absolutely free from any defect and shall not have a slope of grain more than 1 in 20 parallel to its longitudinal edges. The end planes of the specimen shalll be perfectly at right angles to the length of the specimen, (where a standard size is not obtainable the length of the specimen shall be four times the shorter dimension of the cross-section).

(a) Procedure:

The specimen shall be so placed that the centre of the moveable head is vertically above the centre of the cross-section of the speimcen and a small load of not more than 2.5 KN (250 Kg) is initially applied to set the specimen. It is essential that the end of the rectangular test specimen are smooth and parallel and normal to the axis and that the testing machine is of type that the surface between which the test specimen is placed are parallel to each other and remian so during the whol eperiod of test. Unless these precautions are taken, values which may be obtained will be considerably below the true values.

(b) Rate of Loading:

The load shall be applied continuously during the test to cause the moveable head of the testing machine to travel at a constant rate of 0.03 mm/minute/per cm length of the spedcimen (that is 0.6 mm/minute in the case of the standard text specimen of 50 × 50 × 200 mm).

(c) Measurement of Loads and Deformation :

Deformation under compression shall be measured correct to 0.02 mm by means of a suitable compressometer over a central gauge length of 150 mm. Where possible direct points shall be obtained on a graph sheet. The readings at the maximum load shall be recorded. It would be preferable to remove the compressometer before the maximum load. The deformation shall be read at load intervals of 10 KN (1000 Kg.)

(d) Record of Failures :

To obtain satisfactory and uniform results the failure may be made to develop on the body of the specimen by continuing to run the machine for a longer time or by any other method. Compression failure shall be classified according to the appearance of the fractured surface. In case two or more kind of failures develop, they shall be described in order of their occurance (for example, shearing, followed by brooming). The failure shall be sketched on the data sheet.

A.4. Observations :

Size of sample in mm.	*Area in mm²*	*Max. failure load in KN(t)*
Sample No. 1	....	....
2.	....	....
3.	....	....

Load (tonnes)	Deformation Sample No.			Strain $\left(\frac{\Delta}{L}\right)$ Sample No.			Stress $\frac{P}{A}$ N/mm² (Kg/cm2)	Modulus of Elasticity $\left(\frac{LP}{\Delta . A}\right)$ N/mm²(Kg/cm²)			Compressive Stress at max. load $\frac{P}{A}$ N/mm² (Kg/cm²) Sample No.		
	1	*2*	*3*	*1*	*2*	*3*		*1*	*2*	*3*	*1*	*2*	*3*
0													
1													
2													
3													
4													
5													
6													
7													
8													
9													
10													

B. Compression Perpendicular to Grain

B. 1. Apparatus :

The test shall be carried out on suitable testing machine. The load shall be applied througth metal bearing plate 50 mm in width of at leat 15 mm thickness placed centrally across the upper surface of the specimen at equal distance from the ends and at right angles to the length.

B. 2. Test Specimen :

Test for compresson prependicular to the grain shall be made on the central portion of the specimen 50 × 50 × 150 mm in size. The spcimen shall be free from defects. The various characteristic shall be determined by the following formulae :

Sr. No.	*Characteristic*	*Unit*	*Formula*
1.	Compressive stress at limit of proportionality	N/mm^2 (Kg/cm^2)	$\frac{P}{A}$
II.	Compressive stres at compression of 2.5 mm	N/mm^2 (Kg/cm^2)	$\frac{P'}{A}$
III.	Crushing strength at maximum load	N/mm^2 (Kg/cm^2)	$\frac{P_o}{A}$
IV.	Modulus of elasticity in compression perpendicular to gbrain	N/mm^2 (Kg/cm^2)	$\frac{P}{A} \times \frac{h}{\Delta}$

Where,

P = Load of limit of proportionality in N (Kg)

A = Area of the cross section normal to the direction of load in mm^2 cm^2) (50 × 50 mm plate)

P′ = Load at 2.5 mm compression in N (Kg)

Po = Maximum load if reached at a compression less than 2.5 mm in N (kg.)

h = height of the specimen in mm (cm)

Δ = Deformation at the limit of proportionality in mm (cm)

B. 3. Procedure :

(a) Placing the Specimen :

Unless otherwise required specifically the specimen shall be so placed that the load will be applied thgrough the bearing plate to a radial surface.

(b) Rate of Loading :

The load shall be applied continuously throughout the test such that the movfeable head of the machine travels at a constant rate of 0.6mm/minute.

(c) Measurement of Load and Deformation :

The deformation shall be measured correct to 0.02 mm by means of dial gauge or mirror and scale technique at regular load interval of 2KN (200Kg.) and is continued upto a deformation of 2.5mm. Should a definite maximum be reached at some lesser value of compressive deformation, the maximum load and its associated deformation shall both the recorded.

B. 4. Observations and Calculations :

Size of sample *(mm)*	Are of the cross-section *normal to the direction of load (mm²)*	Maximum load if reached *at a compression less than 2.5 mm (tones)*
Sample No. 1	....	....
2.	....	....
3.	....	....

Load (Tones)	Defomration (upto 2.5 mm deformation)			Strain $\left(\frac{\Delta}{h}\right)$ Sample No.			Stress $\left(\frac{P}{A}\right)$ N/mm²(Kg/cm²) Sample No.			Modulus of Elasticity $\left(\frac{P}{A} \times \frac{h}{\Delta}\right)$ Sample No.			Crushing strenth at maximum load $\frac{P_o}{A}$ N/mm2 (Kg/cm2)
	1	2	3	1	2	3	1	2	3	1	2	3	
0													
0.2													
0.4													
0.6													
0.8													
1.0													
1.2													
1.4													
1.6													
1.8													

2. Precautions :

(a) The load should be applied continuously and at constant rate.

(b) Deformations should be recorded very accurately and to the nearest 0.02mm.

3. Discussion of Result :

Comment on the results obtained by you and compare these values with those of IS specifications.

4. Questions :

(a) Why do you perform compression test ?

(b) What do you mean by conversion of timber ?

(c) What are various market forms in which the timber is cut and sold.

(d) Name of various uses of timber in Civil Engineering Construction.

(e) The compressive strength of timber is dependent on the orientation of grains comment on it.

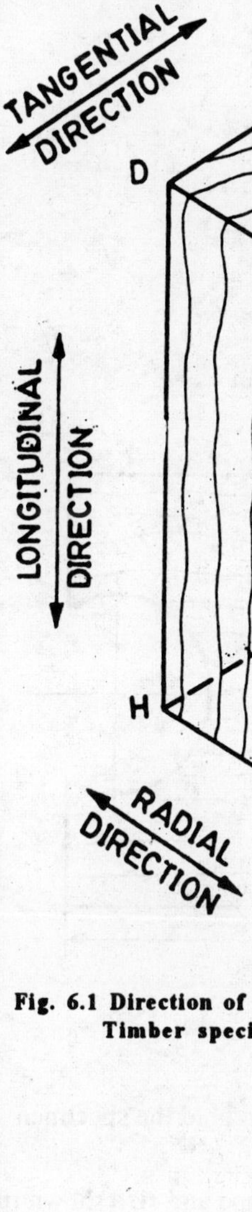

Fig. 6.1 Direction of Testing Timber specimens.

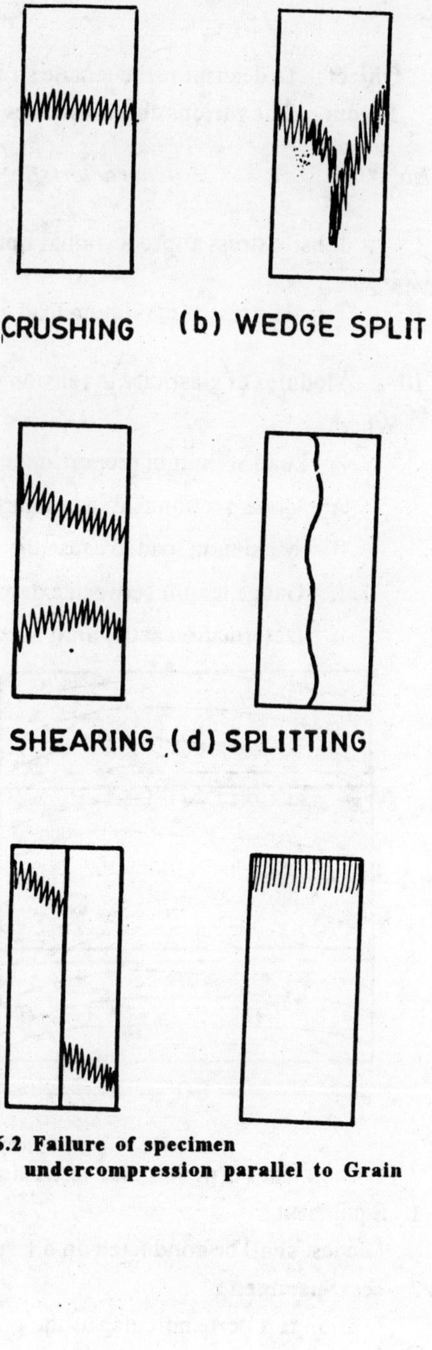

Fig. 6.2 Failure of specimen undercompression parallel to Grain

EXPERIMENT NO. 6/3

TENSILE STRENGTH

1. **Object**—To determine the tensile strength of timber perpendicular to grain and parallel to grain.
2. **Theory**—The various characteristics shall be determined by the following formula.

Sr. No.	*Characteristic*	*Unit*	*Formula*
I.	Tensile stress at proportional limit	N/mm^2 (Kg/cm^2)	$\frac{P}{A}$
II.	Tensile stress at maximum load	N/mm^2 (Kg/cm^2)	$\frac{P'}{A}$
III.	Modulus of elasticity in tension parallel to grain.	N/mm^2 (Kg/cm^2)	$\frac{LP}{\Delta A}$

Where,

P = Load at limit of proportionality in N(Kg.)

A = Cross-sectional area in mm^2(cm^2)

P′ = Maximum load to cause the failure of the specimen in (N(Kg.)

L = Gauge length between extensometer points in mm (cm)

Δ = Deformation at the limit of proportionality in mm (cm)

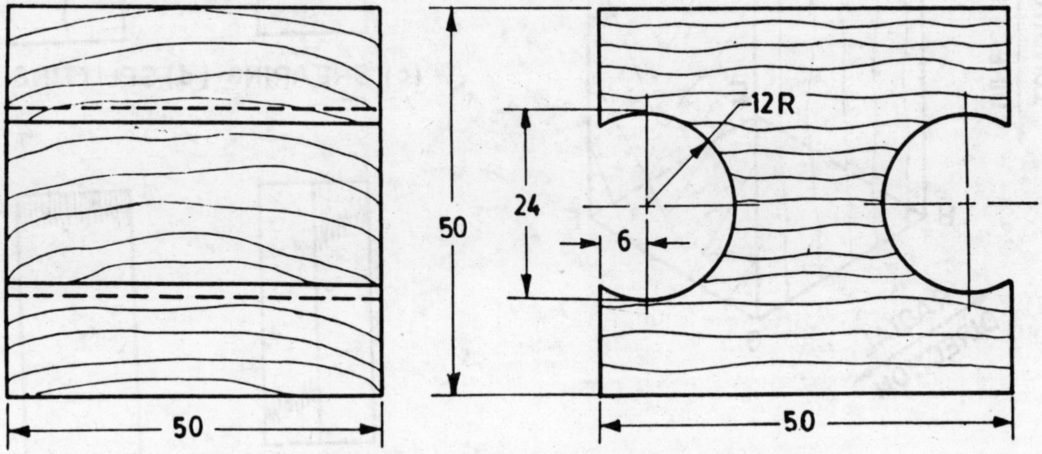

Fig. 6.3 Test specimens for tension perpendidcular to grain.

A. Tension test Perpendicular to Grain:

A. 1. Equipment:

The test shall be conducted on a testing machine provided with suitable grips to hold the specimen.

A. 2. Test Specimen:

Tension test perpendicular to the grains shall be made on a specimen of the shape and size shown in Fig. 6.3. The Specimen shall be free from all defects. The notches shown in the figure shall be so made as to produce a failure on 50 × 20mm area in the radial tangential surface as desired.

A. 3 Procedure:

(a) Placing the Specimen:

The specimen shall be accurately measured at its minimum section and placed in the grips.

(b) Rate of Loading:

The load shall be applied continuously throughout the test so that the moveable head moves at a constant rate of 2.5 mm per minute until the maximum load is reached.

(c) Recording of Data and Computations:

The maximum load required for failure across fibre shall be recorded. The load divided by the area gives the maximum tensile stress across the fibre in the concerned plane (radial or tangential). The average of the two planes shall be taken as tensile stress across the grain.

(d) Record of Failure:

A sketch shall be made of the specimen under test indicating the orientation of rings at the cross section of the piece and the failure recorded on the sketch according to its appearance and development.

A. 4. Observations and Calculations:

Sample No.	*Length × thickness of minimum section (mm)*	*Area (sq. cm.)*	*Load N(Kg.)*	*Tensile Strength* $\frac{P'}{A}$ *N/mm²(Kg/cm²)*
1.				
2.				
3.				

B. Tension Test Parallel to Grains:

B.1. Equipment same as A. I

B.2. Test Specimen:

Tension test parallel to grains shall be made on a specimen of the shape and size shown in Fig. 6.4 so as to have a gauge length of 50mm and minimum cross section of 7 × 7mm at centre. The specimen shall be absolutely free from all defects and shall have the annular rings on the ends perpendicular to the greater cross sectional dimensions. The cross sectional dimension at the centre of the specimen (minimum section) shall be measured correct to 0.1 mm.

B.2 Procedure:

(a) Placing the Specimen:

The specimen shall be held firmly in the **grips** and a suitable elongation measuring device shall be attached to the gauge length.

(b) Rate of Loading:

The load shall be applied continuously throughout the test at a rate of motion of the moveable cross head of one millimetre per minute.

(c) Measurement of the Load and Elongation:

Elongation under tension shall be measured on a central gauge length of 50mm on all specimens.

Elongation shall be measured correct to 0.002mm by means of a calibrated extensometer, or by mirror and scale or by any other device at regular load intervals of 500 N(50Kg.)

Readings shall be continued well beyond the proportional limit and the final reading of load at failure be recorded. It is preferable to remove the extensometer before the maximum load is reached.

(d) Record of Failure:

A sketch shall be made of the specimen and the failure recorded in the sketch according to its appearance and developments.

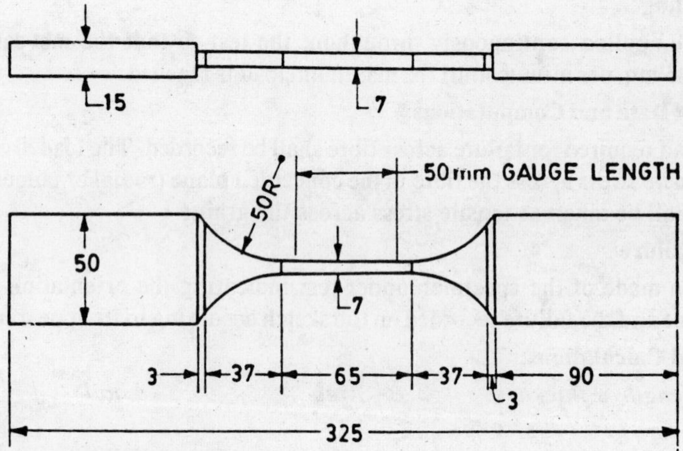

Fig.6.4 Specimen for Testing Tesion Parallel to Grain.

B.4 Recording of the Data and Computations :

The readings of elongation and the load shall be recorded. The load elongation curve shall be drawn. The corresponding load and elongation at proportional limit shall then be read accordingly.

Observations and Calculations:

Sample No.	*Length × thickness at minimum section*	*Area $mm^2(cm^2)$*	*Max. Load N(Kg)*
1.			
2.			
3.			

Sr. No.	*Deformation*			*Strain* $\frac{\Delta}{L}$			*Stress* $\frac{P}{A}$ $N/mm^2(Kg/cm^2)$			*Modulus of Elasticity* $\frac{LP}{\Delta A}$ $N/mm^2(Kg/cm^2)$			*Tensile strength at max. load* $\frac{P'}{A}$ $N/mm^2/(Kg.cm^2)$		
	Sample No.			*Sample No.*			*Sample No.*			*Sample No.*			*Sample No.*		
	1	2	3	1	2	3	1	2	3	1	2	3	1	2	3
0															
50															
100															
150															
200															
250															
300															
350															
400															

3. Precautions :

(a) The cross sectional dimensions of the specimen should be measured very accurately.

(b) The load should be applied continuously and at a constant rate.

4. Comments :

Comment on the results obtained by you and compare with those advocated by IS code.

5. Questions :

(a) What is the importance of this test ?

(b) What are the common diseases of timber ?

(c) What are the various methods of preserving timber ?

(d) Name atleast ten common trees of India.

(e) Differentiate between Veneers and Plywood.

EXPERIMENT NO. 6/4

BRITTLENESS OF TIMBER (IZOD AND CHARPY'S TEST)

1. **Object**—To determine Brittleness of timber (Izod and Charpy test).

2. **Test Specimen :**

   The test specimen for Izod test shall be 22 × 22mm in cross-section and 125–150mm in length with any type of notch shown in fig. 6.5 is recommended. The specimen for the charpy test shall be 12.5 ×12.5mm in cross section, 125mm in length with notch cut as shown in fig. 6.5. The notch shall be on the radial faces so as to produce the maximum concentration of impact stress on a cross-section of 22 × 12mm at a distance of 75 mm from one end for the Izod specimen and 10 × 12.5mm at the centre of the specimen for the charpy test.

3. **Equipment :**

   The test shall be conducted on any swinging pendulum machine with suitable devices to hold the specimen tightly as a cantilever for the Izod specimen and freely on simple support for the chapry specimen. The equipment shall here a calibrated dial on the scale as to give direct recordings of the energy absorbed in breaking the specimen on a single blow. The initial position of pendulum shall be so fixed at position (usually 45°, 90°, or 180°) that there is complete failure of the specimen in one single blow itself.

   On release of the pendulum from its initial position it shall strike the specimen at the lowest point of the swing.

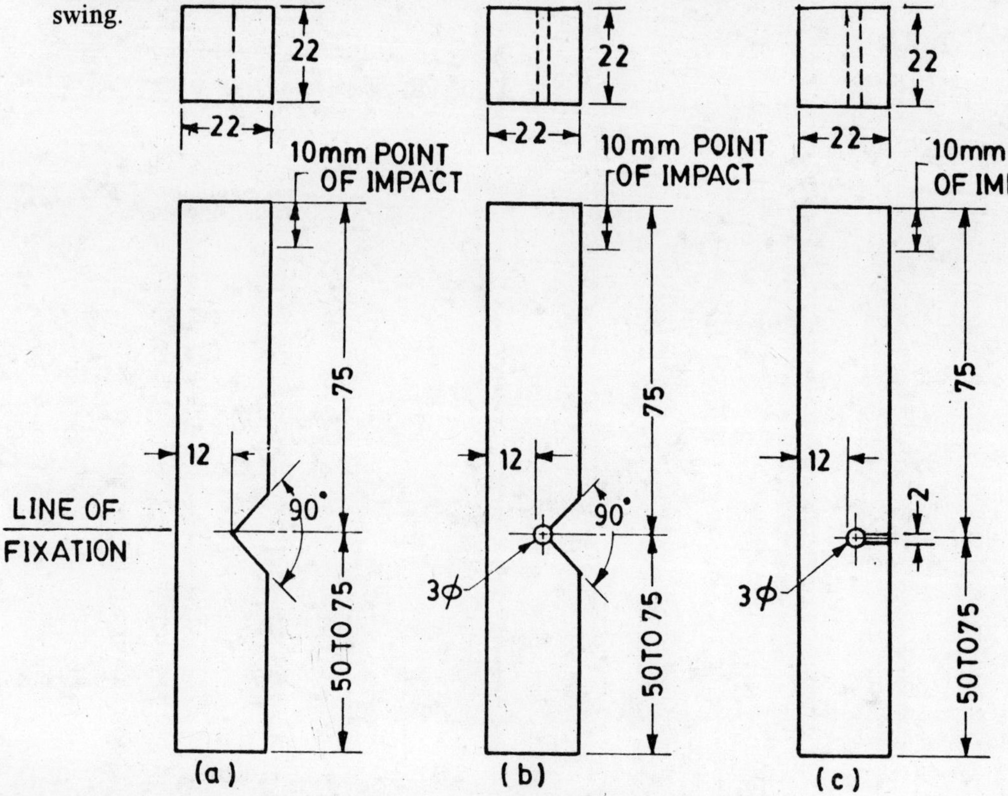

ALL DIMENSIONS IN MILLIMETRES

Fig. 6.5—Specimen for Brittleness Test (Izod Test).

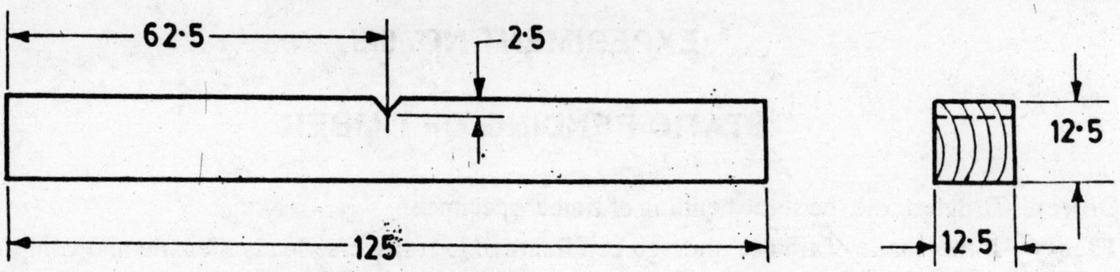

Fig. 6.6—Specimen for Brilleness Test (Charpy Test)

4. **Procedure :**

The cross sectional dimensions of the specimen shall be measured accurately at the section of notch, correct to 0.1mm and the specimen shall be so placed that the blow is given in the tangental direction on the side of notch in the case of Izod specimen and on the opposite side in the case of the chapry specimen.

The impact blow shall be given by releasing the pendulum and allowing the same to fall freely.

The reading in Nmm (Kg. cm) as indicated on the calibrated dial shall be recorded.

5. **Observations and Calculations :**

Sample	*Dimensions (mm)*	*Readings on dial-gauge without specimen (A)*	*Reading on dial-gauge after fracture of test Specimen (B)*	*Impact energy absorbed by the specimen specimen (A-B) Nmm(Kg.cm)*
Izod Test				
1.				
2.				
3.				
Charpy Test				
1.				
2.				
3.				

6. **Precautions :**

(a) Measurement of cross sectional dimensions of the specimen should be correct to 0.1mm.

(b) Allow the pendulum load to fall freely.

7. **Comments :**

Comment on the results obtained by you and compare with standard results recommended by Bureau of Indian Standards New Delhi.

8. **Questions :**

(a) Why do you perform this test ?

(b) Mention the names of timbers suitable for following uses :

 (a) Agriculture tools
 (b) Cart Wheels
 (c) Furniture
 (d) Railway Sleepers
 (e) Scaffolding
 (f) Sports goods.

(c) What is the basic difference between Izod and charpy test.

EXPERIMENT NO. 6/5

STATIC BENDING OF TIMBER

1. **Object**—To determine the static bending of timber specimen.

2. **Theory**—Joints made of timber undergo bending due to transverse loads. Tensile and compressive stresses develop along the grain direction and under this condition of loading shear stress also develop. The behaviour of the beam is not elastic but, upto a limit, is nearly so. This is called the proportional limit.

Timber beams can exhibit relatively large deflections as loads are increased beyond proportional limit before failure. This capacity to be 'ductile' is characteristic of timber, as a material.

Moisture content of timber also influences its properties, particularly when the moisture content changes below fibre saturation points (FSP). Timber, as it comes to the market is already seasoned to a moisture content below FSP but can loose further moisture if the environment is less humid or dry or gain moisture if environment is wet.

Bending tests reveal information regarding the limit of proportionality, flexrual rigidity, failure mode, strain energy absorption characteristic and probably maximum shear stress under the given conditions of loading. These are required in order that timber beams can be designed adequately for both service-loads and ultimate loads.

3. **Apparatus**—Universal testing machine. jig for applying central point load, weighing balance with accuracy upto 0.001gm, electric oven, deflectometer, dial gange etc.

The specimen size is either 50mm × 50mm in cross-section and 750 mm in length or 20mm × 20mm in the cross-section and 300mm in length. The specimen shall be defect free and shall not have a slope of grain more than 1 in 20 parallel to longitudinal edges.

4. **Procedure**

(1) The bottom surface of the loading block shall be cylindrical having a radius equal to 75 mm in case of 50 × 50 × 750mm and 300mm in case 20 × 20 × 300mm specimens (Fig. 6.7)

Load shall be applied centrally on a span of 700 mm (280 mm for smaller size). Thin metal sheets shall be placed between the loading block and the specimen.

(2) Rate of loading at a constant rate of 2.5 mm per minute. (1.0mm per minute for the smaller sized specimens) is applied.

(3) Deflections of the neutral plane at the midspan shall be measured with a suitable deflectometer.

(4) Load intervals 100 to 500 N(10-50kg) shall be such that about 8-10 readings are available upto the limit of proportionality. Loads and deflections shall be measured beyond this limit at suitable intervals till maximum load is reached.

(5) If the beam has not failed completely, deflections may continued to be measured upto 150mm or 60mm, depending on the size of the specimen.

(6) The load and deflection at first failure, the maximum load and points of sudden changes in deflection and loads shall be recorded even if these do not occur at the regular intervals.

Observations and Calculations

(1) While drawing a load-deflection curve-the following rules shall be adopted:

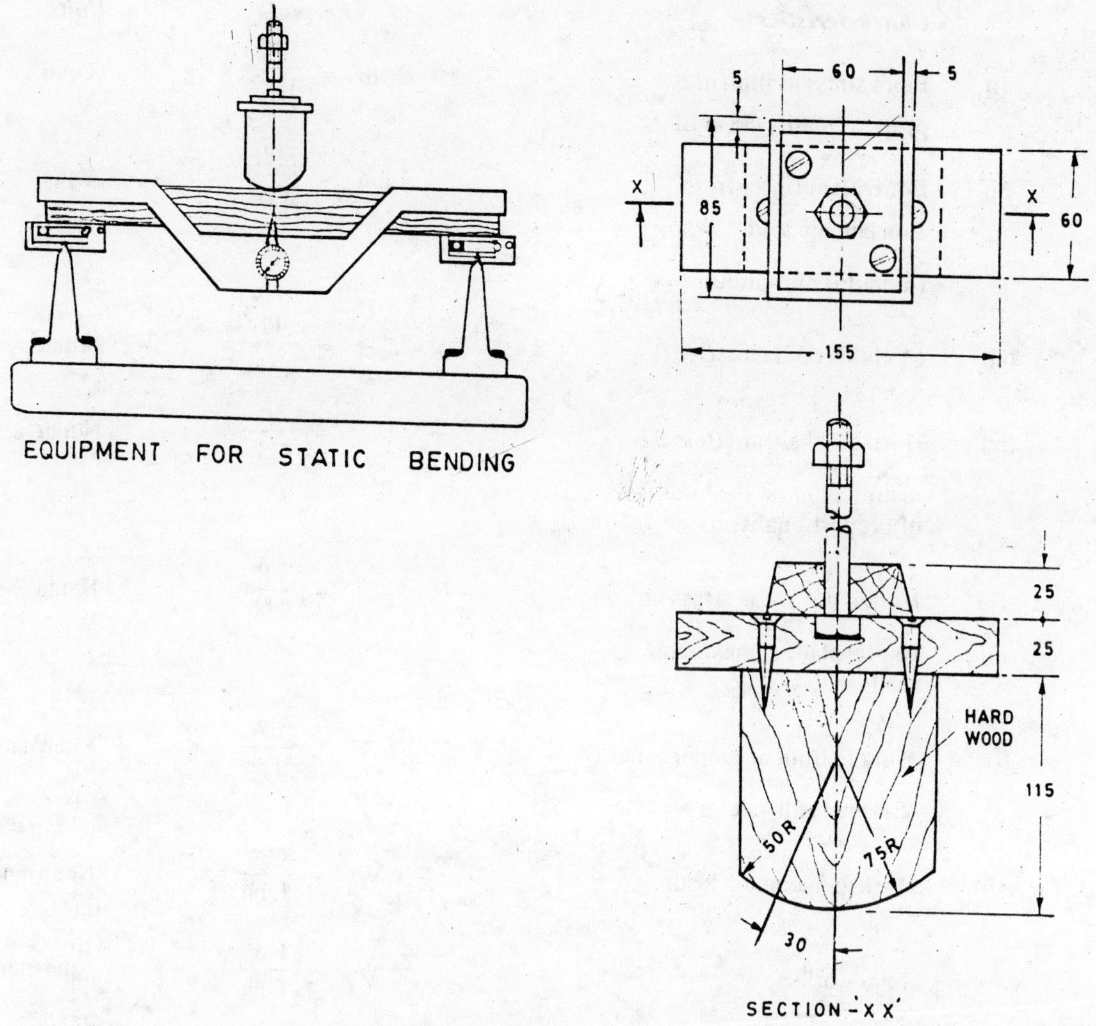

Fig. 6.7

The straight line of proportionality shall be drawn in such a way that maximum number of points shall be on the straight line or nearest to the same. No consideration shall be given to the initial two or three points.

When the straight line does not pass through the origin, a parallel line shall be drawn through the origin. The deflection and load at the limit of proportionality shall be measured on this line. If a planimeter is used for finding the areas at the maximum load or the final load, the planimeter shall pass through the point where the load deflection curve actually ends, and then extended in a line parallel to the Y axis until it cuts the abscissae.

The points beyond the elastic limit and upto maximum load shall be connected by a smooth curve but point to point for evaluating total work.

(ii) The various characteristics shall be determined by the following formulae and the load deflection curve. The area shall be measured directly or by calibrated planimeter.

	Characteristics	*Formula*	*Units*
(i)	Fibre stress at limit of proportionality-FS at LP	$fb = \frac{3PL}{2bh^2}$	N/mm²
(ii)	Equivalent fibre stress at maximum load (modulus of rapture)	$fbu = \frac{3P'L}{2bh^2}$	N/mm²
(iii)	Modulus of elasticity(Et)	$Et = \frac{PL^3}{4\Delta bh^3}$	N/mm²
(iv)	Horizontal shear stress on neutral plane at the limit of proportionality	$= \frac{3P}{4\,bh}$	N/mm²
(v)	Horizontal shear stress on ventral plane at maximum loads.	$= \frac{3\,P'}{4\,bh}$	N/mm²
(vi)	Work to limit of proportionality (Elastic resilience)	$W = \frac{CA}{L\,bh}$	Nmm/mm²
(vii)	Work to maximum load	$W_u = \frac{CA'}{L\,bh}$	Nmm/mm²
(viii)	Total work	$W_T = \frac{CA''}{L\,bh}$	Nmm/mm²

Where:

P–Load in Newtons at the limit of proportionality

L–Span of the test specimen in mm

h–breadth and depth of the test specimen in mm.

p′– maximum load in Newtons.

Δ–deflection in mm at the limit of proportionality

C–Area constant in Newtons mm

A–area in mm² of load-deflection curve to limit of proportionality.

A′–Area in mm² upto maximum load and

A″–area in mm² upto the final reading when total work is required.

(iii) **Ratio :**

For purposes of comparison of results of tests on 50 × 50mm to 20 × 20mm cross-section the following ratio apply:

Fibre stress at limit of proportionality = 0.92

Modulus of Rupture = 0.93

Modulus of Elasticity = 1.06

6. Results

1. **Fibre stress at limit of proportionality =**
2. **Equivalent fibre stress at maximum load =**
3. **Modulus of elasticity =**
4. **Horizontal shear at neutral Plane at the limit of proportionality =**
5. **Horizontal shear stress at neutral plane at maximum load =**
6. **Work to limit of proportionality =**
7. **Work to maximum load =**

7. Precautions

1. **The dimensions of the specimens should be carefully measured.**
2. **Load should be applied gradually and at uniform rate.**
3. **Test specimens should be free from defects.**

8. Questions

(a) **Why this test is performed ?**

(b) **Differentiate between elastic limit and limit of proportionality ?**

(c) **What do you understand by elastic resilience ?**

(d) **P - D curve is a measure of work done. Comment.**

(iii) When the straight line does not pass through the origin, a parallel line shall be drawn through the origin and deflection and the load at the limit of proportionality shall be measured on this line.

(iv) If a planimeter is used for finding the areas at maximum load or at the final load, the planimeter shall pass through the point where the load deflection curve actually ends and then extended in a line parallel to y-axis until it cuts the abscissa.

(v) The points beyond the elastic limit and upto maximum load may be connected by smooth curve but the joints beyond the maximum load shall be joined from point to point for evaluating total work.

5. Observations and Calculations

From the graph, the various characteristics shall be determined by the following formulae:

		Formula	*Unit*
(i)	Standard "maximum height of drop"	H	mm
(ii)	Standard height of drop at limit of proportionality	H'	mm
(iii)	Fibre stress at limit of proportionality	$\frac{3H'WL}{bh^2\Delta}$	N/mm^2
(iv)	Modulus of elasticity(E)	$\frac{H'WL^3}{2bh^3\Delta^2}$	N/mm^2
(v)	Work to limit of proportionality	$\frac{H'W}{L\,bh}$	Nmm/mm^3

Where:

H - Maximum height of drop in mm under the given weight

H′ - height of drop in mm at limit of proportionality, read from the curve.

W - Weight of hammer used in Newtons

L - Span of the test specimen in mm

b - breadth of the test specimen in mm

h - depth of the test specimen in mm

Δ - (x + y) at limit of proportionality from the curve.

6. Results

(1) Fibre stress at limit of proportionality =

(2) Modulus of Elasticity (E) =

(3) Work to limit of proportionality =

7. Precautions

(1) Place the specimen in such a way that hammer falls at the centre of the specimen.

(2) The actual deflection (y) should be measured properly with the help of pair of dividers.

(3) While plotting the graph the straight line of proportionality should be drawn in such a fashion that most of the points should lie on the straight line.

8. Questions

(a) Explain the importance of this test.

(b) Differentiate between flexural bending and impact bending.

(c) Explain the term toughness of a timber specimen.

(d) Explain the term dynamic modulus of elasticity.

EXPERIMENT NO. 6/7

HARDNESS OF TIMBER

1. **Object**—To measure the hardness of timber by indentation test.
2. **Theory**—The indentation test assesses the hardness of timber by the determination of the load necessary to force a standard bar with, hemispherical end to a specified extent. Since the hardness of spring wood and summer wood is different, their indentation loads are also different for the same timber. This implies that the hardness is also a structure-sensitive property.

   Both resistance to indentation and resistance to scratching are important properties in timber used for furniture and for finishing. These properties together with the ability to wear without splintering determine wearing resistance of timber for floors and pavements. This test gives an index for the evaluation of such properties. Experience shows that woods like pine and oak having marked difference between summer wood and spring wood. were best when laid with edge of grain exposed to wear.
3. **Apparatus**—The testing machine equipped with a special tools is shown in fig. 6.8. The tool consists of either a micro-switch or a mechanical collar to enable the determination of the penetration of the tool.

   Specimen shall be 50 × 50 × 150 mm or 20 ×20 × 100 mm. It is shall be free from any defect and the faces shall approach closely to the true radial and tangential directions.
4. **Procedure**

   (1) If a specimen of size 50 × 50 × 150 mm is used, it is so placed that two penetration are made on the radial face two on the tangential face and one on each end. But if 20 × 20 × 100mm size of specimen is used then one penetration shall be made on tangential and one on radial face.

   (2) Apply load continuously such that the moveable cross head travels at a constant rate of 6 mm per minute.

   (3) The load giving the 5.64 mm penetration i.e., penetration of the tool to a depth of half the diameter of the hemispherical end shall be noted down as the hardness.

   (4) The average of the loads required to produce two penetrations on each surface and also of the two penetrations one at each of the two ends are taken as hardness figures of the respective surfaces (also called side hardness) are taken.
5. **Observations and Calculations**

   Size of specimen (mm) =

   Rate of loading = 6 mm per minute

S.No.	*Orientation*	*Indentation load N(kg)*
1	Tangential 1.	
	2.	
2	Radial 1.	
	2.	
3	Side surface 1.	
	2.	

6. **Results**

   Average tangential hardness = N(kg)

   Average Radial Hardness = N(kg)

   Average side Hardness = N(kg)

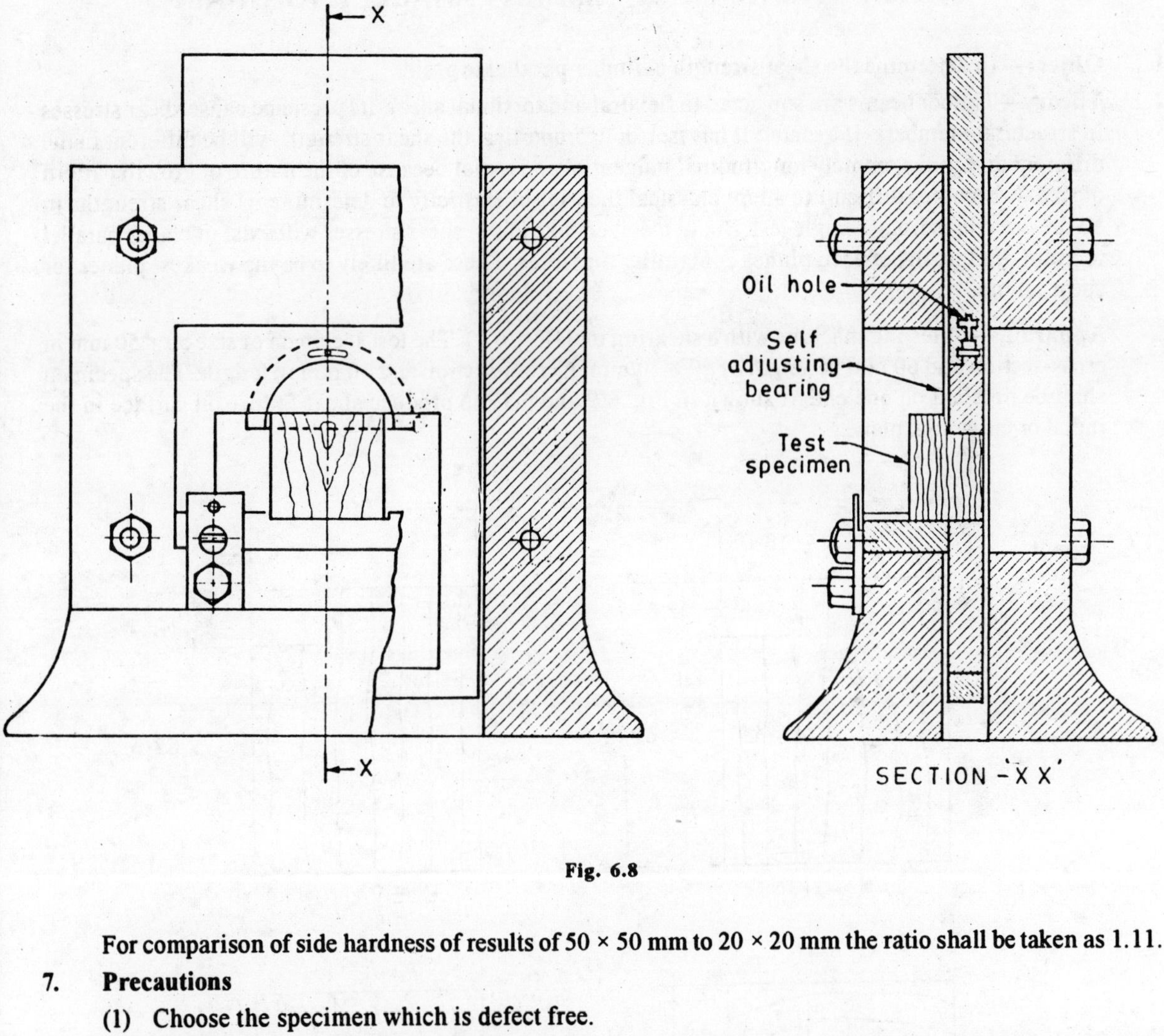

Fig. 6.8

For comparison of side hardness of results of 50 × 50 mm to 20 × 20 mm the ratio shall be taken as 1.11.

7. **Precautions**

(1) Choose the specimen which is defect free.

(2) The radial and tangential indentation faces chosen for the test shall approach closely to the true radial and tangential directions of the grains.

(3) For every indentation, place the specimen in correct position.

(4) Take care of rate of loading for every indentation.

8. **Questions**

(a) What do you mean by hardness of timber ?

(b) What is the effect of seasoning on the hardness of timber ?

(c) How the tested specimens are to be used to have maximum resistance against wear ?

(d) How can we relate hardness with compressive strength of timber ?

(e) Comment on the isotropicity of the tested timber specimens from the hardness measurements.

EXPERIMENT NO. 6/8

SHEAR STRENGTH OF TIMBER PARALLEL TO GRAIN

1. **Object**—To determine the shear strength of timber parallel to grain.
2. **Theory**—Timber beams are subjected to flexural and torsional shear. Its presence cause shear stresses in structural members. If a material has isotropic properties, the shear strength will be different in the different directions, namely longitudinal tangential and radial because of the nature of growth pattern of tree. It becomes difficult to adopt classical theories of elasticity to determine its shear strengths in all the directions from a single test. But in members like joists, shear stresses will exist in planes parallel to grain, that is, in between planes containing the fibres. These are likely to be the weakest planes for shear failure.
3. **Apparatus**—A testing machine with a shearing tool (Fig. 6.1). The test specimen of size 50 × 50 mm in cross-section and 60 mm in length or 20 × 20 mm in cross-section and 30 mm in length. The specimen shall be notched on one end as shown in Fig. 6.9 and 6.10 to produce shear failure on surface in the radial or tangential plane.

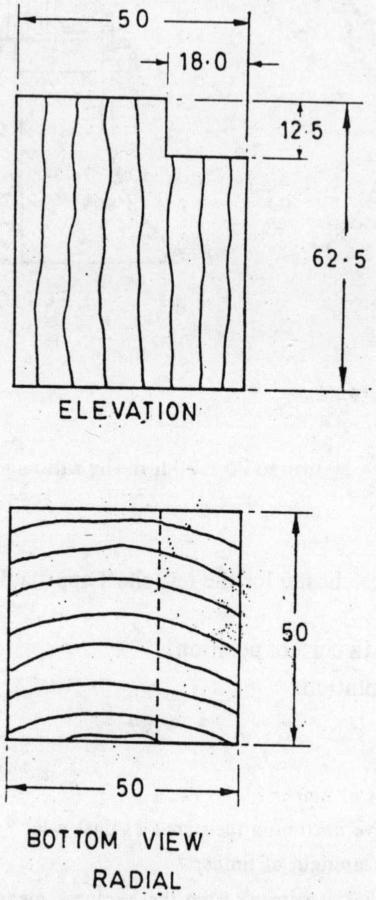

Fig. 6.9.

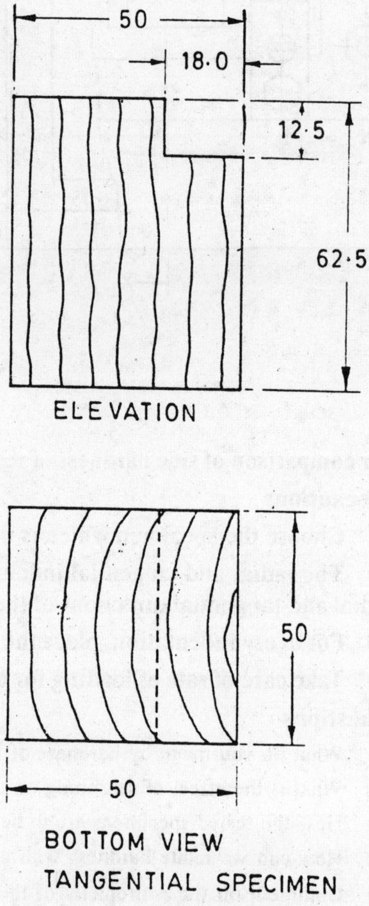

Fig. 6.10.

4. Procedure

(1) Support the specimen in the rig by means of a cross bar such that the edges of the specimen are vertical and the part of the end surface not to be sheared off, rests on the support throughout the test. The shearing tool shall rest on the notch. The direction of shearing shall be parallel to the longitudinal direction.

(2) Rate of loading shall be such that the moveable head travels at a constant rate of 0.4 mm per minute.

5. Observations and Calculations

Shearing area =

(a) Failure surface in the tangential direction:

S.No	Failure load N(kg)	Shear strength (τ_{TL}) N/mm²(kg/cm²)
1.		
2.		
3.		

Mean shear strength (N/mm²(kg/cm²)

(b) Failure surface in the radial direction :

S.No	Failure load N(kg)	Shear strength (τ_{RL}) N/mm²(kg/cm²)
1		
2		
3		

Mean shear strength N/mm²(kg/cm²)

(c) Average shear strength parallel to grain $= \dfrac{\tau_{TL} + \tau_{RL}}{2}$

6. Results

(1) Mean shear strength (in Radial Direction =

(2) Mean shear strength (in Tangential Direction) =

(3) Average shear strength parallel to grain =

7. Precautions

(1) Specimen should be notched properly.

(2) Specimen should be free from any defect.

(3) Rate of loading should be constant.

(4) Place the specimen in right position, for every reading.

8. Questions

(a) Define the terms shear stress and shear strength.

(b) Compare the shear strength obtained with the allowable shear stress in timber structures. What is the F.O.S. as obtained from laboratory data ?

(c) Quote the instance where you feel the experiment is relevant in practice.

REFERENCES

1. I.S. 287-1973 Recommendations for maximum permissible moisture content for timber used for different purposes.
2. I.S. 1708-1969 Methods of testing small clear specimens of timber.
3. I.S. 2191 (Pt. I.-1973) Specifications for wooden flush door shutters.
4. Building Materials by N. Chowdhuri-Bani Book C0. Calcutta.
5. Engineering Materials by Sushil Kumar, Metropolitan Book Co. Pvt. Ltd. Delhi.
6. Basic construction Materials by Charles A Herubin and Theodore W. Marutta. Reston Publishing Co. Restun, Virginia, U.S.A.
7. I.S.. 883-1970 Design of Structural Timber in buildings.

PART VII
STEEL

EXPERIMENT NO. 7/1

TENSILE TEST OF STEEL

1. **Object**—To conduct tensile test (i) M.S. Bar (ii) M.S. Flat (iii) M.S. wire and to determine its yield strength, ultimate tensile strength, percentage reduction in area, percentage elongation and modulus of elasticity.

(i) M.S. BAR (ii) M.S. FLAT

2. **Apparatus**—Suitable tensile testing machine which shall be calibrated in accordance with IS: 1828-1961, suitable extensometer, screw gauge, vernier calipers, scale.

3. **Theory :**

(a) Yield Strength N/mm² (Kg/cm²) $= \dfrac{\textit{Yield load in N (Kg)}}{\text{Area cross section (original) in mm}^2 (\text{cm}^2)}$

(b) Ultimate tensile Strength N/mm² (Kg/cm²) $= \dfrac{\textit{Maximum load in N(Kg.)}}{\text{Area of cross section (original) in mm}^2\ \text{cm}^2)}$

(c) Percentage elongation $= \left(\dfrac{L_u - L_o}{L_o}\right) \times 100$

(d) Percentage reduction in area $= \dfrac{(S_o - S_u)}{S_o} \times 100$

Where

L_u = Final gauge length after fracture

L_o = Original gauge length = $5.65 \sqrt{S_o}$

S_o = Original cross sectional area of the gauge length

S_u = Minimum cross sectional area after fracture

(e) Proof Stress (R_p)—A steel which did not show yield phenomenon, its proof stress shall be determined.

This proof stress is determined from a stress-strain diagram on which a line is drawn parallel to the straight portion of the curve and at a distance from it by an amount representing an increase of strain equal to the required non-proportional amount for example 0.2 percent. The point at which the line cuts the curve represents the required proof stress (i.e. point corresponding to 0.2 percent strain).

The curve may be obtained by either automatic or manual methods. An accurate determination of the stress-strain diagram can be made by the direct method using an extensometer. However, the use of a proof stress indicator without the production of an actual stress-strain diagram is permitted.

4. **Test Piece**—The cross section of the test piece may be circular, square, rectangular or, in special cases, of other form. For test pieces of rectangular section it is recommended that a ratio of width to thickness of 8:1 should not be exceeded.

Test pieces shall generally be made to the dimensions given in table 7.1 and 7.2. The M.S. flat of width

TABLE 7.1 Dimension of circular section test pieces gauge length $L_o = 5.65\sqrt{S_o}$

Cross-sectional area (S_0)	*Diameter (d)*	*Gauge Length (L_o)*	*Minimum Parallel Length (L_u = 5.5.d)*	*Minimum transition radius (r)*
(mm²)	*(mm)*	*(mm)*	*(mm)*	*(mm)*
400	22.56	113	124	23.5
200	15.96	80	88	15
150	13.82	69	76	13
100	11.28	56	62	10
50	7.98	40	44	8
25	5.64	28	31	5
12.5	3.99	20	22	4

Note (a)—The gauge length is given to the nearest 1 mm and the minimum parallel length is adjusted accordingly.

Note (b)—Test pieces with diameter other than those given in this table may be used provided that the gauge length $L_u = 5.65\sqrt{S_o}$

TABLE 7.2 Dimension of Rectangular section test pieces

Width (b) (mm)	*Gauge Length (L_o) (mm)*	*Minimum Transition radius (r) (mm)*	*Approximate total length (L_t) (mm)*
40	200	25	450
20	200	25	375
15	100	25	300
12.5	50	25	200
6	24	12	100
3	12	6	50

Note (a)—Not withstanding the above, test pieces having a gauge length equal to $5.65\sqrt{S_o}$ are permitted.

(b) For any width from 3 to 25 mm a gauge of 50 mm may be used and total length being adjusted accordingly.

(c) A straight, parallel test piece without enlarged ends is permissible for any size.

5. **Procedure :**

(a) Cross Sectional area of the test piece shall be measured (Fig. 7.1)

(b) Original gauge length can be rounded off to nearest 5 mm and marked by means of fine mark or a scribed line.

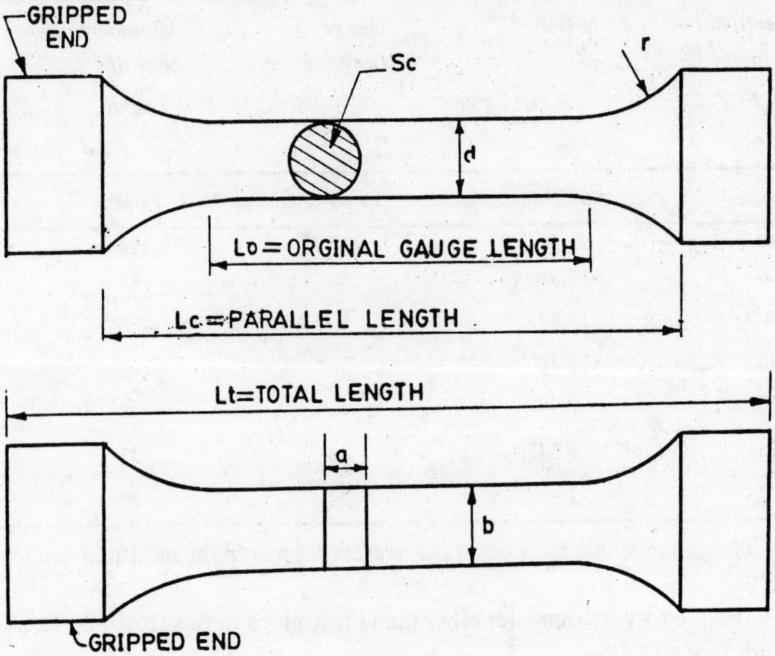

Fig. 7.1—Test Piece, of Circular and Rectangular Sections

(c) Test piece should be held in the testing machined. Every effort should be made to ensure that test pieces are held in such a way that the load is applied as axially as possible.

(d) For determining the value of young's modulus (E), the elongations are recorded by means of extensometer upto the yield point of the material at suitable increment.

(e) When determining the yield stress, the test piece shall be so loaded that the stain rate during elastic range is controlled and shall not exceed 0.15/min. If this rate of straining cannot be achieved directly, it should be obtained by controlling the rate of loading just before yield commences.

(f) While determining the tensile strength the speed of testing should be uniform as possible and the change of speed from one range to the other should be made gradually and without shock.

(g) Tensile strength is determined as the maximum load divided by the original cross sectional area of the test piece.

(h) The percentage elongation after fracture should be expressed to the nearest 1% and is determined as permanent elongation of the gauge length after fracture (L_u-L_o) expressed as a percentage of the original gauge length L_o.

(i) The percentage reduction in area is determined as the ratio of the maximum change in the cross sectional area, which has occurred during the test (S_o-S_u), to the original cross sectional area S_o, expressed as percentage.

(j) Knowing extension on the extensometer gauge length for the increment of loading, stress and corresponding strain can be calculated. Plot the stress-strain curve upto yield stress, the slope of the line shall give the value of E.

6. Observations and Calculations

TABLE 7.3 Recording of observations for stress-strain curve

Sample No. 1

Load N(Kg.)	*Extensometer reading mm(cm)*	*Stress = Load / Area of cross section*	*Strain = Change in length / Original gauge length*
1.			
2.			
3.			
4.			
5.			
6.			
7.			
8.			
9.			
10			
11			
12			
13			
14			
15			
16			
17			
18			
19			
20.			

TABLE 7.4

Sample No.2

Load N(Kg.)	*Extensometer reading mm(cm)*	*Stress = Load / Area of cross section*	*Strain = Change in length / Original gauge length*
1.			
2.			
3.			
4.			
5.			
6.			
7.			
8.			
9.			
10			
11			
12			
13			
14			
15			
16			
17			
18			
19			
20.			

TABLE 7.5.

Sample No.	Identification	Length (mm)	Weight N (Kg)	Average dia (mm)	Size (mm)	Area (mm^2)	Yield load N(Kg.)	Yield stress N/mm^2 (Kg/cm^2.)	Max load N(Kg.)	Ultimate tensile strength N/mm^2 (Kg/cm^2)	Percen- elonga- tion	Percentage reduction in area
I												
II												

7. **Results :**

TABLE No. 7.6

Sample No.	Type of specimen	Dia size (mm)	Yield stress N/mm^2 (kg/cm^2)	Ultimate tensile Strength N/mm^2 (Kg/cm^2)	Percentage elongation (Kg/cm^2)	Percentage reduction in area	Modulus of Elasticity (E) N/mm^2 (kg/cm^2)
I							
II							

8. **Precautions :**

(a) Measure the cross sectional dimensions of the test piece very accurately.

(b) Ensure that the test piece has been held in the machine as axially as possible.

(c) Speed of testing should be as uniform as possible.

9. **Comments :**

Comment on the results obtained by you in the laboratory. Compare these results with those recommended by Bureau of Indian Standards, New Delhi.

10. Questions :

(a) Why is tensile test required to be performed? What is its significance ?

(b) What do you understand by the proof stress ?

(c) What is the least count of the screw gauge and extensometer used by you ?

(d) Does the original gauge length depend on the original diameter of the specimen ?

(e) Differentiate between upper and lower yield points.

(f) Does the specimen fracture at maximum load ? If not, why.

(g) Is the ultimate load greater than maximum load ?

(h) How do you define the modulus of elasticity of steel ?

(i) How does mild steel differ structurally from cast iron.

(j) Mild steel is equally strong in compression as well as in tension, comment.

(iii) M.S. WIRE

1. **Apparatus**-Tensile Testing machine, screw gauge, extensometer, test pieces.

2. **Test piece**-Test piece, shall be prepared from the products which have usually been cold worked and are of constant cross section, either round, square, rectangular or any other special shape. the dimensions of cross section are always very small compared with the usual length produced and for wires of rectangular cross section the ratio of width to thickness is generally less than 4.

   The cross section of the test piece shall be that of the wire. The usual gauge length adopted is 100 or 200 mm. For the diameters of 3mm and greater, the minimum practical gauge length is 10d(d=diameter). However gauge length of 50mm and 250mm are also permitted. The distance between grips should be at least 50mm greater than the gauge length if possible, the test piece should not be straightened before testing. If straightening is necessary this should be done by hand if practicable, but otherwise a hammer having a head of wood should be used, the wire being supported on a flat surface of wood.

3. **Procedure :**

   (a) Diameter of the wire shall be measured within 1% error.

   (b) When the elongation is to be determined, the test piece shall be marked throughout the length between grips, except for a distance of at least 2d, with gauge marks spaced at intervals equal to half the gauge length to an accuracy of + 0.5 mm.

   (c) The test piece shall be held by wedge grips which will produce the minimum depth of notch in the wire and it shall be ensured that the load is applied as axially as possible.

   (d) The testing machine shall be caliberated in accordance with IS: 1828-1961. The increment of the extensometer shall not exceed 5% of the value of the elongation for which the stress value is obtained.

   (e) Draw the stress strain diagram from the observations of the extension made at the sequence of increasing the load during the tensile test.

4. **Observations :**

TABLE 7.7-Recording of observations for stress-strain curve.

Sample No.1

Load *N(Kg.)*	*Extensometer reading*	*Stress* $= \frac{Load}{Area\ of\ cross\ Section}$ *N/mm²(Kg/cm²)*	*Strain* $\frac{Change\ in\ length}{original\ gauge\ length}$
1.			
2.			
3.			
4.			
5.			
6.			
7.			
8.			
9.			
10			
11			
12			
13			
14			
15			
16			
17			
18			
19			
20			

TABLE 7.8 : Sample No.2

Load *N(Kg.)*	*Extensometer Reading*	*Stress* $= \frac{Load}{Area\ of\ cross\ Section}$ *N/mm² (kg/cm²)*	*Strain* $= \frac{Change\ in\ Length}{Original\ Guage\ Length}$
1.			
2.			
3.			
4.			
5.			
6.			
7.			
8.			
9.			
10.			
11.			
12.			
13.			
14.			
15.			
16.			
17.			
18.			
19.			
20.			

TABLE 7.9.

Sample No.	Identi-fication	Length (mm)	Weight N (Kg)	Average dia (mm)	Size (mm)	Area (mm^2)	Yield load N(Kg.)	Yield stress N/mm^2 (Kg/cm^2.)	Max load N(Kg.)	Ultimate tensile strength N/mm^2 (Kg/cm^2)	Percen-elonga-tion	Percentage reduc-tion in area
I												
II												

5. **Results :**

TABLE 7.10

Sample No.	Type of specimen	Dia (mm)	Yield stress N/mm^2 ($Kg./cm^2$)	Ultimate tensile strength (N/mm^2) (Kg/cm^2)	Percentage elongation	Percentage reduction in area	Modulus of lasticity (E) N/mm^2 (Kg/cm^2)
I							
II							

6. **Precautions :**

(a) Diameter of the wire should be measured atleast at six locations and average taken.

(b) Load should be applied axially.

7. **Comments :**

Comment on the results obtained by you and compare your values with the values of Indian standards.

8. **Questions :**

(a) What is the difference between the test performed on M.S. wire and M.S. flat ?

(b) Explain the significance of gauge length.

(c) How does the test piece is prepared for M.S. wire ?

(d) How you will determine 0.2 percent proof stress of high tensile wire ?

(e) Why do you perform this test ?

EXPERIMENT NO. 7/2

IMPACT TEST OF STEEL

1. **Object**—To determine the impact strength of notched mild steel test piece using (i) chary test (ii) Izod Test.

(A) CHARPY TEST

2. **Apparatus**—Test piece notched in the middle, Impact testing machine.
3. **Theory**—The test consists of breaking by one blow from a swinging hammer under prescribed conditions, a test piece U notched in the middle and supported at each end. The energy absorbed is determined, from which the impact values is obtained.

Impact strength of U notched specimen =

$$= \frac{\text{Energy absorbed in kgfm}}{S_o}$$

Where S_u = cross sectional area of test piece below the notch, measured in mm^2 (cm^2) before the test.

4. **Test Specimen**—Test specimen shall be 55 mm long and of square section with 10 mm sides. In the centre of the length, there shall be a U notch 5 mm deep (unless otherwise specified) rounded off at the base with a radius of 1.0 mm. The notch shall be carefully prepared so that no grooves appear at the base of the notch. The following dimensions are permitted.

Length 55 mm ± 0.6 mm

Thickness(a) 10 mm ± 0.11 mm

Depth below the Notch 5 mm ± 0.09 mm

Root radius of notch 1 mm ± 0.07 mm

Distance of notch from ends of the test piece 27.5 mm ± 0.42 mm.

Angle between plane of symmetry of notch and longitudinal axis of test piece 90° ± 2°.

5. **Testing Machine**—The testing machine shall comply with the following requirements :

Distance between supports	= 40 ± 0.5 mm
Radius of curvature of the support	= 1 mm
Tapers of support	= 1.5

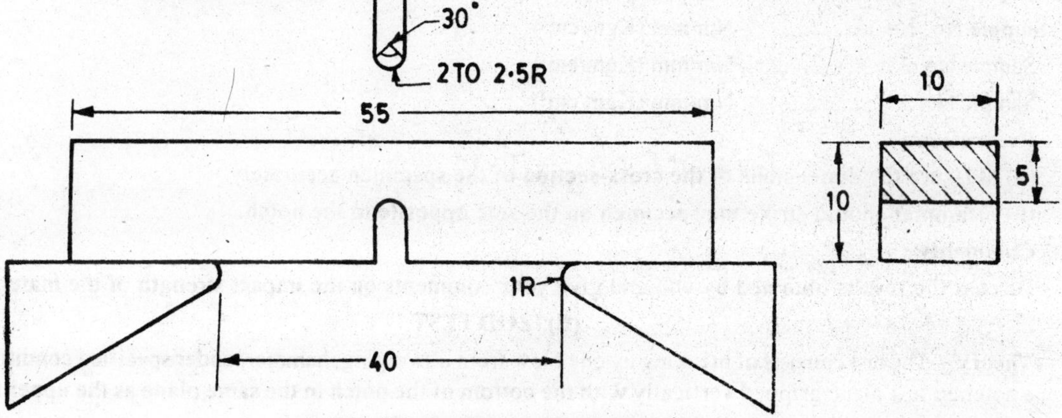

Fig. 7.2. Test Piece for Charpy Test

Angle at tip of the hammer = 30° ± 1°
Radius of curvature of the tip of the hammer = 2 to 2.5 mm
Speed of hammer at the instant of striking = 4.5 to 7 m/s

For a standard test the striking energy of the testing machine shall be 30 ± 1 Kgfm

6. **Procedure :**

(a) The specimen shall be laid squarely against the supports with the plane of symmetry of the notch within 0.5 mm of the plane midway between them.

(b) Specimen shall be struck by the hammer in the plane of symmetry of the notch and on the side opposite the notch.

(c) The temperature of the specimen shall be taken 27 ± 2°C

(d) If during the test, specimen is not completely broken, the impact value obtained is indefinite.

(e) The energy of the free hammer should be calculated before the striking energy of the specimen is obtained from the test.

7. **Observations and Calculations:**

Sample No. 1				Sample No. 2				Sample No. 3			
S_o	Energy of Hammer without specimen (A)	Energy of hammer after breaking the test piece (B)	Energy absorbed in Kg fm $= \frac{A-B}{S_o}$	S_o	(A)	(B)	$\frac{A-B}{S_o}$	S_o	(A)	(B)	$\frac{A-B}{S_o}$

S_o = Cross-sectional area of test piece below the notch, measured in mm²(cm²) before the test.

8. **Result:**

Impact strength of U notched Specimen by charpy's test

Sample No. 1 = ... Nm/mm²(Kgm/cm²)

Sample No. 2 = ... Nm/mm²(Kgm/cm²)

Sample No. 3 = ... Nm/mm²(Kgm/cm²)

9. **Precautions :**

(a) Measure the dimensions of the cross-section of the specimen accurately.

(b) Hammer should strike the specimen on the side opposite to the notch.

10. **Comments:**

Discuss the results obtained by you and give your comments on the impact strength of the material.

(B) IZOD TEST

1. **Theory**—The test consists of breaking by one blow from a swinging, hammer, under specified conditions, a notched test piece gripped vertically with the bottom of the notch in the same plane as the upper face

of the grips. The hammer is struck at a fixed position on the face having the notch. The energy absorbed is determined as the difference of energy of hammer before and after striking and is taken as the energy required to smash the specimen.

2. **Tests Specimen**—Specimen shall be 75 mm long and of square or circular section with 10 mm sides. At 25 mm from one of the ends, a V notch of 2 mm depth shall be cut for a square specimen. The notch shall be carefully prepared so that no grooves appear at the base of notch.

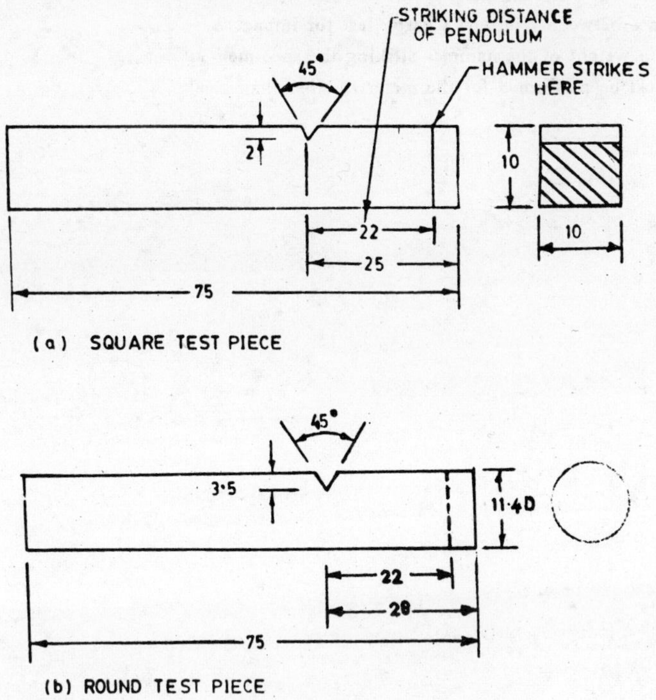

Fig. 7.3. Test Piece for Izod Test

3. **Procedure:**

Procedure shall be same as for Charpy's test.

4. **Observations and Calculations:**

Sample No. 1				Sample No.2				Sample No.3			
S_o	(A)	(B)	$\frac{A-B}{S_o}$	S_o	(A)	(B)	$\frac{A-B}{S_o}$	S_o	(A)	(B)	$\frac{A-B}{S_o}$

5. Results:

Impact value of specimen No. 1 = ... Nm/mm^2 (Kgm/cm^2)

2 = ... Nm/mm^2 (Kgm/cm^2)

3 = ... Nm/mm^2 (Kgm/cm^2)

6. Precautions:

Same precautions as for Charpy's test

7. Comments

Comment on the result obtained by you in the Laboratory.

8. Questions:

(a) What is the impact strength of the specimen ?

(b) Differentiate between Izod and Charpy test for impact ?

(c) What is the weight of the hammer striking the specimen ?

(d) Can this test be performed for the material other than steel ?

EXPERIMENT NO. 7/3

HARDNESS TEST OF METALS

1. **Object**—To determine Hardness number of various materials viz, mild steel, cast iron, brass and aluminium specimen.
2. **Apparatus**—Brinell Hardness testing machine, microscope.
3. **Theory**—The best consists in forcing a steel ball diameter D under a load F into the specimen and measuring the mean diameter *d* of the impression left in the surface after removal of the load as shown in Fig. 7.4.

$$\text{Brinell Hardness HB} = \frac{F}{\frac{\pi D}{2}\left(D - \sqrt{D^2 - d^2}\right)} = \frac{\text{Test load}}{\text{Surface area of indentation}}$$

Where D = diameter of ball (mm)

F = test load (Nf)

d = mean diameter of Indentation (mm)

$$h = \text{depth of indentation} = \frac{D - \sqrt{D^2 - d^2}}{2}$$

Test Specimen—The contact surface of test piece shall be free from foreign mater like oil, dirt etc. Specimen shall be placed on a rigid support. Specimen should be firmly on the support so that the displacement cannot occur during the test. The surface of the test piece shall be smooth to measure the diameter of indentation accurately. Specimen shall be so prepared to avoid any change in condition due to heating and cold working.

4. **Testing Ball** :

Usually a ball of 2.5 mm nominal diameter shall be used. Balls of 1.2 and 5 mm are also used but in no case balls less than one milimeter shall be used. The balls shall be of hardened and tampered steel with a hardness of at least 850 HB. It shall be polished and free from surface defects. Any ball with surface defects shall be rejected.

5. **Procedure**:

(a) Thickness of specimen shall not be less that 8 × h. Following table shows minimum thickness for various ball diameters, loads and hardness values.

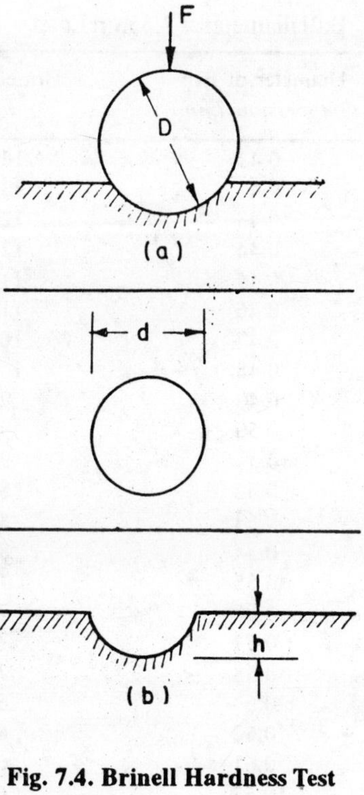

Fig. 7.4. Brinell Hardness Test

Ball dia-meter (mm)	Load (Nf)	Brinell Hardness value (HB)				
		100	200	300 (minimum thickness (mm))	400	450
1	300	0.76	0.38	0.25	0.19	0.17
2	1200	1.52	0.76	0.51	0.38	0.23
2.5	1875	1.91	0.95	0.64	0.48	0.42
5	7500	3.81	1.90	1.27	0.97	0.84
10	30000	7.64	3.81	2.54	1.90	1.70

(b) Test shall be carried out at the ambient temperature.

(c) Specimen is placed in the machine such that the distance of the centre of indentation from the edge of the specimen shall be atleast 2.5 × diameter of indentation and the distanced of centre of two adjacent indentations shall be atleast 4 × dia of indentation.

(d) Ball is placed against the surface of the specimen and the pressure is gradually applied until the test load of $F = 30D^2$ is attained. This load shall be maintained for a min. of 10 seconds.

(e) Diameter of each indentation shall be measured in two perpendicular directions and the mean value of the two readings shall be taken for the purpose of determining hardness number. The measuring microscope shall be capable of measuring the diameter of indentations with an accuracy of ± 0.25% of the diameter of ball.

(f) The Brinell Hardness for different ball diameters and loads shall be determined from the following table.

Brinell Hardness Charts

Ball diameter = 2.5 mm Load = 1875 N (187.5 Kg)

Diameter of ball *impression (mm)*	Brinell Hardness *number*	Diameter of Ball *impression (mm)*	Brinell Hardness *number*
0.41	1411	0.65	555
0.42	1344	0.66	538
0.43	1282	0.67	522
0.44	1223	0.68	507
0.45	1169	0.69	492
0.46	1119	0.70	477
0.47	1071	0.71	464
0.48	1027	0.72	451
0.49	985	0.73	438
0.50	945	0.74	426
0.51	908	0.75	415
0.52	873	0.76	404
0.53	840	0.77	393
0.54	809	0.78	383
0.55	780	0.79	373
0.56	752	0.80	363
0.57	725	0.81	354
0.58	700	0.82	345
0.59	676	0.83	337
0.60	653	0.84	329
0.61	632	0.85	321
0.62	611	0.86	313
0.63	592	0.87	306
0.64	573	0.88	298

Diameter of ball *impression (mm)*	Brinell Hardness *number*	Diameter of Ball *impression (mm)*	Brinell Hardness *number*
0.89	292	1.24	145
0.90	285	1.25	143
0.91	278	1.26	140
0.92	272	1.27	138
0.93	266	1.28	135
0.94	260	1.29	133
0.95	255	1.30	131
0.96	249	1.31	129
0.97	244	1.32	127
0.98	239	1.33	125
0.99	234	1.34	123
1.00	229	1.35	121
1.02	219	1.36	119
1.03	215	1.37	117
1.04	211	1.38	115
1.05	207	1.39	113
1.06	202	1.40	111
1.07	198	1.41	110
1.08	195	1.42	108
1.09	191	1.43	106
1.10	187	1.44	105
1.11	184	1.45	103
1.12	180	1.46	101
1.13	177	1.47	99.9
1.14	174	1.48	98.4
1.15	170	1.49	96.9
1.16	167	1.50	95.5
1.17	164	1.51	94.1
1.18	161	1.52	92.7
1.19	158	1.53	91.3
1.20	156	1.54	90.3
1.21	153	1.55	88.7
1.22	150		
1.23	148		

6. **Results:**

(1) Hardness value of Mild Steel

Specimen No. 1 =

2 =

3 =

(2) Hardness value of cast iron

Specimen No. 1 =

2 =

3 =

(3) Hardness value of Brass

Specimen No. 1 =

2 =

3 =

(4) Hardness value of Aluminium

Specimen No. 1 =

2 =

3 =

7. Precautions:

(a) Diameter of each indentation should be measured in two perpendicular directions and mean should be taken.

(b) Pressure on the specimen should be applied gradually.

8. Questions:

(a) Why do you perform this test ?

(b) How do you define hardness of a material.

EXPERIMENT NO. 7/4

COLD BEND TEST OF STEEL

1. **Object**—To conduct cold bend test on steel bar.
2. **Test Piece**—The bar of large dia should be reduced to a convenient size between 20 and 50 mm in diameter. Bar of less than 20 mm dia shall be tested without reduction in dia.
3. **Apparatus**—Suitable testing machine and bend test fixtures.
4. **Procedure:**

(a) Lay the test piece on two parallel supports and bend it in the middle by means of a mandrel to the specified angle. The width of the supports and of the mandrel should be greater than that of the test piece.

(b) If it is necessary to observe the point at which cracking begins, the outer surface of the test piece should remain clearly visible in the portion being bent while conducting the test.

(c) The radius of the supports and the mandrel and the distance between the supports shall be as specified in the material specifications. If the distance between the supports is not specified in the material specifications, this distance should be taken as approximately $D + 3a$.

Where,

D = Dia of mandrel

a = Angle of bent

5. **Observations :**

After bending, the sides and the outside of the bent portion should be examined.

6. **Result:**

Report the result if any crack or defect observed.

7. **Precautions:**

(a) Measure the diameter of the specimen at six locations and take the mean.

(b) Apply the bending force uniformly.

8. **Questions:**

(a) What is the importance of this test ?

(b) Sketch the mandrel used for bending.

REFERENCES

1. I.S. 1608-1972 Method for tensile testing of steel products.
2. I.S. 1521-1972 Method for tensile testing of steel wire.
3. I.S. 1499-1959 Method for charpy impact test (U Notch) for steel.
4. I.S. 1500-1968 Method for Brinell Hardness for steel.
5. I.S. 1586-1968 Method for Rockwell hardness test (B and C scale) for steel.
6. I.S. 1599-1960 Method for Bend test for steel products other than sheet, strip wire and tube.

PART - VIII

BUILDING LIME

EXPERIMENT NO. 8/1

CHEMICAL ANALYSIS OF BUILDING LIME

1. **Object**—To determine the following of building lime :
   (a) Insoluble Residue
   (b Loss of ignition
   (c) Insoluble Matter
   (d) Silicon-di-oxide
   (e) Ferric and aluminium Oxide
   (f) Calcium Oxide
   (g) Magnesium Oxide.

2. **Theory**—Lime is not generally found in nature in the free state, but it is obtained by burning lime stone, a raw material found in limestone hills or lime stone boulders found in the beds of old rivers or kankar found below ground or shells of sea animals. White chalk is pure lime stone and kankar is an impure lime stone.

Chemically lime is oxide of calcium (CaO). It is the product obtained by the calcination of limestones or other calcarious substances, the effect of which is to drive off the carbonic acid and moisture they contain

$$CaCo_3 = CaO + CO_2$$

$$\text{(Lime stone)} = \text{(QuickLime)} + \text{(Carbondioxide)}$$

Thus Quicklime or Caustic Lime (CaO) is the resulting lime as left immediately after calcination of a comparatively pure lime stone. It is amorphous, highly caustic, absorbs moisture quickly and has no effinity for carbonic acid. It remains in this state only for a short time unless kept in a dry place.

Slaked lime or hydrate of lime ($Ca\,(oH)_2$) is the product formed by the absorption of required quantity of water by quicklime. It is the ordinary purelime which is available in the market.

$$\underset{\text{(Quicklime)}}{CaO} + \underset{\text{(Water)}}{H_2O} = \underset{\text{(Hydrate of Lime)}}{Ca\,(0H)_2}$$

In this state it has the power of absorbing Carbonic acid from the atomosphere in presence of moisture and forms particles of carbonate of lime, setting free the moisture absorbed lime. So lime should be used as fresh as possible.

Chemical analysis of lime is done to find the cementation and hydraulic properties of the sample. The limits for various values are given in table E.1 in Appendix-E, specification for lime.

3.1 A-Determination of Insoluble Residued

3.1.1 Apparatus :

(1) Dilute hydrochloric acid 1:1 (v/v). It shall be prepared by diluting hydrochloric acid of specific gravity 1.16 and conforming to IS:265 - 1962 (Specifications for hydrochloric acid) with an equal volume of water.

(2) Sodium carbonate solution. It shall be prepared by dissolving 5 gm of sodium carbonate conforming to IS:296 1965 (Specifications for sodium carbonate anhydrous) in 100 ml of water.

3.1.2 Procedure :

(a) Weigh 1gm of the sample in a 250 ml beaker. Add 10 ml of water to the lime in beaker and make the contents into a slurry. Then add 20 to 25 ml of dilute hydrochloric acid and digest the contents for half an hour with occasional gentle agitation. Rinse the sides of the beaker with hot water thus diluting the solution to about 100 ml. Redigest the contents at a temperature just below the boiling point for about 15 minutes. Filter the contents of the beaker through a filter paper and wash the residue and filter paper twice with dilute hydrochloric acid and then with hot water till they are free from chlorides.

(b) Transfer the filter paper along with the residue to a porcelain dish and add 30 to 40 ml sodium carbonate solution. Cover the dish and digest its contents for about half an hour at a temperature just below the boiling point. Add hot water in small quantities during digestion to make up the loss of volume caused by evaporation. Decant off the supernatant liquid through a filter paper and wash the residue in the dish a few times with hot water decanting off the liquid into the filter paper. Cover the residue in the dish with sodium carbonate and digest agina for about 10 minutes. Filter the contents and wash the residue on the filter paper twice with hot sodium carbonate solution and then with hot water till free from alkali. Aagain wash the filter paper and residue twice with dilute hydrochloric acid and then with hot water till free from chlorides.

(c) Transfer the filter paper and the residue to a crucible, dry, ignite and weigh the contents.

3.2 Determination of Loss on Ignition

Place 1gm of the prepared sample in a weighted platinum crusible and cover with a lid. Then ignite it at a temperature not less than 1000°C to a constant mass. The difference between the original mass and the final mass of the sample represents the loss on ignition. This shall be expressed as a percentage of the mass of the sample taken.

3.3 Determination of Insoluble Matter including Silicon Dioxide

3.3.1 Reagents

(a) Concentrated hydrocloric Acid–Specific gravity 1.16 (conforming to IS 265-1962).

(b) Dilute Hydrochloric Acid - 1 : 99 (v/v)

3.3.2 Procedure

(a) Transfer the ignited sample from 3.2 into an evaporating dish and mix with water into a thin slurry. Add about 10 ml of concentrated hydrochloric acid into the dish and digest the contents with the acid by heating and agitating simultaneously until dissolved. Then evaporate the solution to dryness on a water bath. When the sample is nearly dry, place it in an oven for 1 hour. Maintain the temperature of the oven between 110 to 120°C. Take out the sample, cool and add about 10 ml of concentrated hydrochloric acid. Allow it to stand for a few minutes. Add an equal volume of water, cover the dish and place on the water bath for 10 minutes. Filter and wash the residue with hot dilute hydrochloric acid and finally twice with hot water. Evaporate the filterate to dryness and then bake at 110 to 120°C for 1 hour. Extract it with hydrochloric acid as before and filter through a second smaller filter paper. Reserve the filterate for conducting further tests.

(b) Transfer the wet filter papers containing the residue to a weighted platinum crusible, clear without allowing the paper to catch fire and finally ignite to constant mass at 1100°C. This gives the mass of insoluble matter including silicon diaoxide in the sample taken.

3.4 Determination Silicon Dioxide

3.4.1 Reagents

(a) Hydrofluoric acid–Approximately 40% (v/v).

(b) Concentrated sulphuric Acid–Specific gravity 1.84 (Conforming to IS : 266 - 1966).

3.4.2 Procedure

Treat the insoluble matter including silicon dioxide obtained under 3.3.2 (a) in the crusible with 5 ml each of water and hydrofluoric acid and one or two drops of concentrated sulphuric acid and then evaporate to dryness. Ignite the residue for 2 to 3 minutes and weight again. Repeat this procedure till the mass obtained is constant within ± 0.1 percent.

3.5 Determination of Ferric and Aluminium Oxides

3.5.1 Reagents

(a) Dilute Hydrochloric Acid - 1:1 and 1:3 (v/v)

(b) Concentrated Nitric Acid - Specific Gravity 1.42 (Conforming to IS : 264-1968)

(c) Concentrated Hydrocholoric Acid - Specific gravity 1.16 (Conforming to IS : 265-1962).

(d) Methyl Red Indicator - 0.1 percent (m/v). It shall be prepared by dissolving 0.1 g of the sodium salt of the methyl red in 100 ml of water. In case the acid is available, 0.1 g is dissolved in 60 ml alcohol and made up to 100 ml, with water.

(e) Ammonium Hydroxide Solution – Specific gravity 0.90 (Conforming to IS : 799 - 1955)

(f) Ammonium Chloride Solution–2 percent (m/v)

3.5.2 Procedure

(a) To the filterate reserved in 3.3.2 (a) add a few drops of concentrated nitric acid and boil the solution until all traces of chlorine are gone. If necessary add 10 to 15 ml of concentrated hydrochloric acid and dilute to 200 ml. Then add a few drops of methyl red solution, heat the solution to boiling and neutralise with ammonium hydroxide (diluted towards the end) until the colour of the liquid changes to district yellow. Boil the solution for 1 to 2 minutes, allow to settle and filter. Wash the precipitate immediately two or three times with hot ammonium chloride solution and dry by suction. Reserve the filterate.

(b) Dissolve the precipitate on the filter paper in hot dilute hydro-chloric acid (1:3) and collect the solution in the beaker in which the precipitation was made. Thoroughly wash the filter paper with hot water into the same beaker. Boil the solution to expel any trace of chlorine and treat the solution with ammonium hydrooxide solution for precipitation. Then filter and wash with hot ammonium chloride solution. Combine this filterate and the one reserved in (a) for the determination of calcium oxide.

(c) Ignite the moist filter paper containing the precipitate in a weighted platinum crucible to constant weight at 1100°C. This gives the mass of ferric and aluminium oxide in the sample taken. The precipitate may contain in case of some limes small quantities of phosphorous pentoxide (P_2O_5), Magnesium oxide (Mn_3o_4) and titanium oxide (T_1O_2).

3.6 Determination of Ferric Oxide

3.6.1 Apparatus

(a) Bunsen valve or Jones' reductor

3.6.2 Reagents

(a) Sodium pyrosulphate ($Na_2S_2O_7$) - Solid. Alternatively potasium pyrosulphate ($K_2S_2O_7$) may also be used.

(b) Dilute sulphuric acid - Approximately 5 N.

(c) Standard potassium permagnate solution (k Mn o_4) - Approximately 0.05 N. It shall be prepared by dissolving 1.6 grams of potassium permangnate in 1000 ml of water. It shall be allowed to stand for a week or more and then filtered through purified asbestos and standardised against standard sodium oxalate solution, prepared by dissolving exactly 0.75 grams of sodium oxalate in 250 ml of water.

(d) Hydrofluric Acid

3.6.3 Procedure

(a) Fuse the combined ferric and aluminium oxides obtained in 3.5.2 (c) in a platinum crucible at a very low temperature with 3 to 4 gm of sodium pyrosulphate. Treat the melt with sufficient dilute sulphuric acid to ensure the presence of not less than 5 gm of absolute acid and enough water to effect the solution on heating. Evaporate the solution and heat until it fumes copiously. After cooling and redissolving in water, filter, wash and ignite the small amount of silicondioxide appearing as precipitate in the solution. Then weigh and correct by volatizing silicon dioxide by treating with hydrofluoric acid and sulphuric acid. Add the mass so corrected to the mass of silicon dioxide previously found and deduct from the gross mass of the ferric and aluminium oxides. The correction for impurities shall not be made when the hydrofluric acid correction of the silicon dioxide determination has been omitted.

(b) Reduce the filterate after removal of silicon dioxide precipitate by zinc using Bunsen valve or Jones reductor. Filter it through whatman No. 41 filter paper, wash with hot water and titrate with 0.05 N potassium permagnate solution.

(c) Evaluation - Once millilitre of the 0.05 N potassium permangnate solution is equal to 0.003992 gm of ferric oxide (Fe_2o_3). Accordingly the ferric oxide content shall be calculated, which shall be expressed as a percentage of the mass of the sample taken in 3.1.2 (a).

3.6.4 Determination of Aluminium oxide—The mass of ferric oxide shall be deducted from the total mass of ferric oxide and aluminium oxides obtained under 3.6.3 (c).

3.7 Determination of calcium oxide content

3.7.1 Gravimetric Method

(a) Dilute Hydrochloric acid - 1 : 1 (v/v). It shall be prepared by diluting hydrochloric acid of specific gravity 1.16 and conforming to IS : 265-1962 with an equal volume of distilled water.

(b) Ammonium hydroxide solution - Sp gr 0.90 approximately

(c) Ammonium oxalate solution - 0.1 percent (m/v) and saturated.

(d) Ammonium chloride solution - 2 percent (m/v)

3.7.1.2 Procedure

(a) The combined filterate reserved under 3.5.2 (b) shall be used. The filterate shall be diluted with distilled water so as to obtain a volume of 500 ml. Use 25 ml of this filterate in the analysis given under 3.7.2.

(b) Add a few drops of ammonium hydroxide solution to the aliquot taken and allow the solution to boil. Add 35 ml of saturated solution of ammonium oxalate to the liquid and continue boiling until the precipitated calcium oxalate assumes a granular form. Then allow to stand for 20 minutes or until the precipitate has settled and the supernatant liquid is clear. Filter and wash it moderately with ammonium oxalate solution (0.1 percent). Reserve the filterate.

(c) Transfer the wet filter paper and precipitate to a weighted platinum crucible. Burn the filter paper gently over a small flame and later ignite at 1100°C until calcium oxalate is converted into calcium oxide. Dissolve the contents in 10 ml of hot dilute hydrochloric acid and make up the volume to 250 ml. Add ammonium hydroxide to the solution in slight excess which is indicated by persistent smell of ammonia and boil the liquid. If a small amount of aluminium hydroxide separat out, filter it, wash with ammonium chloride, ignite and weigh. Add the weight of aluminium oxide so determined to that found under 3.6.4.

(d) After the precipitate settles, filter the solution, wash the residue with ammonium oxalate solution (0.1 percent) and ignite in a weighted covered platinum crusible to a constant mass. The difference shall give the mass of calcium oxide content in the sample. Combine the filterate with that reserved in 3.7.1.2 (b) and reserve for conducting further test.

3.7.1.3 Report of the Test Results

The calcium oxide content shall be reported as a percentage of mass of the sample under 3.3.2 (a).

3.7.2 Volumetric Method

3.7.2.1 Reagents

(a) Ammonium hydroxide - Sp. gr. 0.90 approximately.

(b) Ammonium oxalate solution - Saturated.

(c) Dilute sulphuric Acid - 1 : 10 (v/v).

(d) Standard potassium permangnate solution -It shall be prepared by dissolving 5.634g of potassium permangnate in 1000 ml of water. It shall be allowed to stand for a week or more before use. filtered through a purified asbestos and then standardized against sodium oxalate solution, prepared by dissolving 0.75 gm of sodium oxalate in 250 ml of water.

3.7.2.2 Procedure

(a) Make second half of the filterate [see 3.7.1.2. (a)] alkaline with ammonium hydroxide solution. Boil vigorously and allow to stand until the precipitate has settled. Filter through a filter paper of 110 mm diameter and wash the precipitate ten times with hot water. Alternatively, use a Gooch or sintered glass crucible instead of filter paper. The total quantity of water used for this wash shall not exceed 125 ml.

(b) Transfer the filter paper along with the precipitate to the beaker in which the precipitation was done, speading the paper out against the upper portion of the beaker. Wash the precipitate from the paper with a jet of hot water, fold the paper and leave it adhering to the upper portion of the beaker. Add 50 ml of dilute sulphuric acid to the beaker, dilute the solution to a volume of 250 ml with hot water and then heat to 80-90°C. Titrate it with standard potassium permanganate solution until the pink end point is obtained. Drop the folded filter paper (which has been adhering to the side of the beaker) into the liquid, the pink colour of the latter will be dishcarge. Complete the titration by adding potassium permanganate solution drop by drop until the pink end point is again obtained.

3.7.2.3 Evaluation—One millilitre of the standard potassium pemanganate solution would be approximately equivalent to 0.005 g of calcium oxide.

3.7.3 EDTA Method

For non hydrauli type of lime, EDTA method as mentioned in IS : 5949 - 1970 (Method for volumetric determination of calcium and magnisium using EDTA) may also be used.

3.8 Determination of Magnesium Oxide

3.8.1 Reagents

(a) Dilute hydrochoric acid - 1 : 1 and 1 : 4 (v/v). It shall be prepared by diluting hydrocholoric acid sp. gr. 1.16 and conforming to IS : 265-1962 (Specifications for hydrochloric acid) with an equal volume of distilled water.

(b) Diammonium Hydrogen Phosphate Solution - 25 percent (v/v).

(c) Ammonium hydroxide solution - Sp. gr. 0.90 approximately.

(d) Ammonium Nitrate Wash Solution - It shall be prepared by diluting ammonium hydroxide with distilled water until the solution contains 2.5 percent of ammonia by mass, then adding 3 or 4 drops of concentrated nitric acid (Sp. gr. 1.42).

3.8.2 Procedure

(a) Acidify the combined filterate obtained in 3.7.1.2 (d) with hydrochloric acid and concentrate to about 150 ml. Add 10 ml of diammonium hydrogen phosphate solution and cool it by placing in a beaker of ice water. After the solution cools down add ammonium hydroxide solution drop by drop. stir the contents constantly until crystalline precipitate of magnesium ammonium orthophosphate begins to form. Add excess of ammonium hydroxide solution to the extent of 5 to 10 percent of the volume of the solution. Continue stiring for several minutes. Allow the liquid to stand in a cold atmosphere for 12 to 48 hours and then filter.

(b) Dissolve the precipitate in hot dilute hydrochloric acid (1 : 4) and dilute the solution to about 100 ml. Add 1 ml diammonium hydrogen phosphate solution and then ammonium hydroxide solution drop by drop with constant stiring until the precipitate again begins to form as described in 3.8.2 (a). Add ammonium hydroxide in moderate excess. Allow it to stand in a cold atmosphere for 12 to 48 hours filter and wash with ammonium nitrate wash solution. Burn the filter paper off at a low temperature and finally ignite the residue to constant mass at 1100°C (A).

3.8.3 Report of Test Results

(a) The magnesium oxide content shall be calculated from the following formula -

$$\text{Magnesium Oxide, percent by mass} = \frac{A}{B} \times 36.2$$

Where A = mass of magnesium pyrophosphate

B = mass of the ignited sample represented by the aliquot taken for the estimation of calcium oxide under 3.7.1.2. (a).

(b) the magnesium oxide content shall be expressed as a percentage of mass of the sample taken under 3.3.2 (b).

3.8.4 EDTA Method

For nonhydraulic type of lime, EDTA method as mentioned in IS : 5949 - 1970 (Method for volumetric determination of calcium and magnesium using EDTA) may also be used.

3.9 Precautions

(a) Reagents should be prepared very carefully as per relevant Indian standards.

(b) Filter papers used should be of high quality.

3.10 Questions

(a) What are the different varities in which lime is generally used in civil engineering construction.

(b) What is the chemical composition of lime.

(c) What do you understand by slaked lime. What is the type of lime available in the market.

(d) What do you mean calcining of limestone. what are the different types of products obtained after calcining limestone.

(e) Discuss the Bureau of Indian Standard Classification of lime.

(f) State the characteristics of a good lime.

(g) State the limits of various cementation and hydraulic components in lime as advocated by Bureau of Indian standards.

EXPERIMENT NO. 8/2

DETERMINATION OF CARBON DIOXIDE CONTENT

1. **Object**—To determine carbon diaoxide content of a building lime.

2. **Theory**—Chemically lime is oxide of calcium (Cao). It is the product obtained by calcination of limestones or other calcarious, substances, the effect of which is to drive off the carbonic acid and moisture they contain

$CaCO_3$ =	CaO +	CO_2
(limestone)	(Quicklime)	(Carbon dioxide)

Limestone may be burnt either in clamps or in kilns as in the case of bricks. Hydraulic lime may be manufactured either naturally by burning in kiln an impure limestone such as kankar not containing more than 30% of the clay with coal or charcoal as fuel or artificially by calcining a mixture of limestone and clay in correct proportions in a kiln. If the limestone used in the manufacture of hydraulic lime is soft, it is ground into powder and mixed with correct proportion of clay and then burnt in a kiln.

If the limestone is hard, it is generally burnt and slaked first and then mixed with the correct proportion of clay and reburnt. The burnt product is slaked with water or ground into a fine powder and screened before it is ready for use. A lime that is burnt twice is called twice klinked lime.

3. **Apparatus and Reagents**

(a) a suitable form of apparatus is shown in Fig. (8.1). The system consists of a U-tube A with anhydrous granulated calcium chloride and another U-tube B with soda asbestos, funnel C with a glass stopcock S and a bent inlet glass tube (projecting below the acid level) is used to introduce hydrochloric acid into the generating flask D. Condenser E condenses most of the water and hydrochloric acid. The U-tube F contains zinc pallets to react with residual acid, if any. Bubbler G contains concentrated sulphuric acid to absorb moisture. The U-tube H_1 contains pumice stone, impregnated with anhydrous copper sulphate to remove traces of hydrogen sulphide. Pumice stone is prepared by crushing it to approximately 5 mm size, shifting it free from dust and then transferring 60g of it to a casserole, it is then covered with a concentrated solution of 30 to 35 g of copper sulphate and then evaporated to dryness while stirring constantly. It is then heated for 3 to 4 hours at 150 to 160°C, cooled in a desiccator and preserved in a glass-stoppered bottle. U-tube H contains anhydrous granulated calcium chloride in one limb and anhyrous magnesium perchlorate in the other to remove the last traces of moisture. U-tubes, J_1 and J contain both soda asbestos and anhydrous magnesium perchlorate in each limb to absorb carbon diaoxide. U-tube K contains anhydrous granulated calcium chloride and anhydrous magnesium perchlorate in each limb to protect the end of the train against mosture. U-tubes are suspended from a cross bar N. Two retort stands L and M carry the cross bar N. All joints are made of stout-walled rubber tubing with the ends of the glass tubes touching each other. Means are provided to pass air through the system either under pressure or by suction.

(b) Dilute Hydrochloric Acid-1:4 (v/v). It shall be prepared by diluting hydrochloric acid (sp. gr. 1.16 and conforming to IS : 265-1962) four times its volume with water.

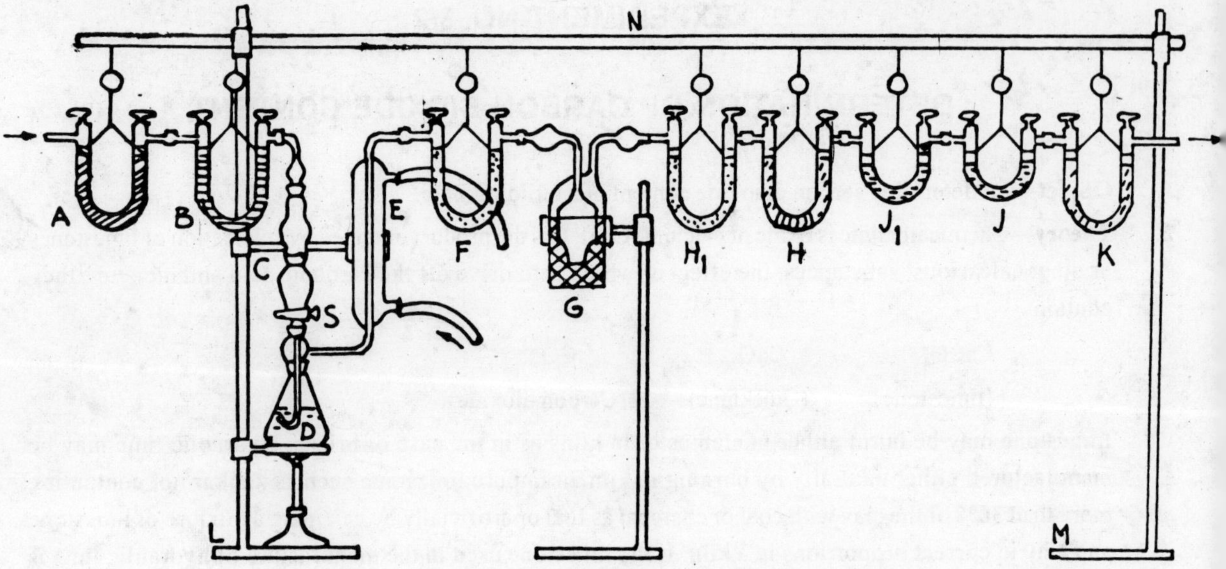

Fig. 8.1

Fig. 8.1

4. Procedure

Accurately weigh about 2.5g of the sample, transfer it into the flask D and add 20 to 40 ml of distilled water. Insert the glass stopper carrying the funnel arrangement and condenser and make sure that the apparatus is air-tight. Pass air through the system until the carbon dioxide absorption tubes, J_1 and J attain constant mass. Close the stopcock S and reconnect in the system the weighed carbon dioxide absorption tubes J_1 and J. Introduce 40 ml of hydrochloric acid into the flask D through funnel C and heat the flask carefully so that the gases pass through the sulphuric acid bubbler at a moderate rate. Allow the contents of the flask to boil after about 30 to 40 minutes. After 2 to 3 minutes of boiling remove the flame and connect the flask to scrubbers A and B by means of stopcock S and pass air through the system for 20 minutes at a moderate rate. Keep the absorption tubes J_1 and J at room temperature for 30 minutes and then weigh. The increase in mass denotes the carbon dioxide content in the sample.

5. Report of the test results

The carbon dioxide content shall be reported as a percentage of mass of the sample taken.

6. Precautions

(a) Prepare the reagents very carefully.

(b) All weighings should be done very accurately.

7. Questions

(a) What is the chemical composition of lime.

(b) How lime stone is burnt?

(c) How do you manufacture hydraulic lime.

(d) What is twice klinked lime.

EXPERIMENT NO. 8/3

SLAKING OF QUICK LIME

1. **Object**—To determine the residue on slaking of quick lime including isothermal slaking of the sample.

2. **Theory**—There are two ways of slaking lime :

(a) By sprinkling water uniformly over the heap of quicklime and then raking the heap thoroughly with kassi or Phaorah.

(b) By dipping quicklime in a basket for required time and throwing it in heaps on level ground.

Fat lime slakes readily and within two or three hours a large quantity may be slaked but hydraulic lime takes 12 to 48 hours in slaking according to the extent of their hydraulic properties. In the case of fat lime all the required water is added in the first instance and then water is added gradually till it slakes thoroughly. The quantity of water required for slaking varies with the purity and freshness of lime and is approximately between one third to one half of its bulk. A fresh lime requires more water than old lime.

3. **Isothermal slaking of sample and preparation of putty**

(a) The sample of quicklime shall be sieved through 2.36 mm IS sieve and the residue, if any, shall be broken in a manner so an to avoid undue production of fines and again sieved through 2.36 mm IS sieve until the whole quantity passes through that sieve. This sample of lime shall be slaked isothermally by immersing in hot water maintained at a substantially uniform temperature during the actual slaking process in accordance with method specified in (b). The quantity of water required for slaking shall be equal to 4 times the mass of quicklime for the majority of limes. However, with certain high calcium limes of high volume yield it may be found necessary to use 8 times the mass of the lime in order to obtain a product which could be conveniently handled.

(b) When a slaking temperature has been specified by the vendor, place a sufficient quantity of water as specified in (a) in a large clean metal vessel (for example, a large circular bin approximately 450 mm in diameter, and 500 mm deep) equipped with a thermometer reading to 1°C and with means for heating. Adjust the temperature of water to within ±2°C of the specified temperature, add 5 kg of the crushed quicklime sample in small quantities at a time, and then stir constantly and thoroughly at such a rate that not less than 5 minutes are required to introduce the whole quantity. During this process and a total period of 1 hours, control the temperature of the mixture to within ± 2°C of the specified isothermal temperature by the addition of cold water or by the application of heat. Spray through a rose, whilst stirring rapidly, any such additional water so as to avoid excessive local chilling of the mixture. Allow the product to stand for 24 hours from the time the quicklime was added to water and allow to cool gradually to room temperature during this period. Thoroughly stir it with a wooden stirrer at least twice during this period. The last stirring shall, however, be done within one hour before the expiration of the 24 hours.

Where a slaking temperature has not been specified by the vendor, carry out slaking on two separate quantities, each of 5 kg of crushed quicklime, but with the temperature of water adjusted to and maintained at 50°C in one case and 100±2°C in the other case.

4. **Procedure**

The product obtained after slaking on expiry of 24 hours shall be used. Sieve first the supernatant liquid and then the remainder after stirring thoroughly with a wooden stirrer through 850 - micron IS Sieve and then throgh 300 - micron IS Sieve into a vessel similar to that used for the slaking. Fit the vessel with a temporary filter cloth such as a rectangular sheet of close woven unbleached calico of

size about 1.0 ×1.5 m which has been previously washed free from dressing. Take special care to see that the contents of the slaking vessel are completely transferred on to the sieves by washing out the slaking vessel with a jet of water. Wash the residues on both the sieves with a moderate jet of water from a flexible tube, the whole operation taking not more than 30 minutes. The residue shall not be rubbed through the sieves. Dry the residue at 100 ± 10°C to constant mass. Weigh separately the residue on each of the sieves.

5. Report of test results

The residues on the respective sieves shall be reported as the percentage of mass of quicklime taken for the test.

6. Precautions

(a) Sieve the sample carefully.

(b) Control the temperature during salking by continuous stirring with a wooden stirer.

(c) All the weighings should be accurate.

7. Questions

(a) What do you mean by slaking of lime?

(b) What are the different methods of slaking

(c) Discuss the slaking properties of fatlime and hydraulic lime.

(e) Differentiate between fresh lime and old lime.

EXPERIMENT NO. 8/4

FINENESS

1. **Object**—To determine the finess of hydrated lime sample.
2. **Theory**—Pure limestones slake readily and fall into powder and are then ready for mixing with other ingredients to make mortar. But impure or hydraulic limes often do not slake at all and have to be ground to poweder after burning before they are used for mortar. Pulverizing may be done by hand using wooden beaters when quantity is small but when a large quantity is required, a mill worked by bullocks or steam power or a machine is usually employed.
3. **Preparation of sample and apparatus**

   (a) The sample for carrying out this test shall be prepared in accordance with clause 7.2 of IS : 712 - 1973 (Specifications for building limes).

   (b) The distilled water shall be used where use of water as a reagent is intended.

   (c) Set of IS Sieves conforming to IS : 460 - 1962.
4. **Procedure**

   The IS Sieves specified in the material specification shall be superimposed, one above the other with the coarser sieves at the top and finer sieves at the bottom. Holding the sieves in both hands, sieving shall be done with a gentle wrist motion, this will involve no danger of spilling the lime which shall be kept well spread out on the sieve. Place 100 g of th› hydrated lime on the top sieve and the material washed through the sieves with a moderate jet of water from a flexible tube, the whole operation shall not take more than 30 minutes. The residue on each sieve shall be dried at 100 ± 10°C to constant mass. The residue on each of the sieves shall be weighed.
5. **Report of test results**

   The result shall be expressed as a percentage of mass of the hydrated lime taken.
6. **Precautions**

   (a) Sieving should be done with a gentle wrist motion to avoid danger of spilling the sample.

   (b) Wash the residue left on the sieves after sieving with a modrate jet of water from a flexible tube.
7. **Questions**

   (a) What is the importance of this test?

   (b) How do you pulverize the lime sample?

   (c) What is the effect of pulverizing on the strength of mortar?

EXPERIMENT NO. 8/5

UNHYDRATED OXIDE CONTENTS

1. **Object**—To determine the unhydrated oxide contents of a building lime sample.
2. **Theory**—Lime obtained by calcining limestones are divided into following classes according to their action in slaking and setting :

(a) Rich, fat, common high calcium, air or pure lime.

(b) Lean, meagre or poor lime.

(c) Hydraulic or water lime :

(i) Slightly hydraulic lime.

(ii) Moderately hydraulic lime.

(iii) Eminently hydraulic lime.

(d) Hydraulic or water cement :

(i) Natural

(ii) Artificial

Pure lime contains clay from 0-5%. It slakes readily. It makes a good pase with water and dissolves in water frequently. Mortar of pure lime will never set or harden under water or in moist places, such as, foundations or interior of thick masonary walls where there is no free access of air.

Hydraulic lime contains clay from 12-25%. It slakes slowly with difficulty according to the clay content in it. It forms a thin paste with water and does not dissolve in water though frequently changed. Mortar prepared out of hydraulic lime will set rapidly in all moist places.

3. **Preparation of sample**

(a) The sample shall be slaked at a specified temperature of 25 ± 2°C. The quantity of water will be sufficient to make a stiff putty. The sample shall then be dried in vacuum till its mass becomes constant.

(b) Before carrying out the analysis, the hydrated lime sample shall be dried. For this purpose about 25gm of the sample shall be required to be kept in vacuum until its mass becomes constant.

4. **Apparatus**

(a) **Thermobalance**—The termobalance shall consist of an arrangement wherein the sample can be heated, automatically weighed at regular intervals and the temperature of heating and the mass of the sample can be automatically recorded.

(b) The arrangement for stopping the temperature rise at any point shall be provided within this set-up,

(c) **Crucible**—The crucible shall be made of a material which does not in any way react with lime up to 1400°C.

(d) **Support**—The support over which the crucible is mounted before sliding over into the furnace shall be made of sintered or fused alumina.

(e) **Furnace**—The furnace should be such that its temperature can be raised at a sufficient controllable rate to 1100°C, preferably 1400°C. This furnace may be raised and lowered as required with the help of a chain arrangement.

(f) **Autoclave**—The autoclave shall be made of a high pressure steam vessel provided with a thermometer well. The autoclave cover lid shall be equipped with a automatic pressure control and a safety valve device. A vent valve shall be provided on the lid of the autoclave so as to allow the steam to escape out whenever required. The pressure gauge shall have a dial with 114 mm diameter and shall be graduated from 0 to 4 N/mm^2 (0-40 kg/cm^2) with scale divisions of not more than 0.05 N/mm^2 (0.5 kg/cm^2). The heating may be controlled such that pressure of 2.1 N/mm^2 (21 kg/cm^2) can be obtained in 45 to 75 minutes. The autoclave shall be designed to permit the gauge pressure to drop from 2.1 N/mm^2 (21 kg/cm^2) to less 0.1 N/mm^2 (1kg/cm^2) in 1½ hours after the supply has been cut off.

5. **Procedure**

(a) Dry the hydrated magnesium lime powder in a vacuum desiccactor for 1 hour at a pressure of 0.00136 N/mm^2 (0.0136 kg/cm^2). Accurately wiegh 1.000g of the sample in a crucible and analyse thermogravimetrically at any heating rate less than 200°C/h. When the temperature reaches 380°C, discontinue the heating programme and keep the temperature constant until no further loss in mass takes place. Restart heating after 10 minutes and continue the programme until the mass finally becomes constant.

(b) Accurately weigh 1.000g portion from the dried hydrated magnesium lime sample in a platinum crucible. Cover this with another loosely fitting crucible. Place inside the autoclave. Heat the autoclave carefully to raise the pressure to 2.0746 N/mm^2 (20.746 kg/cm^2) in about 3 hours and keep it constant for another hour. Release the pressure gradually. Dry the crucible in vacuum, as previously, until the mass becomes constant. Transfer the contents of the platinum crucible into the small crucible quantitatively and analyse thermogravimetrically as before.

6. **Calculations**

(a) [Loss from (280 to 380)] $\frac{111}{100} \times 3.238$ = mass of $Mg(OH)_2$ in the hydrate = A

(b) Mass of $Mg(OH)_2$ in the autoclaved hydrate = B

(c) Increse in mass of $Mg(OH)_2$ = (B-A)

(d) Unhydrated MgO = (B-A) × 0.6920

B-Alternative method based on chemical analysis

1. The amount of unhydrated magnesium oxide in the sample may also be determined by the following alternative procedure.

2. **Principle of Method**

From the percentage of the loss on ignition, calcium oxide, magnesium oxide, carbon dioxide and sulphur trioxide, the value of unhydrated magnesium oxide may be calculated as given below.

3. **Determination of Sulphur Trioxide Content**

(a) Sample for analysis- The sample selected in accordance with 7.3 of IS : 712-1973 (Specifications for building limes) shall be used for analysis.

(b) Reagents

(i) Dilute hydrochloric acid	-	1 : 1 (v/v)
(ii) Barium chloride solution	-	10 percent (m/v)

4. **Procedure**

(a) Accurately weigh about 2.5g of the sample, transfer it into a beaker and add 10 ml of cold water. Stir with a glass rod to ensure that all lumps are broken. Add 20 ml dilute hydrochloric acid and heat carefully until the dissolution is complete. Filter through a small filter paper and wash the residue thoroughly with hot water.

(b) Dilute the filtrate to about 250 ml. Heat this solution carefully and bring it to boiling. Add 10 ml of hot barium chloride solution drop by drop with constant agitation. Boil for further 10 minutes. Stir well and allow to stand for overnight. Filter through filter paper No. 42 Whatman or its equivalent filter paper and wash with boiling water. Place the filter paper along with its contents in a weighed platinum crucible. Slowly incinerate the paper without inflaming. Ignite to constant mass and weigh as barium sulphate ($BaSo_4$). Multiply by 0.343 to get SO_3.

5. **Calculations**

(a) Subtract carbon dioxide from the loss on ignition. this gives the amount of chemically combined water (X).

(b) Calculate the calcium oxide equivalents of carbon dioxide and sulphur trioxide by multiplying their determined values by 1.275 and 0.700 respectively, and subtract the resultants from the total calcium oxide obtained by estimation. Calculate the water equivalent of the remaining calcium oxide by multiplying it with 0.3213 (Y).

(c) Subtract Y from X to obtain the remaining combined water (Z), and calculate the magnesium oxide equivalent to it by multiplying with 2.238.

(d) Subtract Z from the total magnesium oxide obtained by estimation. This gives the percentage of unhydrated magnesium oxide.

7. **Precautions**

(a) The heating should be controlled accurately so that the necessary pressures may be maintained.

(b) All weighings should be done accurately.

(c) Raise the pressure to desired level slowly and gradually.

8. **Questions**

(a) What is the importance of this test.

(b) State the different classes of building limes.

(c) Differentiate between pure lime and hydraulic lime.

(d) Which lime you will prefer, purelime or hydraulic lime.

EXPERIMENT NO. 8/6

VOLUME YIELD OF QUICK LIME

1. **Object**—To determine the volume yield of quicklime.
2. **Theory**—Quicklime or caustic lime (CaO) is the resulting lime as left immediately after calcination of a comparatively pure lime stone. It is amorphous, highly caustic, absorbs moisture quickly and has no affinity for carbonic acid. It remains in this state only for a short itme unless kept in a dry place.
3. **Apparatus**

(a) The Southard viscosimeter (Fig. 8.2) shall be used for adjusting the consistency of the putty and a vessel of the shape and dimensions shown in Fig. 8.4 shall be used for the determination of the volume yield. The Southard viscosimeter consists of the vertical metal cylinder 50 mm internal diameter equipped with a tight-fitting metal piston having a working stroke of 65 mm measured from the upper open end of the cylinder. The piston can be raised, without rotation by a coarse-thread pcam having threads passing through a nut at the lower closed end of the cylinder and gaging the piston on the lower side of the latter. In operation, the piston is lowered to the bottom of its stroke, the cylinder is filled carefully with the putty avoiding the inclusion of air bubbles, and the putty is struck off smooth at the top. The piston is then raised streadily by rotating the screw at the rate of one turn per second for 10 seconds, thus ejecting the contents of the cylinder vertically upwards. The degree to which the ejected cylinder of putty has slumped is then determined by measuring its present height by means of metal bridge or similar device. For this purpose it is convenient to provide the top of the cylinder with an extended external horizontal flange with a plane surface on which the bridge may be applied. The lime putty vessel used for determining the volume yield consists of a tinned iron cylindrical pot 63 ± 1 mm in diameter with a volume of 250 ml with soldered joints and a reinforced rim of brass, the upper edge being made plane.

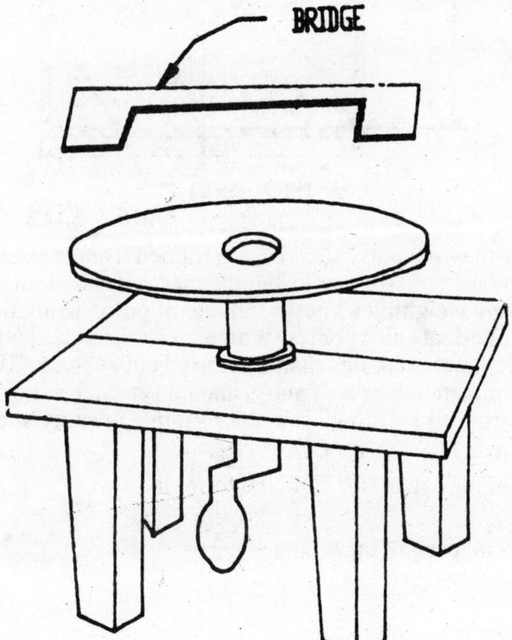

Fig. 8.2 Southard Viscosimeter

(b) Preparations of Sample for Test

Sufficient lime putty for the determination of volume yield be prepared after conducting the test described in (4) in experiment No. 8/3 and the ends of the filter cloth shall be folded together to form a bag and tied. This shall be suspended by cord above the vessel to allow the lime putty to drain. The bag shall be pressed by hand with moderate pressure to accelerate the process. The consistency of the putty adjusted to a standard value such that a slump of 13mm is obtained when tested in the Southard viscosimeter described under 3(a). The consistency of the putty shall be adjusted by trial by adding or substracting water and 'knocking up' thoroughly; mixing and working the material before each trial, and repeating until the required slump is obtained with a permissible deviation of not more than 2mm from the standard slump of 13mm. The viscosimeter shall be washed after each examination. A small mixer shall be used for the 'knocking up' of the material before each determination, the material being passed through twice. When the putty contains more water it shall be removed by placing the putty for a short period on a clean absorbent surface.

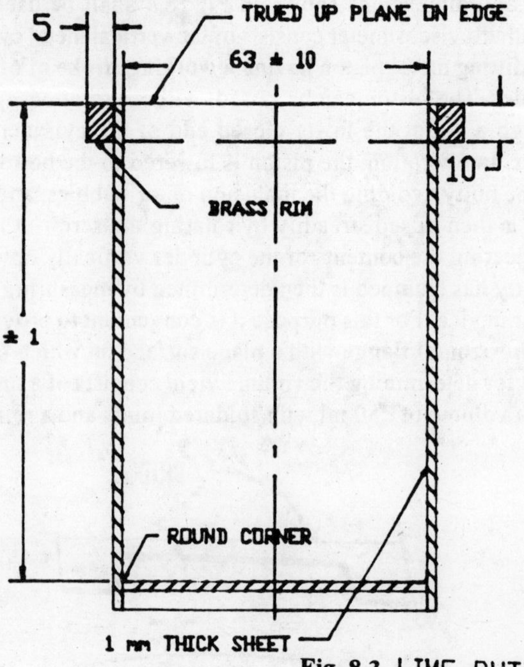

Fig. 8.3 LIME PUTTY DENSITY VESSEL

4. Procedure

The volume yield of the lime putty shall be determined from the density of a portion of the putty when adjusted to the standard consistency in the manner described under 3 (b). The density of the putty shall be determined by weighing a known volume of putty, using the density vessel shown in Fig. 8.3 care being taken to eliminate air bubbles. Where no isothermal slaking temperature has been specified by the vendor, the duplicate slakings shall be carried out at 50 and 100°C and after the determination of volume yields on duplicate samples of putty, that putty which exhibits the higher volume yield shall be chosen for the purpose of recording. The other sample of putty shall be discarded.

5. Report of test results

(a) The volume shall be calculated from the formula :

$$\text{Volume yield in ml per g of quicklime} = \frac{0{\cdot}70}{d-1}$$

where

d = density of the lime putty.

(b) The volume yield shall be expressed in ml/g of quicklime taken. Table 8.1 gives the volume of lime for different densities of lime putty for guidance.

Table 8.1

Volume yield of Quicklime for different densities of lime putty

Density d	Volume yielded	Density d	Volume yielded
(1)	(2)	(1)	(2)
	ml/g		ml/g
1.20	3.50	1.38	1.84
1.21	3.33	1.39	1.79
1.22	3.18	1.40	1.75
1.23	3.04	1.41	1.71
1.24	2.92	1.42	1.67
1.25	2.80	1.43	1.63
1.26	2.69	1.44	1.59
1.27	2.59	1.45	1.56
1.28	2.50	1.46	1.52
1.29	2.41	1.47	1.49
1.30	2.33	1.48	1.46
1.31	2.26	1.49	1.43
1.32	2.19	1.50	1.40
1.33	2.12	1.51	1.37
1.34	2.06	1.52	1.35
1.35	2.00	1.53	1.32
1.36	1.94	1.54	1.30
1.37	1.89	1.55	1.27

6. Precautions

(a) The consistency of the putty should be adjusted to a standard value such that a slump of 13 mm is obtained.

(b) Material should be knocked up in the mixer before each experiment.

(c) Remove air bubbles before starting each experiment.

7. Questions

(a) Explain the importance of this test.

(b) What do you mean by the terms quicklime and fatlime.

EXPERIMENT NO. 8/7

TRANSVERSE AND COMPRESSIVE STRENGTH

1. **Object**—To determine transverse strength and compressive strength of building limes.

2. **Theory**—Concrete is mostly used to resist compressive stresses. This compression may be due to axial compressive loads or compression developed due to end moments or due to the application of transverse loads on the structural elements compressive strength is also used as a measure of overall quality of the concrete and also is an indication of the other properties relating to the deformations and durability.

When concrete is subjected to bending tensile and bending compressive stresses and in many cases, direct shear stresses get developed. The best example is a highway pavement slab which gets subjected to flexure and the strength of concrete for pavements is commonly evaluated by means of bending tests. Bending test gives the flexural strength of the modulus of rupture of concrete in tension. The modulus of rupture of the test specimen is calculated as follows :

$$\sigma_t = \frac{3p \times 1}{2 \ bd^2}$$

Where σ_t = Modulus of rupture in kg/cm^2

P = Breaking loads in kg

1 = Span = 8 cm

b = Breadth of specimen = 2.5 cm

d = Depth of specimen = 2.5 cm

Substituting the above values

$$\sigma_t = \frac{3 \times p \times 80}{2 \times 25 \times (25)^2} = \frac{3 \times P \times 8}{2 \times 2 \cdot 5 \times (2 \cdot 5)^2}$$

$$= 0.768 \text{ P}$$

The value of σ_t should be more than 1N/mm^2 (10kg/cm^2 for class A and more than 0.7 N/mm (7kg/cm^2) for class B respectively.

3. **Preparation of standard lime-sand mortar (1:3)**

(a) The sand employed for the preparation of mortar shall conform to IS : 650-1971 (Specification for standard sand for testing of cement).

(b) The lime used for the preparation of the mortar shall be either hydrated lime or quicklime.

(c) **Adjusted Lime Putty**

(i) When hydrated lime is used, 500 g of the sample shall be throughly mixed with 60 to 65 percent of water for 5 minutes, and the resulting putty shall be passed twice through a mixer of the type shown in fig. 8.3 and used immediately for preparing the standard mortar. Mix 350 g of the putty with an amount of standard cement equal to 3 times the mass of the dry hydrate contained in it, that is, 636g to 656g. The balance of the putty shall be discarded. The lime putty and sand shall be thoroughly mixed for 10 minutes continuously, so as to form a uniform plastic mortar.

(ii) When quicklime is used about 1 kg of the sample shall be crushed to pass through 2.36 mm IS : 460-1962 Specifications for test sieves) and slaked isothermally for 1 hour as described in under (3) in IS sieve conforming to experiment No. 8/3. The resulting putty shall be stirred with a wooden rod and sieved through 850 micron IS Sieve and collected over a filter cloth as described in 3 (b) in experiment No. 8/6. The excess water shall be removed by folding the filter cloth in the form of a gag and pressing

moderately by hand. The consistency of the putty shall be adjusted by trial to a water content of 60 to 65 percent by mass of water of the mass of dry hydrated lime. The adjustment shall be carried out by subtracting any excess water from the filter cloth, for a short time on a clean absorbent surface, or alternatively, if oven dry, by adding a small quantity of water and mixing and knocking up thoroughly.

(iii) The proportion of water present can be determined by drying a weighed portion rapidly in a drying oven at 100 ± 10°C so that no significant amount of carbon dioxide is absorbed in the process, and weighing the dry residue when the loss in mass should be 60 to 65 percent of the mass of the dry residue, or by any convenient alternative method.

(iv) The adjusted lime putty shall be thoroughly mixed and knocked up and passed twice through a mixer and used immediately for preparing the mortar.

(v) Thoroughly mix 350 g of the putty with an amount of standard sand conforming to IS : 650-1971 (specification for standard sand for testing of cement) equal to 3 times the mass of the dry hydrate contained in it, that is, 636 to 656 g. The balance of the putty shall be discarded. The lime putty and sand shall be thoroughly mixed and knocked up for 10 minutes continuously, so as to form a uniform plastic mortar. The mortar so prepared shall be used immediately for filling the moulds for strength tests.

The whole operation starting from the slaking of the quicklime up to the filling of the moulds shall be carried out as expeditiously as possible.

4. TRANSVERSE STRENGTH

4.1 Preparation of test Specimen

(a) Six test specimens each 25 mm square in cross-section and 100 mm in length shall be prepared using the standard lime and mortar specified under 3.0. The mould used shall be an individual or gauge-mould of bronze or other suitable non-corrodible metal, and of internal dimensions 25 mm square and 100 mm long, the inner surface of the mould shall be carefully machined to a tolerance of ± 0.02 mm and the mould shall be so constructed that the specimens can be removed without the mould being tapped. The mould shall be well greased with petroleum jelly before use, and shall rest on a well-greased non-corrodible plate during the filling operations. The mould shall be filled by hand, the mortar being pressed in with the thumb, lightly tamped, and then smoothed off with two or three strokes of palette knife.

(b) The filled mould together with its base plate and covered on the top with a similar plate shall be stored for a period of 28 days undisturbed in a suitable container in a atmosphere at least 90 percent RH and at a temperature of 27 ± 2°C. A record shall be made of the temperature of storage on at least 24 days of the 28 days period. The maximum and minimum temperatures shall be read from time to time, in order to check any possible wide variations of temperature that may have occured whilst the apparatus was not under direct observation.

4.2 Procedure

After the expiry of the period of storage specified under 4.1 (b) the specimens shall be removed from the mould, care being taken not to injure them in any way during this process, and immersed in water for a period of half an hour. They shall be then removed and tested immediately for transverse strength. The specimens to betested shall rest symmetrically on their sides on two parallel metal rollers 40 mm in diameter and spaced at 80 mm centres. The load shall be applied through a third parallel roller of the same size at a point midway between the other two. No packing shall be used between the rollers and the specimen. The load shall be applied streadily and uniformly, starting from zero, and increased at a rate of 15 kg/min ± 10 percent.

4.3 Evaluation and Report of Test Results

(a) The modulus of rupture of the specimen is obtained by the formula :

$$\sigma_t = kP$$

where σ_t is the modulus of rupture, P is the total load and k is a facctor. The value of k is equal to 0.768 when the modulus of rupture is expressed in kg/cm² P in kg and the dimensions of the specimen in cm.

(b) The average of the 6 test specimens shall be taken as the modulus of rupture of the mortar and the result shall be expressed in N/mm²

5. COMPRESSIVE STRENGTH

5.1 Preparation of Test Specimens

Twelve cubes with side 50 mm shall be prepared from standard lime-sand mortar specified under 3.0 using bronze or other non-corrodible metallic moulds which shall be so designed as to prevent spreading during moulding. The inner surface of the moulds shall be carefully machined to a tolerance of ± 0.02 mm and the moudls shall be so constructed that the specimens can be removed without tapping them. The moulds shall be filled by hand, the mortar being pressed in with the thumb, lightly tamped, smoothed off with two or three strokes of the twoel or palette knife stored undisturbed in a suitable container for a period of 72 hours in an atmosphere of at least 90 percent RH and at a temperature of 27 ± 2°C. After the expiry of this period the specimens shall be taken out of the moulds and placed in the air in the laboratory for 4 days. When 7 days old, the specimesn shall be immersed in clean water and left there until just prior to testing for its strength in the testing machine. The water shall be renewed every 3 days maintained at a temperature of 27 ± 2°C.

5.2 Procedure

(a) After 7 days of storage in water (and in the case of Class B limes, under moist sand) 6 of the cubes shall be taken out of water, wiped surface-dry and tested for compressive strength in a compression testing machine. This gives the strength at 14 days. Those faces of the cube specimen which when moulded were in contact with the sides of the mould shall be placed in contact with the surface through which load is applied. There shall be no packing between the cube and steel platens of the testing machine. One of the platens shall be carried on the ball and shall be self adjusting. The load shall be steadily and uniformly applied, starting from zero increasing at the rate of 15 kg/min.

(b) The remaining 6 test specimens shall be taken out after 21 days and similarly tested thus determining the compressive strength at 28 days.

5.3 Evaluation and Report of Test Results

The crushing load divided by the area over which the load is applied denotes the Compressive strength of the mortar. The average strength of the six specimens shall be taken as the compressive strength of the mortar and the result expressed in kg/cm².

6.0 Precautions

(a) The samples while under curing in water should not be disturbed till the time of testing.

(b) Why building lime should be tested for transverse strength ?

(c) Why do you test building lime for compression?

(d) What are different classifications of building lime as per Bureau of Indian Standards?

(e) What is the period at which building lime is tested :

(i) For compressive strength

(ii) For Transverse strength

(f) Quote the standard values for the above two strengths as advocated by the relevant Indian Standard Code.

EXPERIMENT NO. 8/8

TEST FOR WORKABILITY

1. **Object**—To determine workablity of building lime.

2. **Theory**—Concrete is said to be workable if it can be easily mixed, placed, compacted and easily finished. A workable concrete should not show any segregation or bleeding. Segregation is said to occur when coarse aggregate tries to separate out from the finer material and coarase aggregate gets concentrated at one place. This results in large voids, less durability and less strength. Bleeding of concrete occurs whenexcess water comes up at the surface of the concrete. This creates small pores in the concrete mass and should be avoided.

   Flow table method specifies the procedure for the use of the flowtable to determine the fludity of concrete. It also gives an indication of the consistency of concrete and its tendency to segregation by measuring the spread of a pile of concrete subjected to jolting. It is with regard to segregation that the flow test is of greatest value but it also gives a good assessment of consistence of stiff, rich and rather cohesive mixes.

   In the field this test can be performed by throwing a handful of mortar on the surface where it is to be used. The area covered by the mortar and the amount of mortar picked up gives the indication of the suitability of various ingredients in lime mortar namely lime, sand and water with or without cement, surkhi etc.

3. **Apparatus**

   (a) The apparatus shall consist of a standard flow table and a truncated conical metallic mould (See Fig. 8.4). The standard flow table shall consist essentially of a horizontal smooth table top made of mild steel, ground and polished on the surface. The table top shall be 300 mm diameter and 3 mm thick mounted on a vertical shaft, which can be raised and then allowed to fall freely by a cam, the fall being exactly 12.5 mm. A cast iron rim 25 mm square in cross-section and 30 mm external diameter shall have securely fixed under the edge of the table top with 6 rivets spaced symmetrically apart. Three circles having diameters of 70, 110 and 190 mm respectively shall be engraved on the surface of the table and concentric with it. The engraved lines shall be filled with wax polished flush with the surface of the metal. The length of fall shall be as defined by a shoulder on the shaft coming in contact with the top of the cast iron to steel body of the instrument, the contact being, therefore, metal to metal. The total mass of the moving part (table top, loading rim, shift, etc) free to fall, shall be approximately 7 kg. The mass of the body, with cam shaft and cam handle, etc. shall be approximately 19 kg.

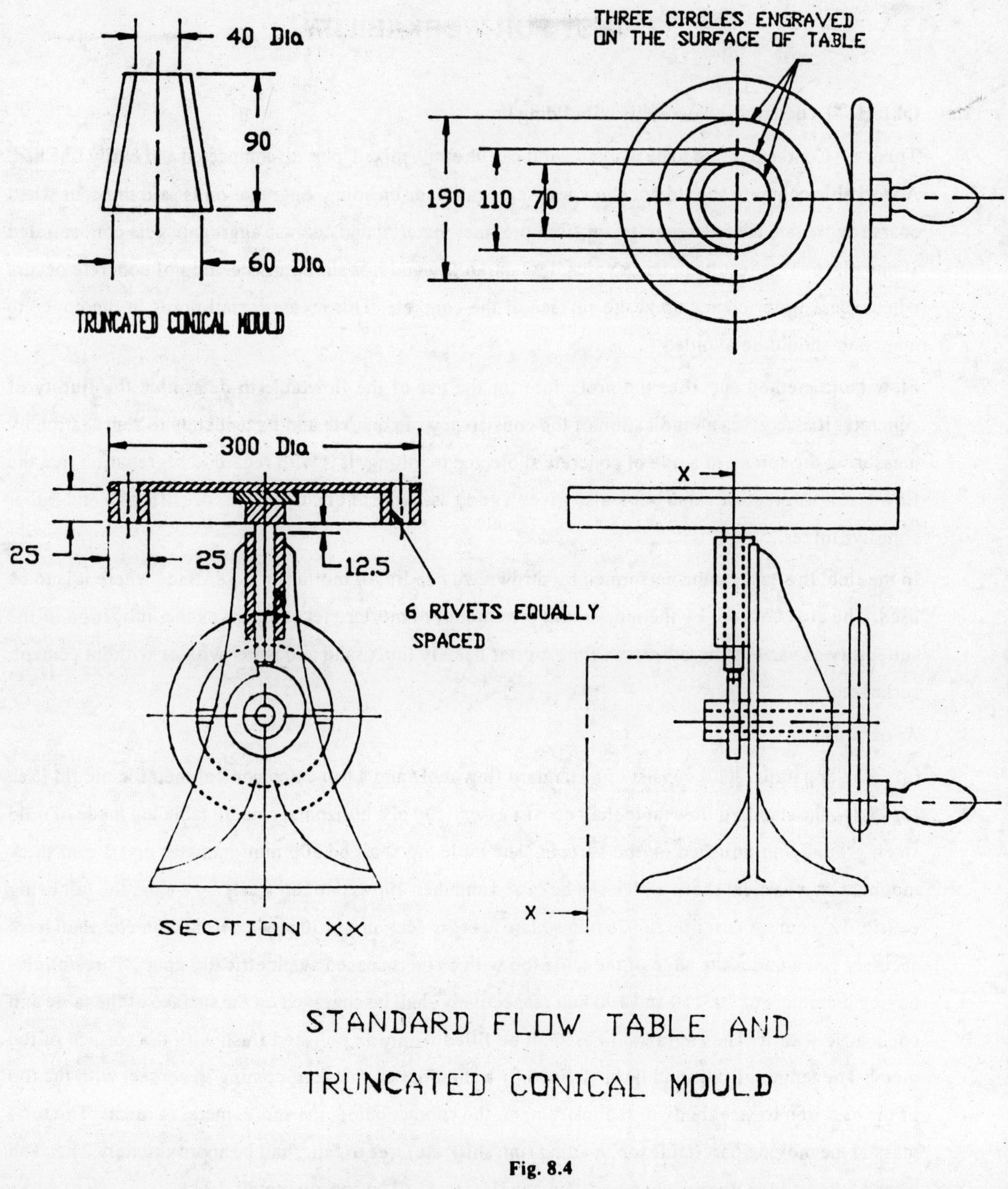
40 Dia
90
60 Dia
TRUNCATED CONICAL MOULD
THREE CIRCLES ENGRAVED
ON THE SURFACE OF TABLE
190 110 70
300 Dia
25
25
12.5
6 RIVETS EQUALLY
SPACED
X
SECTION XX
X
STANDARD FLOW TABLE AND
TRUNCATED CONICAL MOULD

Fig. 8.4

(b) The flow table shall stand unattached in the centre of a brick, stone of concrete pier at least 350 mm square, built on a firm foundation, and upon which the base of the table shall stand firmly without any trace of rocking or chattering. The height of the pier shall be 800 mm and its top shall consist of 50 mm thick sand-cement mortar (3:1) with its surface finished smooth with a steel trowel.

(c) The mould for preparing the test specimen shall consist of a truncated conical mould of sheet metal with internal diameter of 40mm at its narrower end, an internal diameter of 65 mm at its wider end and 90mm in height. Its inside and the ends shall be smooth. In addition, the ends shall be plane.

4. Preparation of sample

(a) In case of quicklime the putty shall be prepared in accordance with 3 (b) of expriment No. 8/6.

(b) In the case of hydrated lime, the lime putty shall be prepared by thoroughly mixing the hydrated lime with an equal mass of clean water at a temperature of 27 ± 2°C, 24 hours before the subsequent operations. A convenient quantity of hydrated lime to be taken for this purpose shall be 500 g. At the expiry of 24 hours the soaked material shall be thoroughly mixed and knocked up to produce a plastic putty. A mixer shall be used for the 'knocking up', the material beign passed twice through this mixer.

(c) The specimen of material for testing shall be prepared by filling the metallic mould specified under 3 (c) such that no air bubbles or voids are retained inside. Before each test the mould shall be rinsed out with clean water, allowed to drain and shaken to remove superfluous water.

(d) The lime putty prepared in accordance with 4 (a) and 4 (b) shall be adjusted to standard plastering consistency, which shall be that indicated by an average spread of the lower part of the lime putty to 110 mm with a permissible deivation of not more than 1 mm when subjected to one bump on the standard flow table. When first tested, if the consistency is too stiff, more water shall be added, and if too wet, a small portion of the water shall be withdrawn by placing the material for a short period on a clean absorbent surface. The test for workability shall then be carried out immediately as described in 6.0.

5. Temperature for testing

The temperature of the material under test and of the flow table and immediate surroundings shall be maintained at 27 ±2°C during the test.

6. Procedure

(a) The shaft and shoulder of the standard flow table shall be carefully wiped clean and the shaft oiled with a few drops of thin mineral oil. The top of the table shall be clean and completely dry. The cone of material prepared in accordance with 4 (c) shall be applied to the centre of the table with the aid of the mould and the mould carefully withdrawn. No substantial amount of the material under test shall remain adhering to the interior of the mould after removal. Otherwise the test shall be invalidated and shall be repeated.

(b) The handle of the flow table shall be turned steadily and evenly at the rate of approximately one turn per second, without jerking or lingering at any point in a revolution. The average spread of the material shall be determined by measuring three diameters at approximately 60° apart and taking the average. Care shall be taken to avoid any undue exposure of the material.

7. Evaluation

The workability shall be estimated by noting the number of bumps required to attain an average spread to 190 mm, the material having been already adjusted to standard consistency as indicated under 4 (d) by the spread after one bump to 110 mm

8. Precautions

(a) The shaft and shoulder of the standard flowtable shall be carefully wiped clean.

(b) The shaft should be oiled with a few drops of thin mineral oil.

(c) The top of the flow table shall be clean and completely dry before starting the experiment.

(d) No substantial amount of the material under test shall remain adhering to the interior of the mould after removal.

9. Questions

(a) What do you understand by the term workability?

(b) Explain the importance of this test.

(c) Differentiate between workability, flowability and consistency.

EXPERIMENT NO. 8/9

TEST FOR SOUNDNESS

1. **Object**—To determine soundness of a building lime sample.

2. **Theory**—Unsoundness of building lime may be due to general expansion caused by the inclusion of a large number of fine particles of slow slaking materials. These materials slake and expand slowly and so produce an increase in volume.

   In the soundness test, the test specimen of building lime, cement and standard sand is exposed to steam for a fixed time so that any tendency to expand is speeded up and can be detected.

3. **Apparatus**

   The appratus for conducting the 'Le-Chatelier' test shall as shown in Fig 1.3.

4. **Preparation of sample for test**

   A suitable amount of hydrated lime shall be mixed with one-third its mass of Portland cement and 4 times its mass of standard sand. The ingredients shall be mixed dry and then gauged and mixed with 12 percent by mass of water calculated on the dry mixture. It shall then be used for conducting the test.

5. **Procedure**

   Three 'Le-Chatelier' moulds shall be used for conducting the test. These shall be well greased internally. Each mould shall be placed upon a small non-porous plate and filled with the mortar under test, care being taken to keep the edges visibly open. The mould shall then be covered with another non-porous plate, upon which a small weight shall be placed. The 3 moulds shall be left undisturbed for 1 hour. At the expiration of this period the distance separating the indicator points shall be measured and these moulds transferred to a damp air cupboard for a period of 48 hours. They shall then be removed, with covers in place, from the damp air cupboard and placed in a suitable steam boiler, in which water is already boiling vigorously, and subjected to the continuous action of saturated steam at atmospheric pressure for a period of 3 hours; but is shall not be immersed in water. At the end of this period, the moulds shall be removed from the steam and allowed to cool and the distances between the indicator points again measured. The increase, if any, over the former measurement shall in no case exceed 10 mm after the deduction of 1 mm (to allow for the expansion of the added cement) from the measured expansion. The figure so obtained shall be recorded as the net expansion due to lime.

6. **Report of test result**

   Soundness of the sample = minutes.

7. **Precautions**

   (a) Moulds should be well greased internally.

   (b) Measure the distance between the indicator points accurately.

8. **Questions**

   (a) What is the importance of this test?

   (b) What is the Indian Standard value for soundness for building limes ?

   (c) Do we mix cement while casting the sample for this test.

   (d) How do you account for the cement which was added at the time of casting, when you calculate soundness.

   (e) Why do you say, the building lime sample is not sound.

EXPERIMENT NO. 8/10

TEST FOR POPPING AND PITTING

1. **Object**—To determine popping and pitting of a building lime sample.
2. **Theory**—This test is also a measure to study the unsoundness of building limes. Popping, pitting and blowing are due to the presence of coarse unslaked or only partially slaked particles. On final slaking, these cause dislodgement of pieces on the surface of the plaster, usually in the form of a cone.

   In this test pats are prepared by mixing 70 gms of hydrated lime with 70 ml of water and 10 gms of plaster of paris. They are subjected to steam action and examined for disintegration, popping and pitting. Any of these occurances is an indication of unsoundness of lime.
3. **Preparation of sample**

   Gauging Plaster

   The gauging plaster used for popping and pitting test when gauged with 50 percent of its own mass of distilled water and tested by the Vicat needle shall have an initial setting time of not less than 15 minutes. The gauging plaster shall be free from pops and pits. Fresh, fine, white and good quality plaster of Paris which shows no pops or pits when tested without lime may be used.
4. **Procedure**

   (a) Four test specimens shall be separately prepared in the manner described under.

   (b) Mix thoroughly 70 g of the hydrated lime under test with 70 ml of clean water at a temperature 27 ± 3° and allow to soak for 2 hours.

   (c) At the expiration of 2 hours, the lime putty thus obtained shall be thoroughly mixed and 'knocked up' with a twoel, if necessary, with a small additional amount of clean water, so as to obtain a plastic mass; it shall then be spread out on a non-porous surface. 10 g of approved grade plaster of Paris shall then be added, the plaster being scattered evenly over the putty, and the whole shall be mixed with the trowel rapidly and thoroughly for 2 minutes.

   (d) A flat pat shall then be formed by pressing the gauged material into a ring mould 100 mm in diameter and 5 mm deep, greased inside and resting on a well greased non-porous plate. One gram of petroleum jelly, perpat is suitable for greasing when renewed each time.

   (e) The gauged putty shall be pressed in small quantities at a time, with the aid of a broad palette knife or spatula, in such a manner as to avoid air bubbles. It shall then be smoothed off in level with the top edge of the ring with not more than 12 strokes of the knife, any excess material being removed in this process. The total time shall not exceed 5 minutes from the time of adding the plaster of Paris to the last stroke of the knife for any one pat.

   (f) The 4 pats thus formed shall be left to set for half an hour. They shall then be transferred on their base-plates with or without their ring mould to a well ventilated drying-oven maintained at a temperature between 35 and 45°C to be well dried. A period or periods amounting to a total of 16 hours should be ample for this purpose but a minimum of 4 hours suffices in many cases.

   (g) The pats may be left in the oven either before drying or between the periods of drying.

   (h) Any test pats which show shrinkage cracks before steaming shall be rejected and replaced by fresh pats.

   (i) The 4 pats, still on their base-plates, shall be placed horizontally in a suitable steam boiler in which the water is already boiling, and subjected to the action of saturated steam at atmospheric pressure for a period of 3 hours. The steaming vessel shall be so arranged that condensed water cannot drip back on to the face of the pats.

5. Report

The pats shall then be examined in a good light for disintegration, popping or pitting.

6. Precautions

(a) Ring mould and non porous plate should be greased uniformly with petroleum Jelly.

(b) Press the putty in the ring mould with a broad spatula avoiding the entry of air bubbles.

7. Questions

(a) What do you understand by popping of building lime?

(b) Explain the term pitting of building lime?

(c) Why do you perform this test?

EXPERIMENT NO. 8/11

INITIAL AND FINAL SETTING TIMES

1. **Objects**—To determine the initial and final setting times of hydrated lime.
2. **Theory**—It is essential that lime sets neither too rapidly nor too slowly. Setting of paste undergoes, as time passes. It should not gain in mechnical strength after the paste has solidified. The setting test measures the time taken for the lime paste to offer a certain degree of resistance to the penetration of a special attachment pressed into a lime paste. Two periods of lime are used to assess the setting behaviour. These are called initial setting time and the final setting time.
3. **Apparatus**-The vicat apparatus as shown in Fig. 1.2 shall be used.
4. **Procedure**

(a) The sample shall be in the form of putty and shall be prepared in accordance with 4 (d) of experiment No. 8/8.

(b) Fill the vicat mould E with this paste, the mould resting upon a non-porous plate. After completely filling the mould, smooth off the surface of the paste, making it level with the top of the mould. The mould shall be slighlty shaken to expel the entrapped air.

(c) Clean appliances shall be used for gauging and the temperature of lime, water and that of the test room at the time when above operations are performed shall be 27 ±2°C and in an atmosphere of at least 90 percent relative humidity and away from draughts.

(d) **Determination of Initial Setting Time**

Place the test block prepared in accordance with 4 (a) under the rod bearing the needle (C); lower the needle gently in contact with the surface of the test block and quickly release, allowing it to penetrate into the test block. In the beginning, the needle will completely pierce the test block. Repeat this procedure until the needle, when brought in contact with the test block and released as described above, fails to pierce the block by 5 ± 0.5 mm measured from the bottom of the mould. The period elapsing between the time when water is added to the lime and the time at which the needle fails to pierce the test block by 5 ± 0.5 mm shall be the initial setting time.

(e) **Determination of Final Setting Time**

Replace the needle (C) of the Vicat apparatus by the needle with an annular attachment (F). The lime shall be considered as finally set when, upon applying the needle gently to the surface of test block, the needle makes an impression on the surface of test block while the attachment fails to do so shall be the final setting time. In the event of a scum forming on the surface of the test block, use the underside of the block for the determination.

5. **Results**

(a) Initial setting time of lime = Mints.

(b) Final setting time of lime = Mints.

6. **Precautions**

(a) Release the initial and final setting time needles gently.

(b) The experiment should be performed away from vibrations and other disturbances.

7. **Questions**

(a) Explain the importance of above tests.

(b) What are the IS Specifications for initial and final setting times for building lime.

(c) Differentiate between setting and hardening.

REFERENCES

1. IS : 6932 (Part-I) - 1973 - Methods of tests for determination of (i) insoluble residue (ii) loss on ignition (iii) silicon dioxide, (iv) Ferric and aluminium oxide (v) Calcium oxide and (vi) Magnesium oxide. Bureau of Indian standards (BIS), New Delhi.
2. IS : 6932 - (Part-II) - 1973 - Method of test for determination of carbon dioxide content of building lime. BIS, New Delhi.
3. IS : 6932 (Part-III) - 1973 - Method of test for determination of residue on slaking of quicklime including isothermal slaking of the sample. BIS, New Delhi.
4. IS : 6932 (Part-IV) - 1973 - Procedure for determination for fineness of hydrated lime. BIS, New Delhi.
5. IS : 6932 (Part V) - 1973 - Method of test for determination of unhydrated oxide cotents of building lime. BIS, New Delhi.
6. IS : 6932 (Part VI) - 1973 - Method of test for determination of volume yield of quicklime. BIS, New Delhi.
7. IS : 6932 (Part-VII) - 1973 – Method of test for determination of compressive and treansverse-strength of building lime. BIS, New Delhi.
8. IS : 6932 (Part-VIII) - 1973 - Method of test for determination of workability of building lime. BIS, New Delhi.
9. IS : 6932 (Part-IX) - 1973 - Method of test for determination of soundness of building limes. BIS, New Delhi.
10. IS : 6932 (Part-X) - 1973 - Method of test for determination of propping and pitting of hydrated lime. BIS, New Delhi.
11. IS : 6932 (Part-XI) - 1973 - Method of test for determination of setting times of hydrated lime. BIS, New Delhi.
12. IS : 712 - 1973 - Specifications for building limes. BIS, New Delhi.
13. IS : 1070 - 1960 - Specifications for water, distilled quality. BIS, New Delhi.
14. IS : 265 - 1962 - Specification for hydrochloric acid. BIS, New Delhi.
15. IS : 296 - 1965 - Specification for sodium carbonate anhydrous. BIS, New Delhi.
16. IS : 266 - 1966 - Specification for sulphuric acid. BIS, New Delhi.
17. IS : 264 - 1968 - Specification for nitric acid. BIS, New Delhi.
18. IS : 799 - 1955 - Specification for ammonia, liquor, technical. BIS, New Delhi.
19. IS : 5949 - 1970 - Method for volumetric determination of calcium and magnesium using EDTA. BIS, New Delhi.
20. IS : 460 - 1962 - Specification for test sieves. BIS, New Delhi.
21. IS : 1625 - 1971 - Code of practice for preparation of lime mortar for use in buildings. BIS, New Delhi.
22. IS : 650 - 1971 - Specification for standard sand for testing of cement. BIS, New Delhi.
23. IS : 5514 - 1969 - Specification for apparatus used in Le-Chatelier test. BIS, New Delhi.
24. IS : 269 - 1967 - Specification for ordinary, rapid hardening and low heat portland cement. BIS, New Delhi.
25. IS : 4031 - 1968 - Methods of physical tests for hydraulic Cement. BIS, New Delhi.
26. K.P. Roy Choudhary - Engineering Materials. Published by Oxford and IBH Publishing House Co. Pvt. Ltd. New Delhi.
27. S. Rajaraman - "Building Materials". Published by Modern Book stall, Poona.

APPENDIX—A

1. SPECIFICATIONS FOR CEMENT—Physical requirements as per Indian Standard Specifications

Type of cement		Ordinary Portland	Rapid Hardening	Low heat Portland	Portland Blast furnace Slag	Portland Pozzolana	High Alumina	Super Sulphate	High Strength Ordinary Portland
1	2	3	4	5	6	7	8	9	10
Details of test	Specification	269-1976	804 IE—76	269-1976	455-1967	1489-1976	6452-1972	6909-1973	8112-76
Fineness	Residue by weight on 90 micron IS sieve-Not more than %	10	—	—	10	—	—	—	—
	Min specific Surface (Blain's air permeability) cm^2/gm	2250	3250	3250	2250	3000	2250	4000	3500
Soundness	Expansion (Lechatelier) Not more than mm	10	10	10	10	10	5	5	10
	Auto clave-Not more than %	0.8	0.8	0.8	0.8	0.8	—	—	0.8

1	2	3	4	5	6	7	8	9	10
Min Compre-ssive strength N/mm^2 (Kg/cm^2)	24 Hours	–	16(160)	–	–	–	30(300)	–	–
	72 Hours	16(160)	27.5(275)	10(160)	16(160)		35(350)	15(150)	23(230)
	168 Hours	22(220)	–	16(160)	22(220)	22(220)	–	22(220)	33(330)
	672 Hours	–	–	35(350)	–	31(310)	–	30(300)	43(430)
Setting time	Initial (min.) Final (Max.)	30 600	60 600	60 600	30 600	30 600	30 600	30 600	30 600
Heat of Hydration	–	–	–	Heat of hydration to be not more than 65 cal/gm at 7 days and 75 cal/gm at 28 days.	–	Average drying shrinkage of moretars to be not more than 0.15%	–	–	–
Specific gravity	3.15	–	–	–	–	–	–	–	–

2.0 Indian Standard specifications for cements (Chemical requirements)

Type of cement	*Ordinary and rapid-hardening Portland*	*Low heat Portland*	*Portland blast-furnace slag*	*Portland pozzolana*	*High alumina*	*Supersulphated*
Indian Stardard	*269-1967*	*269-1967*	*455-1967*	*1489-1967*	*6452-1972*	*6909-1973*
			Maximum permissible values			
Insoluble residue	2.0%	2.0%	$(x'+0.025)+2.0$	$x^{*}+\frac{2.0(100-x)}{100}$	—	4%
Magnesia (Mg0)	6%	6%	8%	6%	—	10%
Sulphur as sulphuric anhydride ($S0_3$)	2.75%	2.75%	3%	2.75%	—	6%
as sulphide (S)	—	—	1.5%	—	—	1.5%
Magnacie oxide (Mn_20_3)	—	—	2%	—	—	—
Loss on ignition	4%	4%	4%	5%	—	—

* where x is the declared percentage of pozzolana in the given cement.

x' is the declared percengate of granulated blastfurnace slag in the cement.

Chemical composition

(a) Ordinary and rapid-hardening Portland

$$\frac{Ca0 - 0.7\ S0_3}{2.8\ Si0_2 + 1.2Al_20_3 + 0.65\ Fe_20_3} \ngtr 1.02, \nless 0.66$$

The percentage of alumina to that of iron oxide to be not less than 0.66 per cent.

(b) Low heat Porland

$$\frac{Ca0}{2.4Si0_2 + 1.2Al_20_3 + 0.65\ Fe_20_3} \ngtr 1.0$$

$$\frac{Ca0}{1.9Si0_2 + 1.2Al_20_3 + 0.6\ Fe_20_3} \nless 1.0$$

Ca0 representing the percentage of lime after deducting that necessary to combine with the sulphuric anhydride ($S0_3$) percent.

The percentage of alumina to that of iron oxide to be not less than 0.66 per cent.

(c) Portland blastfurnance slag

The chemical composition of the Portland cement clinker portion of the mixture of comply in all respects with the requirements of IS : 269-1967.

The chemical composition of granulated blast-furnace slag to be such as to satisfy the following formulae :

$$\frac{CaO + MgO + \frac{1}{3}Al_2O_3}{SiO_2 + \frac{2}{3}Al_2O_3} \geq 1$$

$$\frac{CaO + MgO + Al_2O_3}{SiO_2} \geq 1$$

$$\frac{CaO + CaS + \frac{1}{2}MgO + Al_2O_3}{SiO_2 + MnO} \geq 1.5$$

The proportion of slag to be not less than 25 per cent and not more than 65 per cent by weight of cement.

(d) Portland-Pozzolana

The Portland cement clinker used in the manufacture of Portland-pozzolana cement to comply in all respects with the chemical requirements of IS : 269-1967. When Portland-pozzolana cement is obtained by blending pozzolana with Portland cement, the latter will comply with the requirements of IS : 269-1967

The pozzolanic constituents to be not less than 10 per cent and not more than 25 percent by weight of Portland-pozzolana cement.

(e) High alumina

The total alumina content (Al_2O_3) to be not than 32 percent by weight.

(f) Supersulphated

The chemical composition of granulated blastfurnace slag to be such as to satisfy the formulae under (c) above, for which silicon dioxide (SiO_2) ranges from 27 to 32 percent, aluminium oxide (Al_2O_3) from to 31 percent, ferrous oxide (FeO) from 0 to 1 percent, calcium oxide (CaO) from 30 to 40 percent, magnesium oxide (MgO) from 0 to 17 percent, and sulphide sulphur (S) from 0 to 2 percent.

3. Specific gravity, Bulk Density and Voids of Different types of Aggregates.

(a) Specific Gravity

(i) Trap	2.9
(ii) Granite	2.8
(iii) Gravel	2.66
(iv) Sand	2.63

(b) Bulk Density (Kg./litre)

(i) River sand	
(a) Fine	1.44
(b) Medium	1.52
(c) Coarse	1.60
(ii) Beach or river Shingle	1.60
(iii) Broken Stone	1.60
(iv) Stone screenings	1.44
(v) Broken granite	1.68

(c) Voids (Percent)

(i) Cement 50

(ii) River Sand

(a) Fine 43

(b) Coarse 35

(c) Mixed and dry 30

(d) Mixed and Moist 38

(iii) Broken Stone graded

(a) 25mm maximum size 46

(b) 50mm maximum size 45

(c) 36mm maximum size 41

(iv) Stone screeings 48

4. Surface Water and Absorption of Aggregates

(a) Surface Water in Aggregates :

The approximate quantity of surface waer in 1 kilo litre of average aggregates may be assumed to be as follows :

(i) Very wet sand 120 to 160 litres

(ii) Moderatly wet sand 80 litres

(iii) Moist sand 40 litres

(iv) Moist gravel or crushed rock 20 to 40 litres

The coarser the aggregate, the lesser the free water carried by it.

(b) Absorption of Aggregates :

The approximate quantity of moisture absorbed by weight by various aggregates may be assumed as follows :

(i) Average sand 1.0 percent

(ii) Pebbles and crushed lime stone 1.0 percent

(iii) Trap rock and granite 0.5 percent

(iv) Porous sand stone 7.0 percent

Very light and porous aggregates may absorb as much as 25 percent of moisture by weight.

(c) Bulking of Sands for various Moisture contents :

Moisture Percent	*Percentage bulking in*		
	Fine Sand	*Medium Sand*	*Coarse Sand*
1	16	8	6
2	26	16	12
3	32	22	15
4	36	27	17
5	38	29	18

Percent	Fine Sand	Medium Sand	Coarse Sand
6	37	28	18
8	35	26	16
10	32	22	12
12	28	19	8
15	22	12	2
17	18	7	0
20	9	0	0
27	0	0	0

5. Recommended Mixes for various Types of Constructions

Sr. No.	*Type of work*	*Recommended mix by volume*
1.	Long span arches, heavily loaded columns	1:1:2
2.	Heavily stressed members, small precast works such as posts and poles for fencing, telegraphs, signals, garden furniture and decorative and other items of work of very thin sections, water tight construction for high heads, long piles etc.	1:2:2
3.	Columns and members subjected to medium loads, Walls and floors of reservoirs and tanks, cisterns, sewers, well kerbs, platforms and other water tight constructions for moderate heads, non-surfaced roof slabs, concrete desposited under water	1:2:3 or 1:1.67:3.33
4.	General building work subjected to ordinary stresses such as beams, slabs, columns panel walls, basement and retaining walls, stairs, lintels and sills, roads, pavements drive ways and side walls, floors, steps, bunkers and silos, bridges, dams and piers etc. exposed to action of water and frost, machine foundations, subjected to vibrations, footings, piles.	1:2:4
5.	Mass concrete work in culverts, retaining walls, compound walls and ordinary machine bases, foundation walls which need not be water tight	1:3:6
6.	Mass concrete for heavy walls, foundations under column footings and under heavy duty floors	1:4:8

6. Precentage Strength of Concrete at various Ages

The strength of concrete increases with the age of concrete. This increase in strength may continue even upto one year, but the basis of design is usually considered as the strength obtained at the age of 28 days after placing the concrete.

The precentages increase in strength for ordinary portland cement concrete at different ages in comparison with the strength at 28 days are approximately as follows :

Sl. No.	*Age of Concrete*	*Strength (Percent)*
1	1 day	16
2	3 days	40
3	7 days	67
4	28 days	100
5	3 months	122
6	6 months	146
7	1 year	155

7. Estimation of Quantities for a concrete mix.

The quantities of dry materials are calculated on the basis that the volume of concrete to be produced will be equal to the sum of volume of water and volume of solid matter contained in cement and aggregates. The amount of water to be added is estimated from the following thumb rule provided the concrete is to be compacted by hand.

$$\text{Weight of water} = \frac{1}{3}\text{ (Weight of cement)} + \frac{1}{20}\text{ (combined weight of dry aggregates)}$$

If the mix is to be compacted by using a vibrator, use 15% less water.

Example—Calculate the quantities of materials for a nominal mix of 1:2:4 to be prepared and compated by hand. The percentage of voids to total volume of cement, sand and broken stone having maximum size 25 mm may be taken as 50%, 43% and 46% respectively. The sand is damp and contains 2% moisture and the stone ballast contains 1% moisture by weight.

Solution :

For one bag of cement weighing 500 N (50 kg.) (35.4 litre or 0.0354 cubic meter), the quantities of ingredients are :

Total number of parts = 1+2+4 = 7.

Total volume of dry material = 35.4×7 = 247.8 litres.

Total volume of wet concrete is taken 67% of total volume of dry mixture for 1:2:4 mix

$$\text{Therefore total volume of wet mix} = \frac{2}{3} \times 247.8 = 165.2 \text{ litres}$$

For one cubic meter of wet concrete amount of

$$\text{Cement required} = \frac{1000{,}000}{165.2 \times 100} = 6.05 \text{ bags say 6 bags.}$$

Weight of dry aggregates = 6×50 = 300 Kg. (i.e. 100 kg. of sand and 200 kg. of coarse aggregate)

$$\text{Weight of water} = \frac{1}{3}\text{ (weight of cement)} + \frac{1}{20}\text{ (weight of aggregates)}$$

$$= \frac{1}{3} \times 50 + \frac{1}{20} \times 300$$

$$= 16.67 + 15.00 = 31.67 \text{ kg. } (316.7\text{N})$$

Amount of water present in sand $= \frac{2}{100} \times 100 = 2$ Kg. (20N)

Amount of water present in C.A. $= \frac{1}{100} \times 200 = 2$ Kg. (20N)

Total water present in the mix = 4Kg. (40N)

Amount of extra water needed = 31.67–4.00 = 27.67 Kg. (276.7N)

$$\frac{W}{C} \text{ ratio} = \frac{27.67}{50} = 0.55$$

Thus the mix by weight contains

Cement = 50 Kg. (500 N)

Sand = 100 Kg. (1000 N)

Stone ballast = 200 Kg. (2000 N)

Water = 27.67 Kg. (2767 N)

If the broken stone ballast has to be used as coarse aggregate, the above quantities may be increased by 4 to 5%.

APPENDIX-B

SPECIFICATIONS OF STEEL

1. MILD STEEL (Standard quality as per IS : 226-1969

1. CHEMICAL COMPOSITION :

(a)	Ladle analysis :	% Max
	Carbon (for thickness/dia upto 20 mm)	0.23
	Carbon (for thickness/dia over 20 mm)	0.25
	Sulphur	0.055
	Phosphorous	0.055
(b)	Finished products of mild steel :	% Max
	Carbon (for thickness/dia upto 20 mm)	0.02
	Carbon (for thickness/dia over 20 mm)	0.03
	Sulphur	0.005
	Phosphorous	0.005

II. MECHANICAL PROPERTIES :

Sl. No.	*Class of Steel*	*Thickness/dia mm mm*	*Tensile strength Kg/mm²*	*Yield stress minimum Kg/mm²*	*% Elongation on minimum gauge length= $5.65\sqrt{S_0}$*
1.	Plates, sections for example, angles, tess etc.	*Below 6 mm	Bend test only shall be required		
		6 to 20 mm	42 to 54	26.0	23
		20 to 40 mm	42 to 54	24.0	23
		Over 40 mm	42 to 54	23.0	23
2.	Bars (Round, square and hexgonal)	+ Below 10 mm	Bend test only shall be required		
		10 and upto and including 20 mm	42 to 54	26.0	23
		Over 20 mm	42 to 54	24.0	23

*In case of plates below 6 mm, the yield shall be assumed to be atleast the same as that for thickness 6 and 20 mm

+In case of bars 10 mm dia the yield stress shall be assumed to be atleast the same as for bars of dia between 10 and 20 mm.

Note—The weight of steel plates sections, flats and bars shall be calculated on the basis that steel weighs = 7.85 gms/cm^3.

S_o = original cross Sectional area of test piece.

III. Mechanical (tensile) properties of Bars

(Mild steel and Medium tensile steel) as per I.S : 432 (Part-I)—1966.

Sl. No.	Property	Normal size of Bars	Mild steel Grade I	Mild steel Grade II	Medium tensile steel
1.	Ultimate tensile stress Kg/mm²	All sizes	42	38	55
2.	Yield stress Kg/mm² (Min)	For bars upto and including 20 mm.	26	23.5	36
		For bars over 20 mm and upto and including 40 mm	24	21.5	34.5
		For bars over 40 mm	24	21.5	32
3.	% Elongation (Min. on gauge length $5.65\sqrt{S_o}$	For bars under 10 mm	20%	20%	17%
		For bars 20 mm and over.	23%	33%	20%

IV. SPECIFICATIONS OF HARD DRAWN STEEL WIRE : IS : 432 (Pt-II)–1966

This wire of medium strength is used as reinforcement in concrete.

Physical Requirements Min.

(a) Ultimate tensile strength Kg/mm² 58

(b) Proof stress (0.2%) kg/mm² 49

(c) % Elongation over a guage length of 8D (where D is the dia of wire) 7½%

V. COLD TWISTED STEEL BARS :

(a) Chemical composition—As per IS : 256-1962

(b) Physical requirements

The tensile strength, proof stress and % elongation for all sizes of twisted bars, whether plain or deformed, determined in accordance with I.S. 1608-1960 shall be as given below :

(1) Tensile strength, Kg/mm² Min 49.5

(2) 0.2% proof stress Kg/mm² Min 42.5

(3) % Elongation Min (On gauge length $5.65\sqrt{S_o}$) 14.5

VI. MECHANICAL PROPERTIES OF HIGH TENSILE STEEL BARS

(USED IN PRESTRESSED CONCRETE)

	Characteristics	Requirement
(1)	Tensile strength, Min	100 Kg/mm2 = 100,00 Kg/cm2
(2)	Proof stress	Not less than 80% or more than 90% of its ultimate strenght
(3)	% Elongation at rupture on a gauge length $5.65\sqrt{A}$ Mim (Where A is area of cross section)	10%
(4)	Young's Modulus	16×10^3 to 21×10^3 Kg/mm²

VII. HOT ROLLED DEFORMED BARS : IS : 1139-1966

(a) CHEMICAL COMPOSITION :

(1) Mild steel deformed bars upto 20 mm dia shall have the chemical composition as per I.S. 226-1962 and over 20 mm as per 2062-1962.

(2) Medium tensile steel deformed bars must meet the requirements of steel designation St 55-HTW of I.S. : 961-1962.

(b) PHYSICAL PROPERTIES OF HOT ROLLED DEFORMED BARS :

I.S. 1139-1966

Sl. No.	*Property*	*Nominal size of bars*	*Mild steel bars*	*Medium tensil bars*	*High Yield strength steel bars*
(1)	Tensile Strength Kg/mm^2, Min	All sizes	42	55	15% greater than the measured Yield stress
(2)	Yield stress kg/mm^2, Min.	For bars upto and including 20 mm	26	36	42.5
		For bars over 20mm upto and including 40 mm	24	34.5	42.5
		40mm and over	24	33	42.5
(3)	% Elongation Min on gauge length 5.65 $\sqrt{S_o}$	All sizes	23	20	14.5

Note : Tensile Test shall be conducted as per I.S. 1608-1960.

APPENDIX-C

Specification for Timber
Table -1

DEFECTS PERMISSIBLE FOR DIFFERENT GRADES OF TIMBER FOR STRUCTURAL PURPOSES

(As per IS : 883-1970)

Selected Grade	*Grade I*					*Grade II*
	B	C		D	θ	
		C_1	C_2			
1	*2*	*3*	*4*	*5*	*6*	*7*
	mm	*mm*	*mm*	*mm*		
Knots, checks and shakes shall be of half the size for grade I	5	19	19	25	1 in	Knots, checks and shakes shall be 1.5 the size for grade
	100	25	25	35	15	
	150	38	38	50	for	
Slope of grain shall be not more than 1 in 20.	200	44	50	65	all	Slope of grain shall be not more than 1 in 12
	250	50	57	81		
	300	54	75	100		
	350	57	81	115		
	400	63	87	131		
	450	66	93	150		
	500	69	100	165		
	550	72	103	181		
	600	75	106	200		

where,
B = width of face
C = Location and sizes of lives knots
C_1 = Narrow face and (¼) of the width of wide face close to top and bottom edges
C_2 = Central half of the width of wide face
D = Depth of checks and shakes
θ = Slope of grain.

TABLE 2
FACTORS OF SAFETY TO BE APPLIED TO BASIC STRESS TO OBTAIN SAFE WORKING STRESSES

S. No.	Stress	Standard Grade		
		Inside location	*Outside location*	*Wet location*
1.	Fibre stress in beams for broad leaved species, max.	5	6	7.5
2.	Fibre stress in beams in conifers, max.	6	7	8.5
3.	Shear along grain	7	7	7
4.	Horizontal shear in beams	10	10	10
5.	Compressive stress parallel to grain	4	4.5	5.5
6.	Compressive stress perpendicular to grain, max	1.75	2.25	2.75
7.	Modulus of elasticity of calculation of allowable deflection in beams	1.25	1.75	2

TABLE 3
SAFE WORKING STRESSES FOR INDIAN TIMBERS

S.No.	*Trade Name of Timbers*	*Average unit weight at 12% moisture content kg/cm³*	*All grades, all locations modulus of elasticity tonnes/cm²*	Working stress in kg/cm² for Standard Grade (Grade I)										
				Bending and Tension along Grain (Extreme fibre stress)			*Shear*		*Compression*					
							1 Horizontal	*2 along gain*	*Parallel to grain*			*Perpendicular to grain*		
				Inside location	*Outside location*	*Wet location*	*All Locations*	*All locations*	*Inside location*	*Outside location*	*Wet location*	*Inside location*	*Outside location*	*Wet location*
1	2	3	4	5	6	7	8	9	10	11	12	13	14	15
	Group A													
1.	Bullet wood	1105	174	228	190	152	15	21	144	126	102	112	88	71
2.	Ballagi	1135	163	226	186	152	15	22	148	130	106	87	67	55
3.	Dhaman	785	148	182	152	124	13	19	120	106	88	60	46	38
4.	Kala Siris	735	136	186	154	126	15	22	134	120	94	72	56	46
5.	Sal	865	127	168	140	112	9	13	106	94	78	45	35	29
	Group B													
1.	Indian Oak	865	125	148	124	98	12	17	92	80	66	45	35	29
2.	Bullet wood	880	124	172	144	116	13	18	108	98	80	55	43	35
3.	Dhaman (U.P., M.P.)	770	120	155	130	102	14	20	91	81	67	41	32	26
4.	Eucalyptus	850	115	166	138	108	12	17	112	102	80	76	59	48
5.	Jaman	850	112	151	126	102	12	17	91	84	67	58	45	36
6.	Babul	785	108	182	154	124	15	22	112	102	80	65	50	41

1	2	3	4	5	6	7	8	9	10	11	12	13	14	15
7.	Teak	640	96	140	116	94	10	14	88	78	64	40	31	25
	Group C													
1.	Indian chestnut	640	98	106	88	70	8	12	64	56	46	26	20	17
2.	Deodar	545	95	102	88	70	7	10	78	70	56	26	21	17
3.	Rose wood	755	93	168	140	112	12	17	106	92	78	54	50	41
4.	Sissoo	785	89	152	126	102	12	17	94	84	66	46	36	29
5.	Safed Siris	640	90	134	112	88	10	14	84	78	64	43	33	27
6.	Chir	575	98	84	70	60	6	9	64	56	46	22	17	14

Note 1. The values of horizontal shears are to be used for beams.

2 In all other cases, the shear along grains are to be used.

TABLE 4
PERMISSIBLE STRESSES FOR GRADE I TIMBER

S. No.	*Types of stress*	*Permissible stress in kg/cm²*		
		Group A	*Group B*	*Group C*
1	2	3	4	5
1.	**Bending and tension along grain**			
	(*i*) Inside location	182	123	84
	(*ii*) Outside location	152	102	70
	(*iii*) Wet location	120	81	60
2.	**Shear**			
	(*i*) Horizonal* all locations	12	9	6
	(*ii*) Along grain** all locations	17	13	9
3.	**Compression parallel to grain**			
	(*i*) Inside location	120	70	64
	(*ii*) Outside location	106	63	56
	(*iii*) Wet location	88	58	46
4.	**Compression prependicular to grain**			
	(*i*) Inside location	60	22	22
	(*ii*) Outside location	46	18	17
	(*iii*) Wet location	38	15	14

Note. *The values of horizontal shears are to be used for beams.

** In all other cases, the values of shear along the grains are to be used.

Modifications factors for permissible stresses

The permissible stresses given in Table 4 are modified by multiplying with the modification factors for folloing :

(*i*) **For change in slope of grain**. When the timber has major defects like slope of grains, knots, and checks or shakes (but not beyond permissible value), the permissible stresses given in Table 4 are multiplied by the modification factor K_1 for different slopes of grain as given in Table 5 as per IS: 883-1970

TABLE 5

MODIFICATION FACTOR k_1 TO ALLOW FOR CHANGE IN SLOPE OF GRAIN

Slope	K_1	
	Strength of beams; Joists *and Ties*	Strength of Posts or Columns
1	2	3
1 in 10	0.80	0.74
1 in 12	0.90	0.82
1 in 14	0.98	0.87
1 in 15 (and flatter)	1.00	1.00

TABLE 6

MODIFICATION FACTOR K_2 FOR CHANGE IN DURATION OF LOADING

S. No.	*Duration of loading*	K_2
1	2	3
1.	Continuous	1.0
2.	Two months	1.15
3.	Seven days	1.25
4.	Wind and earthquake	1.33
5.	Instantaneous or impact	2.00

(ii) **For change in the duration of load.** For duration of design load other than continuous, the permissible stresses given in Table 4 are multiplied by the modification factor K_2 given in Table 6 as per IS : 883-1970.

BEARING STRESS IN TIMBER

The bearing stress or compressive stress on a surface depends upon the inclination of surface with the direction of grains, bearing length, and distance from the end of a structural member. At any bearing of the side grain of timber, the permissible stress in compression perpendicular to the grain f_{cn} is dependent on the length and position of bearing. The permissible stresses given in Table 4 for compression perpendicular to the grain are also the permissible stresses for bearings of any length at the ends of members and for the bearings 150 mm or more in length at any other position. For the bearings less than 150 mm in length and located 75 mm or more from the end of a member, the permissible compressive stress perpendicular to the grain may be multiplied by the modification factor K_7 given in Table 7 as per IS: 883-1970. The allowance is not made for difference in intensity of the bearing stress due to bending of a beam. For the bearing stress under washer or a small plate, the same co-efficient recommended in Table 7 may be taken for bearing with a length equal to the diameter of the washer or the width of the small plate.

TABLE 7

MODIFICATION FACTOR k_7 FOR BEARING STRESSES

Length of bearing in mm	Co-efficient
15	1.67
25	1.40
40	1.25
50	1.20
75	1.13
100	1.10
150	1.00

APPENDIX-D

INDIAN STANDARD SPECIFICATIONS FOR BUILDING LIMES USED FOR CONSTRUCTION PURPOSE

D.1 CLASSIFICATION

1.1 Building limes shall be classified as follows:

Class A—Eminently hydraulic lime used for structural purposes.

Class B—Semi-hydraulic lime used for masonry mortars, lime concrete and plaster undercoat.

Class C—Fatlime used for finishing coat in plastering, whitewashing, composite mortars, etc. and with addition of pozzolanic materials for masonry mortar.

Class D—Magnesium/dolomitic lime used for finishing coat in plastering, white washing, etc.

Class E—Kankar lime used for masonry mortars.

Class F—Siliceous dolomitic lime used for under-coat and finishing coat of plaster.

Lime shall be available either in hydrated or quick form, except that of classes A and E which shall be supplied in hydrated form.

D.2 CHEMICAL REQUIREMENTS

2.1 Building limes shall conform to the requirements given in Table D.1.

D.3 PHYSICAL REQUIREMENTS

3.1 Building limes shall conform to the requirements given in Table D.2.

D.4 PACKING

4.1 The hydrated lime shall be supplied, in suitable containers, such as jute bags lined with polythene or high density polythene woven bags lined with ploythene or craft paper bags, preferably containing 50 kg of lime. If the hydrated lime can be used within 30 days, use of liner may be dispensed with.

4.2 The quick lime shall be supplied in containers like metal containers or similar suitable containers preferably containing 50 kg of lime.

D.5 MARKING

5.1 The lime packages shall bear the type and class of lime, the brand name of manufacturer, date of manufacture and the net weight; in case of quick lime the slaking temperature shall be indicated.

5.2 Lime packages may also marked with the ISI Certifications Mark. The use of the ISI Certification Mark is governed by the provisions of the Indian Standards Institution (Certification Marks) Act and the Rules and Regulation made thereunder. The ISI Mark on products covedred by an Indian Standard Conveys the assurance that they have been produced to comply with the requirements of that standard under a well defined system of inspection, testing and quality control which is devised and supervised by ISI and operated by the producer. ISI marked products are also continuously checked by ISI for conformity to that standard as a further safeguard. Details of conditions under which a licence for the use of the ISI Certification Mark may be granted to manufacturers or processors,, may be obtained from the Indian Standards Institution.

6. STORAGE

6.1 The lime shall be stored in such a manner as to permit easy access for proper inspection and in a suitable building to protect the lime from the dampness and to minimize warehouse deterioration. Quicklime deteriorates rapidly, and therefore, should used as quickly as possible.

7. SAMPLING AND CREITERION FOR CONFORMITY

7.1 The procedure of sampling and criterion for conformity shall be as follows.

7.2 Samples for Testing

7.2.1 The samples for testing shall be taken by the pur:haser or his representative at the manufacturer's works.

7.2.2 Procedures for Sampling

(a) Sampling shall be carried out at quickly as possible so that the material does not deteriorate. The total time occupied in mixing and quartering down the composite samples, and the preparation of the final test samples from this shall not exceed two hours. The final samples shall be three in number and shall be placed immediately in clean, dry and air-tight containers.

Table D.1

CHEMICAL REQUIREMENTS

Sl. No.	Characteristics	Class										Method of test, Ref to
		A	B		C		D		E	F		
		Hydrated	Quick	Hyd.	Quick	Hyd.	Quick	Hyd.	Hyd.	Quick	Hyd.	
(1)	(2)	(3)	(4)	(5)	(6)	(7)	(8)	(9)	(10)	(11)	(12)	(13)
i)	Calcium and magnesium oxide, percent, Min (on ignited basis)	60	70	70	85	85	85	85	50	70	70	IS: 6932 (Part I)-1973
ii)	Magnesium oxides, percent on ignited bases)	6	6	6	6	6	-	-	6	-	-	IS: 6932 (Part I)-1973
	Max, Min	-	-	-	-	-	6	6	-	6	6	IS: 6932 (Part I)-1973
iii)	Silica, alumina and ferric oxide, percent, Min (on ignited basis)	20	10	10	-	-	-	-	20	10	10	
iv)	Unhydrated magnesium oxide, percent, Max (on ignited basis)	-	-	-	-	-	8	8	-	8	8	IS: 6932 (Part 5) 1973
v)	Insoluble residue in dilute acid and alkali, percent, Max (on ignited basis)	15	10	10	2	2	2	2	25	10	10	IS: 6932 (Part 1) 1973
vi)	Carbon dioxide, percent Max (on oven dry basis)	5	5	5	5	5	5	5	5	5	5	IS: 6932 (Part2)-1973
vii)	Free moisture content percent, Max	-	2	-	2	-	2	2	-	2		IS: 1514-1959
viii)	Available lime CaO_3 percent, Min (dry basis)	-	-	-	75	75	-	-	-	-	-	IS: 1514-1959

TABLE D. 2
PHYSICAL REQUIREMENT

Sl. No.	Characteristics	Class										Method of test Refer to
		A	B		C		D		E	F		
		Hydrated	Quick	Hyd.	Quick	Hyd.	Quick	Hyd.	Hyd.	Quick	Hyd.	
(1)	(2)	(3)	(4)	(5)	(6)	(7)	(8)	(9)	(10)	(11)	(12)	(13)
i)	Fineness :											
	a) Residue on 2.36 mm IS Sieve percent, Max	Nil	-	Nil	-	Nil	-	Nil	Nil	-	Nil	IS : 6932 (Part-4)-1973
	b) Residue on 300 micron IS Sieve, percent, Max	5	-	5	-	Nil	-	Nil	5	-	5	
	c) Residue on 212 micron Max	-	-	-	-	10	-	10	-	-	Nil	
ii)	Residue on slaking :											
	a) Residue on 850 micron	-	10	-	5	-	5	-	-	10	-	IS : 6932 (Part 3) 1973
	b) Residue on 300 micron IS Sieve, percent, Max	-	-	-	5	-	5	-	-	-	-	
iii)	Setting time :											
	a) Initial set, Min, h	2	-	-	-	-	-	-	2	-	-	IS : 6932 (Part 2) 1984
	b) Final set, Max, h.	48	-	-	-	-	-	-	48	-	-	
iv)	Compressive strength : Min, N/mm² :											
	a) at 14 days	1.75	1.25	1.25	-	-	-	-	1.0	1.25	1.25	IS : 6932 (Part 7)-1973
	b) at 28 days	2.8	1.75	1.75	-	-	-	-	1.75	1.75	1.75	
v)	Transverse strength at 28 days, N/mm², Min	1.0	0.7	0.7	-	-	-	-	0.7	0.7	0.7	IS : 6932 (Part 7)-1973
vi)	Workability bumps, Max	-	-	-	12	10	12	10	-	-	-	IS : 6932 (Part 8)-1973

vii)	Volume yield ml/g, Min	-	-	-	1.7	-	1.4	-	-	-		IS : 6932 (Part 6)-1973
viii)	Soundness, Le Charterlier expansion mm. Max	5	-	5	-	-	-	-	10	-	10	IS : 6932 (Part-9)-1973
ix)	Popping and pitting	Free from pop and pits	-	Free from pop and pits		Free from pop and pits	-	Free from pop and pits	-	-	Free from pop and pits	IS : 6932 (Part-10)-

When testing is not to be carried out at once, the samples shall be enclosed, marked and sealed to the satisfaction of all concerned, paying special attention to the air-tightness of the containers. Tools and containers shall be of material free from rust and shall be alkali resistant.

(b) From each lot, three final test samples shall be taken as provided under (c) for quicklime and under (f) for hydrated lime.

(c) Quicklime :—The size of the gross sample for lump quicklime and powderred quicklime from each lot depends on the size of the lot and shall be given in Table D.3 and in (d) and (e).

TABLE D.3

TABLE SAMPLE SIZE

Lot size	Gross sample size for lump quicklime	Gross sample size for powdered quicklime
(1)	(2)	(3)
KN	Kg	Kg
Upto 1000	500	250
1001 to 3000	1000	500
3001 to 5000	1500	750
5001 to 10000	2000	1000

(d) When the lump quicklime or powdered quicklime is available in bulk, the gross sample shall be made up of at least 50 equal portions taken from the lot at equal intervals of loading or unloading to make up the prescribed gross sample size. For stationary lots, the gross sample shall be collected from different parts of the stock pile in not less than 50 equal portion. The gross sample collected in the above manner shall be thoroughly mixed on a clean dry surface to about 20 kg for lump quicklime and 10 kg for powdered quicklime by coning and quartering method.

(e) When the lump quicklime or powdered quicklime is presented for sampling in packages, at least 25 percent of the packages shall be opened and equal portion of the material shall be collected from different parts of the packages to make up the prescribed gross sample size. The gross sample collected in the above manner shall be thoroughly mixed on a clean dry surface to about 20 kg for lump quicklime and 10 kg for powdered quicklime by coning and quartering method.

(f) Hydrated Lime-The final samples, each of not less than 5 kg, shall be taken direct in the same manner as described under (d) and (e) for powdered quicklime.

7.3 Material for Physical and Chemical Tests

Subsequently, at the time and place at which the tests and chemical analysis are to be carried out, the sample taken as described under (c) and (f) shall be crushed to pass through 2.36 mm IS Sieve and thoroughly mixed. Slightly more quantity of lime than is sufficient for conducting the tests shall be taken. For chemical tests only, from the material finally chosen, a small quantity from the sample shall be ground and rejected in order to ensure absence of contamination in the grinding equipment; and then about 100 g of the sample shall be rapidly ground with as little exposure to the air and water vapour as possible to pass through 300 micron IS Sieve and placed in a small air-tight container. The remaining quantity shall be used for physical tests.

7.4 Criterion for Conformity

7.4.1 The test sample prepared for each lot shall be subjected to various physical and chemical tests. The lot shall be declared conforming to this specification only if the sample passes all the prescribed tests.

❑ ❑

EXPERIMENT NO. 6/6

IMPACT BENDING OF TIMBER

1. **Object**—To determine the impact bending of timber specimen.

2. **Theory**—A valued property of timber is its capacity to withstand shocks or repeated blows as evidenced by the use to which timber is put to: examples are fenders for small ships and boats, temporary shock absorbing layers for material handling operations, railway sleepers etc.

Toughness in engineering terms can be measured by the energy absorbed by the material to fail or rupture in a particular mode when subjected to an impact or blow. The energy of rupture due to impact, of timber is usually measured by subjecting a timber beam specimen to impact loads.

Toughness increases generally with increases in the moisture of timber. For a given species of timbers, consistently high values of toughness indicates that, not only the species is useful for the purpose but also the processes of conversion and seasoning have been effective.

3. **Apparatus**

A HATT–TURNER impact machine, dial gauge, defect free standard size beam specimen of 50 × 50 × 750 mm or 20 × 20 × 300 mm which shall not have a slope of grain more than 1 in 20 to the longitudinal edges.

4. **Procedure**

(1) The specimen shall be placed in such a way that the hammer falls on the centre of the specimen. The height of the hammer shall be 250N (25 kg) or 15 N(1.5Kg) for the two sizes respectively. When necessary for stronger specimens, a heavier hammer of double the weight may be used. The spans shall be 700 mm or 280 mm for the smaller size specimen.

(2) Static deflection (x) due to the weight of the hammer be measured at the mid span to the nearest 0.02mm with the hammer resting on the top surface of the specimen.

(3) Marking of datum line and recording of deflection: For recording of deflection a drum shall be provided which can be brought into contact with a stylus attached to hammer and can be rotated on a vertical axis. On the drum a paper be fixed by means of a sticking tape, under which a carbon paper be placed, inverted, for recording the impressions. First, a datum line is marked by placing the hammer to rest on the specimen and rotating the drum with stylus touching it. After that, the hammer shall be dropped from different heights and deflections recorded on the paper fixed on the drum. The first drop of the hammer shall be from a height of 50 mm after which the height of the successive drop shall be increased by 25 mm. Until a height of 250 mm is reached. Thereafter the increments in height shall be 50mm until complete failure occurs or 150 mm or 60 mm deflection is reached for the two sizes respectively.

(4) From the tracing on the graphic drum record, the actual deflection (y) (i.e. distance from the lowest point to the datum line) shall be measured at each drop with the help of a pair of dividers and diagonals scale corrected to 0.1mm.

A graph shall then be plotted with the exact height of drop (i.e. height of drop (+ x + y) as the ordinate and (y + x) as the abscissa. For plotting the graph, the following rules shall be observed.

(i) The straight line of proportionality shall be drawn in such a way that maximum number or points shall be on the straight line or nearest to the same.

The point at which the curve deviated from a straight line is known as limit of proportionality.

(ii) For the above purpose no consideration will be given to the initial two or three points.